The Four Faces of Teaching

GOODYEAR EDUCATION SERIES
Theodore W. Hipple, Editor

CHANGE FOR CHILDREN
Sandra Nina Kaplan, Jo Ann Butom Kaplan, Sheila Kunishima Madsen, Bette K. Taylor

CRUCIAL ISSUES IN CONTEMPORARY EDUCATION
Theodore W. Hipple

EARLY CHILDHOOD EDUCATION
Marjorie Hipple

ELEMENTARY SCHOOL TEACHING: PROBLEMS AND METHODS
Margaret Kelly Giblin

FACILITATIVE TEACHING: THEORY AND PRACTICE
Robert Myrick and Joe Wittmer

THE FOUR FACES OF TEACHING
Dorothy I. Seaberg

THE FUTURE OF EDUCATION
Theodore W. Hipple

MASTERING CLASSROOM COMMUNICATION
Dorothy Grant Hennings

THE OTHER SIDE OF THE REPORT CARD
Larry Chase

POPULAR MEDIA AND THE TEACHING OF ENGLISH
Thomas R. Giblin

RACE AND POLITICS IN SCHOOL/COMMUNITY ORGANIZATIONS
Allan C. Ornstein

REFORMING METROPOLITAN SCHOOLS
Allan Ornstein, Daniel Levine, Doxey Wilkerson

SCHOOL COUNSELING: PROBLEMS AND METHODS
Robert Hyrick and Joe Wittmer

SECONDARY SCHOOL TEACHING: PROBLEMS AND METHODS
Theodore W. Hipple

SOLVING TEACHING PROBLEMS
Mildred Bluming and Myron Dembo

TEACHING, LOVING, AND SELF-DIRECTED LEARNING
David Thatcher

VALUE CLARIFICATION IN THE CLASSROOM: A PRIMER
Doyle Casteel and Robert Stahl

WILL THE REAL TEACHER PLEASE STAND UP?
Mary Greer and Bonnie Rubinstein

SOCIAL STUDIES AS CONTROVERSY
R. Jerrald Shive

A YOUNG CHILD EXPERIENCES
Sandra Nina Kaplan, Jo Ann Butom Kaplan, Sheila Kunishima Madsen, Bette K. Taylor

The Four Faces of Teaching

The Role of the Teacher in Humanizing Education

Dorothy I. Seaberg

Professor of Education

Northern Illinois University

Goodyear Publishing Company, Inc.
Santa Monica, California

In Memory of Arthur
Who helped me in my becoming

Library of Congress Cataloging in Publication Data
Seaberg, Dorothy I.
    The four faces of teaching.

    (Goodyear education series)
    Includes bibliographies.
    1. Teaching—Addresses, essays, lectures. I. Title.
LB1025.2.S37   371.1'02   74-76449
ISBN 0-87620-332-2 (pbk.)

Library of Congress Catalog Card Number: 74-76449

ISBN: 0-87620-332-2

Y-3322-8

Current Printing (last number):
        10 9 8 7 6 5 4 3

Printed in the United States of America

Foreword

Ours is an age of struggle. Man struggles to control the technology he has created, so that it will serve his best interests. He struggles to preserve the resources of Spaceship Earth, which he has despoiled, so as to maintain the good life, and to control Earth's expanding population to a size compatible with available resources.

It is natural that the human feeling of inadequacy during a time of turmoil spawns questions of blame and responsibility for societal problems. In America, where faith in education has been widespread, blame of education has also become widespread.

Educators seek to answer questions of accountability to parents, to the state and national governmental agencies supplying funds, and sometimes to students. They ask, "What is the job of the teacher and how can he or she be held accountable?" Pressure has developed for "competency-based" teacher education with defined competencies which can be assessed. Responses to this pressure have been extremely varied, with major conflict developing between the behaviorists and the humanists over the meaning of accountability, the nature of competence and the whole approach to teaching.

In her book, Dorothy Seaberg contributes significantly to the clarification of this matter and gives teacher educators, students seeking to become teachers, and in-service school personnel a substantive analysis of teacher role and how to achieve it. The author has studied teacher role-function behavior systematically for 16 years while working with teacher education students. She has developed new programs and has tried out with students some of the materials in the book.

Helps for the reader are specific and practical. There are checklists such as the statements to help the reader assess his or her own philosophy. Suggestions of "Things to Do" are given. There is attention to the teacher's work with groups and with individuals, with children progressing well and with those not yet achieving their full potential. The author assumes a teacher who values in a child self-worth, self-reliance, and independence.

This book, with the acknowledgment that there are observable teacher behaviors, takes an open-ended approach to defining them. It gives a model, analyzing four major role-functions and the behaviors involved. Humanistic psychology is the basis for validation.

The author has produced in this book an exciting contribution to educational literature. She speaks meaningfully to student teachers and to the most sophisticated professionals. This book is much needed. It could not come at a better time.

Ruth Ellsworth
Professor of Education
Wayne State University

Preface

Early in my career as a teacher educator, I became convinced that teachers behave according to their conceptualized notions of their role. With this given, then, the proper education of a teacher means helping the neophyte to develop a philosophy of teaching and to conceptualize his role in reference to it. This book is my own view of the role of the elementary-school teacher, which I have conceptualized under the rubrics of "relationship," "mediation," "diagnosis," and "choreography." The overview and plan are presented in the introductory chapter.

In writing a book of this nature, it was necessary to refer to the word "teacher" frequently. In order to simplify my writing, I have used the grammatical purist approach in using the pronoun "he" to indicate that either males or females may be fulfilling the teaching role. Likewise, the masculine gender "he" has been used, meaning either sex, when referring to the child.

I am indebted to many people who have contributed to this work. First, there was the help and inspiration of my late friend and colleague, Arthur T. Allen, and of my mentor and friend, Ruth Ellsworth, Professor of Education, Wayne State University—and there was a class of 22 students who willingly let me "practice" on them. Writings of Marcia Grossman and Corrine Mager have slipped. into this book and I acknowledge their contributions.

I am grateful to Wanna Zinsmaster, Professor of Education, California State University, Los Angeles, who collaborated with me in writing the monograph, *Choreography of Teaching: A Conceptual Model*, while participating in the Tri-University Project at New York University.

Colleagues at Northern Illinois University have also helped. Among these I especially acknowledge Rodney M. Borstad, Mary Louise Seguel, Charles Sloan and Margaret Welsh for contributing ideas and/or reading and reacting to portions of my manuscript; likewise I acknowledge Hazel Huston, Eleanor Price and Ethel Miller for their ideas. There are also students, both graduate and undergraduate, who have given their opinions on selected portions as the book was being developed, and I would like to acknowledge their contributions.

I would like to thank the following students, in particular, who permitted me to use their anecdotal records of classroom experience: Patricia Burnight, Margaret Dodd, Joanne Erickson, Arthur Goodman, Olga Gut, Elizabeth Haubrich, Deborah Johnson, Maurine McDonough, Jean Pickering, Jamie Seiler, Sandra Stanley, Annette Tamraz and Jacqueline Warren. I am indebted as well for the contributions of Florence Forman, Lynn Glaser and Donna Pyfer, all of whom are in-service teachers.

I wish to thank the individuals and publishers who have given me permission to reprint or digest materials from their works. Specific acknowledgments are contained in footnotes throughout the book wherever these references occur.

Then, I wish to thank my sister, Ellen Seaberg Van Laningham, for her encouragement and editorial assistance, and my brother-in-law, Marion M. Van Laningham, for the use of his poem, "The Child." Lastly, I wish to commend my typist, Anne Walton, for her efficiency in meeting my deadlines.

Contents

INTRODUCTION

Roles and Goals of Teachers

To understand life is to understand ourselves, and that is both the beginning and the end of education.
J. Krishnamurti*

*J. Krishnamurti, *Education and the Significance of Life* (New York: Harper and Row, Publishers, 1953), p. 14.

Chapter 1

A Role-Function Model for Teaching

This is a book about the role of the teacher in humanizing education. Its purpose is to analyze and describe the teacher's function in developing the potentials of pupils.

At the outset, a "role" approach may seem confusing or even contradictory in a humanistic model of teaching, for the concept of role has several shades of meaning. Most social psychologists conceive of role as ascribed behavior befitting a position. Glasser, a humanistic psychoanalyst, riding on McLuhan's phrase, "young people are searching for 'roles,' not goals," has popularized "role" to mean "identity." Others see role as putting on a façade and say that the teacher should be an authentic person in the classroom, that the teacher should not play a role, and that any focus on method or technique or specified behavior makes a stilted teacher. A good teacher, they say, is simply a person who lives well with children.

It is the position of this book that teachers do engage in identifiable behaviors that are associated with a teaching role. The teacher has an achieved status; responsibilities are vested in him because of his position. Role theory as a system of analysis is helpful here. In terms of traditional social psychology, role means the behavior appropriate to a given status or position. Role may be thought of as a pattern of activity or appropriate social behavior demanded by a given situation or by the expectations placed upon the behaving person by those in the group. Certain expectations are held for teachers in a given school and by society at large, while at the same time, the teacher's role is interdependent with the pupils in the classroom. However, the teacher does select his behavior even though it is limited by what he is as a human being and what his "self" or his "person" permits him to do. Therefore, any treatment of the role of the teacher must be concerned both with the behaviors appropriate to the teacher's position and with the teacher's identity or the authenticity of his person. This book will attempt to deal with both of these aspects of the teaching role.

EDUCATIONAL ENVIRONMENTS AND TEACHING ROLES

It is an educational axiom that people learn in interaction with their environment. Therefore, any study of teaching must take into account the educational environment of the classroom, which is created to a large degree by the teacher. The universe is the child's teacher, but the classroom teacher has only the school setting in which he can hope to make a difference. Any environment, even a classroom environment, is global and infinitely complex. So is teaching, which makes it difficult to define or describe. Nevertheless, it is our premise that in order to study teaching, the basic dimensions of classroom environment must be identified and matched with corresponding teaching roles. If the teacher can gain a fundamental grasp of his major roles, he will make a giant step in becoming an effective teacher, regardless of subject matter or age group.

The teacher is a creator and arranger of educational environments. This is his global role. At least four educational environments intermingle in the classroom. We can identify these as an interpersonal environment that has political overtones, an environment of planned learning experiences that has a technological character, an environment of each individual's perception that is phenomenological[1] in nature, and an environment of affect or feeling that is aesthetic in its effect. We will refer to these environments as "political," "technological," "phenomenological" and "aesthetic" in later chapters of the book. Within these environments, the teacher functions in the roles of "relator," "mediator," "diagnostician" and environmental "choreographer." These are the "Four Faces of Teaching," matched vis-à-vis the major classroom environments. They are the subject of this book.

As a *relator*, the teacher creates an open or a closed system in the political environment through the way he relates to children. As a *mediator*, the teacher is a go-between or an intervener between the child and the curriculum, as he develops a technology of teaching evolved from what he knows about the nature of the learner and how he learns. As a *diagnostician*, the teacher looks at the child's phenomenal self, to discover his potentials as well as the blocks impeding his growth. As a *choreographer*, the teacher structures, integrates and synchronizes the events within the political, technological and phenomenological environments, inducing an overall harmonious effect that is felt aesthetically by the child. Figure 1 diagrams the "Four Faces of Teaching," showing how the

environments intermingle as one global whole. They are always in the process of emerging.

THE TEACHER BRINGS HIS PHILOSOPHY INTO THE CLASSROOM

In the role-function approach, we are making the assumption that the teacher, although working toward educational goals, adapts his role to achieve his goal—or he interprets his function as a teacher in relationship to his beliefs about the function of education. Although society has certain expectations for schools, it is difficult to control the goals and actions of children, and it certainly is not humanizing to do so. The only actions the teacher can really control are his own; the effects—if he creates any—are indirect and are produced through his own behavior. (All teachers do create effects, but many times these effects are negative!) Thus, the teacher behaves in relationship to the pupil with the expectation that what he does will bring a complementary response. If the teacher behaves as a master, the pupil will respond as a slave; if he behaves as a guide, the pupil will respond as a follower. If he behaves as a catalyst, however, the pupil will respond as a free agent.

As we can see, a teacher may behave in many different ways in fulfilling his role. He may relate either as a benevolent dictator or as a concerned helper and guide. He may mediate in ways that are closed and constrictive or in ways that are open and expansive. He may diagnose and put labels on children or open them to growth. He may treat people as puppets or arrange environments where children pull their own strings. How the teacher behaves depends on his point of view, on his system of belief. It is therefore necessary for the teacher to clarify his beliefs about people and how they learn if he is to behave consistently and in ways that facilitate growth.

In this model, which is developed around a belief system espoused by humanistic psychologists, self-actualization is viewed as the overarching goal of education. Tenets from the humanistic stream of thought are used as validating sources for identifying desired teacher behavior, and ideas have been synthesized from a wide spectrum of sources in humanistic and perceptual psychology,

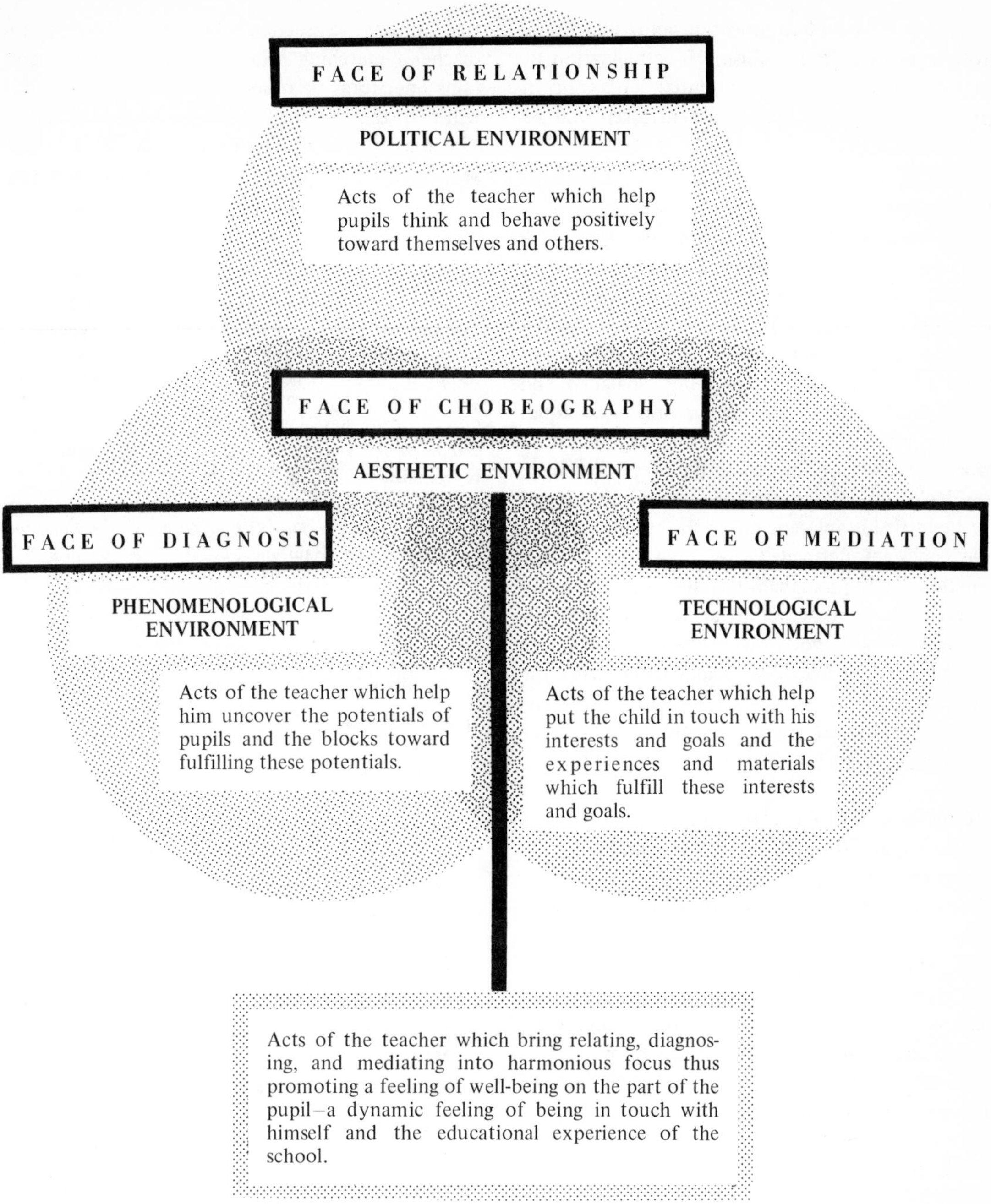

FACE OF RELATIONSHIP

POLITICAL ENVIRONMENT

Acts of the teacher which help pupils think and behave positively toward themselves and others.

FACE OF CHOREOGRAPHY

AESTHETIC ENVIRONMENT

FACE OF DIAGNOSIS

PHENOMENOLOGICAL ENVIRONMENT

Acts of the teacher which help him uncover the potentials of pupils and the blocks toward fulfilling these potentials.

FACE OF MEDIATION

TECHNOLOGICAL ENVIRONMENT

Acts of the teacher which help put the child in touch with his interests and goals and the experiences and materials which fulfill these interests and goals.

Acts of the teacher which bring relating, diagnosing, and mediating into harmonious focus thus promoting a feeling of well-being on the part of the pupil—a dynamic feeling of being in touch with himself and the educational experience of the school.

Figure 1: THE FOUR FACES OF TEACHING: Functions of the Teacher As "Relator," "Mediator," "Diagnostician," and "Choreographer" in Creating Educational Environments.

existential philosophy, education and the helping professions. The focus is on self-actualization or the development of human potential, with concern for the "fully evolved and authentic self and its ways of being."[2]

TEACHING AS ART

In the model, teaching is also viewed as art. All arts have their technologies, and it is the mastery of the technology that frees the artist to work with his media creatively. The composer needs a mastery of notation, the language of music; the plastic artist uses principles of harmony, balance and depth perception. The dancer masters techniques of body movement. But the putting together is up to the artist who is fashioning the event. Teachers, too, have technologies. In this model technologies are identified in relationship to the teacher's major roles and are defined as teaching acts or role-function behaviors that the teacher personally selects and fits together to achieve definite purposes. Actions supported by humanistic theory are offered for the teacher's examination, with the intent that he may become sensitive to his teaching role as he weaves behaviors into his own self-system to create a personal style of teaching.

ORGANIZATION OF THE BOOK

Chapter 2 of "Roles and Goals of Teachers," the introductory section of the book, summarizes the humanistic psychology from which the educational goals of the model are derived. The remainder of the book—Parts I, II, III and IV—is devoted to "relationship," "mediation," "diagnosis" and "choreography"—*the four faces of teaching*—the major roles in which the teacher functions.

Three chapters are devoted to each face. A theoretical chapter delineates aspects of classroom environment, a second chapter deals with the teacher's matching role and a third chapter contains anecdotal or other illustrative material that will help the reader visualize the teacher in action. The inventory of teacher behavior included in each section may be used by the teacher as a self-checklist in analyzing his own teaching.

Notes

[1] The external environment has been called, by some, the phenomenological field. As defined by Syngg, "the phenomenological field is [the] universe, including [the organism], as experienced by the behaver at the moment." See Donald Snygg, "The Need for a Phenomenological System of Psychology," in *The Self in Growth, Teaching, and Learning,* Don E. Hamachek, ed. (Englewood Cliffs, N.J.: Prentice-Hall, 1965), p. 56.

[2] Abraham Maslow, "Existential Psychology—What's in It for Us?" in *The Self in Growth, Teaching, and Learning,* Don E. Hamachek, ed. (Englewood Cliffs, N.J.: Prentice-Hall, 1965), p. 93.

References

Glasser, William. *The Identity Society.* New York: Harper & Row, Publishers, 1972.

Hamachek, Don E., ed. *The Self in Growth, Teaching, and Learning.* Englewood Cliffs, N.J.: Prentice-Hall, Inc., 1965.

Huebner, Dwayne. "Curricular Language and Classroom Meanings." Paper distributed to members of the Tri-University Project seminar, New York University, October, 1967.

Johnson, David W. *The Social Psychology of Education.* New York: Holt, Rinehart and Winston, Inc., 1970.

Seaberg, Dorothy I., and Wanna M. Zinsmaster. *Choreography of Teaching: A Conceptual Model.* Monograph. New York: Tri-University Project in Elementary Education, New York University, 1968.

Chapter 2

Belief Systems of Teachers and Educational Goals

Research of Arthur Combs (1969) in the helping professions—counseling, the ministry, nursing and teaching—has revealed that the system of belief that "helpers" hold about people is a crucial vari-able in their effectiveness with clients. Beliefs, like gyroscopes, keep helpers on course; at the same time, beliefs enable helpers to be spontaneous in their transactions with other people.

As a teacher, what are your basic beliefs about human nature and the motivation of behavior? How are your beliefs acted out in your own teaching role? How are your beliefs reflected in your goals for learners?

Why not check the following statements to help clarify your stand?

Agree	Disagree		I believe that:
_____	_____	1.	Learners need grades, gold stars and other incentives as motivation to learn and to accomplish school requirements.
_____	_____	2.	Learners can be trusted to find their own goals, and that they should have some options or choices in what they do in school.
_____	_____	3.	The teacher is almost helpless in coping with disturbed children, because emotional disturbance results from the early history of the child about which teachers can do little or nothing.
_____	_____	4.	Children should be graded according to uniform standards of achievement which the teacher sets for the class.
_____	_____	5.	Children should be helped to set their own individual standards and should begin to evaluate their own work.
_____	_____	6.	The teacher should discover the unfulfilled needs of the child and help him find ways to fulfill them.
_____	_____	7.	To insure the transmission of the cultural heritage, the program of the school should be organized along subject-matter lines that are carefully sequenced.

Agree	Disagree		I believe that:
_____	_____	8.	Children will learn best if right responses are rewarded and unacceptable responses are ignored.
_____	_____	9.	The teacher can free the child to learn by helping him feel like a worthwhile human being who can do things.
_____	_____	10.	Teachers should not be expected to do very much with disturbed children; after all, teachers are not psychiatrists.
_____	_____	11.	Every child is creative, and the teacher is creative when he unfolds creativity in children by accepting them as they are and by helping them to believe in themselves and in their abilities.
_____	_____	12.	Children should be indoctrinated with a set of values that will govern their behavior toward their fellow man.
_____	_____	13.	The teacher will encourage better work from all children if he posts the best work on the bulletin board.
_____	_____	14.	Teachers help children develop their own values by helping them examine the consequences of their actions.
_____	_____	15.	School experience should help the learner understand himself and find meaningful relationships with his fellow man.

If you agreed with statements 1, 4, 7, 8, 12 and 13, your beliefs about human nature are probably in agreement with the theories of behaviorism. If you agreed with statements 3, 6 and 10, your beliefs are probably Freudian. If you agreed with statements 2, 5, 6, 9, 11, 14 and 15, you are probably attuned to the thinking of humanistic psychologists. If your responses were mixed, then your belief system is a hybrid or a mongrel! Or, in more elegant terms, you are eclectic!

Classroom emphasis on extrinsic rewards—motivation through grades and the gold star, single standards to which pupils must measure up, and external control by the teacher—exemplifies the application of behavioristic theory. Programmed learning and behavior modification through reward are applications of B. F. Skinner's theory of operant conditioning, which holds that reward reinforces and establishes desired behavior and that lack of reward extinguishes behavior. Behavioristic teachers believe in external authority as a guide to values, and they are usually concerned with having students master a body of skills and content, which is prescribed as necessary for fitting the individual into society and making him economically productive.

Reliance on a Freudian or psychoanalytic view of the nature of man has caused some teachers to be overly permissive, to excuse disturbed pupils from responsibility for their actions and to assign failures to reach the child to factors beyond teacher control, because the child's past cannot be retrieved. At best, dedicated Freudian teachers launch out and search for ways to fulfill the child's needs in an attempt to change his future behavior. Freudian beliefs provide a basis of sympathy for the child and his problems, as well as a reprieve from the teachers' own guilt over inability to cope.

In the humanistic classroom, value is placed upon the individual's uniqueness and individuality, upon his potentiality and upon his worth as a person. An open, growth-facilitating environment is the concern of humanistic teachers, who work indirectly to put the child in the driver's seat. They give him opportunities to make choices and to evaluate the consequences of his actions. They are more concerned with the processes of learning than they are with the actual products of learning. Skills are important and basic knowledge is important, as these relate to concerns that the child feels. The humanistic teacher centers on the growing person and that person's needs, trusting that the child will acquire knowledge and skills, and that he also will become creatively productive. The happy man is the one who has developed as an individual, who is saying yes to life. He feels "up to" whatever comes his way and whatever he decides to do.

FINDING A BELIEF SYSTEM
FOR TEACHING

As a teacher, which of these concerns is *your* concern? It is our point of view that both the goals and roles of the teacher need to emerge from a belief system about people, and that the teacher's roles need to be congruent with his goals. Teachers who are ambivalent in their beliefs may become confused about their teaching roles. To gain a clear picture of his role, the teacher needs to clarify his beliefs about people and his beliefs about how they grow.

In this chapter, we will examine the three belief systems about human nature that have been alluded to previously. The major emphasis, however, will be given to the blending of existential thinking and humanistic psychology as a validating philosophy for classroom practice. Existential philosophy deals with the questions and problems of human existence; humanistic psychology deals with the psychology of the self and the development of human potential. These strands are intertwined and really cannot be separated.

Freudianism as a Belief System
About Human Nature[1]

Gathering his data from the emotionally disturbed, Sigmund Freud (1856-1939) called attention to the unconscious mind and its influence on human behavior; to man's basic genetic, or instinctual, drives; and to the conflict that results when man represses these basic instincts to conform to society's imposed customs and moral values. The *id* (man's set of instinctual drives) is at war with the *superego* (the value system imposed by parents and society, which is internalized by the child). The resulting, overt behavior comes from man's *ego,* which combines the forces of the id and superego to determine action. The prime emphasis in Freudian theory is on the influence of early experiences, and the direction of life is assumed to be determined at a very early age (approximately five years). Freudianism—a subjective, deterministic approach to understanding human behavior—

removes responsibility from the behaver, because he is viewed as being controlled basically by unconscious drives. Repressed desire and unfulfilled need lead to guilt and conflict, which are resolved only through insight that is usually gained through therapy. Freudian theory has contributed to the understanding of human behavior, through suggesting that people are motivated to fulfill unmet needs buried in the unconscious. The Freudian defense mechanisms of denying danger (repressing instinctual drives and emotions), externalizing danger (projecting threats to the self onto some other person or object), hiding danger (introjection, or fusing the self with a successful person or group), standing still (fixating self at a given developmental level) and retreating (regressing to an earlier, "safe" level of development) have also shown how man may be self-deceived and thus unfree.

Behaviorism as a Belief System
About Human Nature

Behaviorism, like Freudianism, is a deterministic view of the nature of man. First formulated by John B. Watson (1878-1958), the general theory of behaviorism emerged just after 1900, as the result of endeavors to make the study of man as objective and scientific as possible. Rejecting the subjectivity of Freudianism, the behaviorists asserted that personality can be viewed only as the sum of outward, observable actions. Man's person is expressed in habit systems developed through *conditioning* (Watson, 1930). Behavior, then, is shaped according to external, environmental influences. Man is viewed as "a flexible, malleable, and passive victim of his environment which determines his behavior."[2]

B. F. Skinner, Harvard psychologist, is presently the leading exponent of behaviorism. From his point of view, right and wrong can be determined only in relationship to the survival of culture. Ethics, morals and values are relative and are learned as a result of conditioning influences in the environment. According to Skinner, it must be assumed that man is not free, if human behavior is to be studied scientifically. Skinner, in *Beyond Freedom and Dignity* (1971), advocates that man should not be freed from control but that the kinds of control to which he is exposed should be analyzed and changed. The "good" classroom environment, according to this theory, would be the one in which the teacher (or someone controlling the teacher) decides what behaviors and values are good for children and for society. The teacher then reinforces these behaviors in order to produce a person who will behave well toward himself and his fellows.

The "Third Force" in Viewing
the Nature of Man

Discontent with deterministic views of man as espoused by the Freudians and behaviorists has increased during the past several decades. Man may be viewed as greater than the sum of his parts: He has power of choice, he can take a hand in what he will become, he need not be a helpless pawn in his culture. This third way of looking at human nature has emerged through the blending of existential philosophy, phenomenology and "growth" psychology that has led to the human potential movement. This new view, which is concerned with the psychology of the fully evolved and authentic self and its ways of being,[3] has sometimes been called "existential psychology" but is more frequently termed "humanistic psychology," or the "third force" in viewing the nature of man. Humanistic theory is "centered on man himself—his needs, his goals, his achievements, his success."[4] The humanistic psychologists count among their number Abraham Maslow, Carl Rogers, Rollo May, Erich Fromm, Gordon Allport, Arthur Combs, Clark Moustakas and many others who are often referred to in the educational literature.

Abraham Maslow, in his preface to the revised edition of *Toward a Psychology of Being,* said:

Much has happened to the world of psychology since this book was first published. Humanistic Psychology—that's what it's being called most frequently—is now quite solidly established as a viable, third alternative to objectivistic psychology and to orthodox Freudianism. Its literature is large and is rapidly growing. Furthermore, it is beginning to be used, *especially in education, in industry, religion, in organization and management, in therapy, and in self-improvement and by various other "Eupsychian" (human oriented) organizations, journals and individuals.*[5]

Although many existential philosophers have written pessimistically about the outcome of man and the alienation and "nothingness" he often faces, the major themes have been oriented toward his infinite possibilities. Existential thinkers have dwelt on the themes of the "authentic" person who knows himself, who thus recognizes his complete freedom to choose, who is fully aware of the responsibility that choice places upon him—especially regarding his responsibility to himself and thus, indirectly, to humanity. To exist as a human being, the existentialists say, a person must decide for himself what his life is to be. If he merely copies those around him, he is trying to be something that he is not, and cannot be. He is not authentic.

Third-force psychology is also understood through phenomenology, the handmaiden of existential thinking. In simplistic terms, phenomenology begins with the proposition that all human knowledge is based upon experience that is lived; therefore, it is a science of possibility, of emergence, of the person's coming-into-being. The person's world of subjective experience is viewed as a valid source of knowledge; truth for each of us is relevant when it is lived by us. Kierkegaard, an early existentialist, said: "Truth exists for the individual only as he himself produces it in action" (Gale, 1969).

Behavior, in the phenomenological view, is determined by the person's phenomenological field—the external environment together with the activating organism. Behavior encompasses all the phenomena that the individual is perceiving and is subjectively experiencing as he interacts with his environment in a given moment of time. From a phenomenological view, perception is the key to understanding individual behavior. By trying to view the world from a perspective of the other person and by asking what a given behavior means to that person, it is possible to gain insight into his motivations.

MAJOR THEMES OF
HUMANISTIC PSYCHOLOGY

Humanistic theories are dominated by existential

and phenomenological thinking. Man's own subjective experience is his source of personal validation; his perceptions are the only reality man can know. Humanistic psychology is therefore a "self" psychology; scholars in this field have attempted to evolve a theory of human behavior out of understandings of the development of selfhood. Rather than rejecting completely all the tenets of Freudianism and behaviorism, humanistic psychologists have assessed the useful and meaningful concepts that are applicable to mankind—and from these concepts they have gone on to evolve a psychology of "being." Behavioristic theories, indeed, have been a point of take-off for humanistic psychology, because these theories explain how individuals may become inadequate, unable to function fully within their innate capacities, unable to express their uniqueness. Deterministic theories of psychology hold many answers to the question: "How *does* man become?" but they ignore the question: "What *can* man become?" This, the central question in humanistic psychology, provides the impetus for developing a humanistic theory for educational practice. Man needs to be freed from restraints that have conditioned him into being less than he can be. Deterministic psychology is found wanting, because it is a psychology of "control"; humanistic psychology is a psychology of promise, because it is a psychology of "release."

Persistent themes in humanistic psychology revolve around the ideas of identity and self-awareness—the "Who am I?" question—around individuality and the authentic self. Individuality or sense of self, responsibility for the conduct and outcome of one's life and social integration are basic to the development of personality. Man is a "self" when he is aware of himself as a choosing, free and responsible agent (Morris, 1966).

The question of values is an important issue in existential thinking. Human values come out of the nature of man and are not relative. The individual creates his values through his choices; but to be real, a choice must be made by selecting from alternatives in a state of awareness (Morris, 1966). Rollo May points out in his book *Man's Search for Himself* (1953) that modern man's loneliness, anxiety and hollowness result from a loss of values that can be replaced only through becoming a person in one's own right, through overthrowing psychological hangups that have created dependence, and through exercising the freedom to choose one's self.

Self-actualization (discovering the true self and making one's potentialities real, or actual) is regarded as the *sine qua non* of humanistic psychology. When man is free, self-actualization becomes his primary goal—and self-actualization is possible only if man is free. The self-actualized man is the one who directs his own life to become what he potentially can become. From the existential stance, the person should find out who he is and *be* that person!

Abraham Maslow, a leading third-force psychologist, became intrigued with studying healthy, self-actualized people—the Albert Schweitzers, the Martin Bubers and the Eleanor Roosevelts of society—as opposed to the neurotics who were Freud's subjects. Through his research into the lives of fully mature people, Maslow (1954, 1962) discovered that the self-actualized hold certain characteristics in common: They are open, flexible, humble, spontaneous, courageous people, who are willing to make mistakes. Having a low degree of self-conflict, they are undistorted by desires, fears, unrealistic hopes, false optimism, or pessimism; therefore, they have a superior ability to see life clearly and to express themselves creatively. They possess a healthy respect of self, based on the knowledge that they are competent and adequate; seldom are they confused about what is right or wrong. Dedicated to some work they see important, these people possess a childlike simplicity, a lack of arrogance. Although they are highly independent, they enjoy people and are non-exploitative in their relationships with others. Their excellent perceptions of reality enable them to see both the good and evil in each situation; usually they enjoy solving problems and bringing order out of chaos. Maslow's study of self-actualizing people "refutes the Freudian theory that the human unconscious (id) is only bad, evil, crazy, or dangerous. In self-actualizing people, the subconscious is creative, loving, positive, and healthy."[6]

Needs Theory
and Humanistic Psychology

Maslow believed that in contrast to the self-actualized man, the average person is motivated by deficiencies. He seeks to fulfill his basic needs for safety, belongingness, love, respect and self-esteem, while the healthy man has fulfilled these lower order needs and is primarily motivated by the need to develop and actualize his potentialities fully. Maslow, in his "hierarchy of needs" theory, postulates that man is not free to pursue a higher need until a lower priority is met. Physiological needs come first, then there must be some security or a feeling of safety. When these needs are met, man is able to socialize or interrelate with others, to belong. This ability leads to a feeling of self-worth and self-respect that frees one to achieve or accomplish, to use one's potentialities, to become self-actualized in his own individual way.

Other existential and humanistic thinkers have suggested other needs as contributing to the prime motivation of man. Combs (1959) believes in one basic need, adequacy—the need for the individual to develop and maintain an adequate self. This self is a perceived self, or a phenomenal self—the self known to the individual as experienced by him. In this view, adequacy, like self-actualization, is never sated; it must always be maintained and enhanced.

Morris (1966) proposes an existential need for recognition that is common to all men, a nostalgic yearning for some assurance that our individual existence has been recognized as having occurred in the world. He believes that a craving for ultimate recognition, or the need to believe in the irreplaceability of the individual, is the basic motivation behind all existential striving.

Erich Fromm (1955), a humanistic psychoanalyst, has proposed that the fulfillment of five basic needs of man will produce a "sane society." These fundamental needs, he contends, are universally valid for man, regardless of the given social order. Without coming to grips with these needs, one can find no satisfactory answer to the problem of human existence. Fromm classifies the basic needs and their opposite states as (1) relatedness *vs.* narcissism; (2) transcendence (creativeness) *vs.* destructiveness; (3) rootedness (brotherliness) *vs.*

incest; (4) sense of identity (individualism) *vs.* herd conformity; and (5) frame of orientation and devotion (reason) *vs.* irrationality.

GOALS OF EDUCATION

We are proposing that the only valid source for deriving educational goals is from the fundamental nature of man as viewed from a psychology of the self-actualized person. Humanistic psychology calls for a new kind of education, which will develop responsibility and self-discipline, spontaneity and creativity—along with the more traditional goals of learning to communicate, to think and to solve problems. This "new" education places more emphasis "on the development of the person's potential to be human, to understand self and others and to relate to them."[7] Children in schools must fulfill their basic human needs in order to grow toward self-actualization. An education that is "real" will help the individual become the best person he is able to become.

In this chapter we have been discussing man's existential needs as a basis for deriving educational goals. However, rather than talking about "goals" of education, it may be more appropriate to speak of the "functions" of education, because a person in the process of "becoming" never does fulfill an *ultimate* goal. Good education can, therefore, be viewed as a means of facilitating growth. The teacher functions in ways that release pupils to grow in the direction of self-actualization.

Using Fromm's existential needs as a reference point, the function of education can be conceived as (1) helping individuals to become self-aware, to find identity and to follow their unique patterns of individuation; (2) helping individuals to become related to self and others; (3) helping individuals to develop thinking, problem-solving and creative powers; and (4) helping individuals to become choice makers and to assume responsibility for their own lives. The individual comes to believe: "I am up to whatever comes my way—including what I take on. I have something important to do and be in the world. I can separate what I feel and think from what is actually going on and make a wise decision. I can take responsibility for myself, not the world. I can find out who I am and be it!"

To achieve these personal goals, the *means* of

education must be inseparable from the *ends* of education. The argument of whether the individual should be educated for self-actualization or for fulfilling the needs of society is circuitous. When the existential question of "beingness"—becoming truly human, authentic or growing toward self-actualization—is met constructively, each individual develops into a productive person. The society becomes constructively productive or "sane," because the individuals within it are productive and humane.

Notes

[1] See Frank Goble, *The Third Force* (New York: Pocket Books, 1971) for a very readable and short description of Freudian and behavioristic psychologies. The humanistic stream with major focus on Abraham Maslow is developed in detail in this book. Short quotations from this reference are included in this discussion with the following credits:
From *The Third Force: The Psychology of Abraham Maslow,* by Frank Goble. Copyright 1970 by Thomas Jefferson Research Center, all rights reserved. Reprinted by permission of Grossman Publishers.

[2] Ibid., pp. 7,8.

[3] Abraham Maslow, *Toward a Psychology of Being* (New York: Van Nostrand, 1962), p. 16.

[4] Goble, op. cit., p. xiv.

[5] From *Toward a Psychology of Being* by Abraham Maslow. © 1962 by Litton Educational Publishing, Inc. Reprinted by permission of Van Nostrand Reinhold Company.

[6] Goble, op. cit., p. 36.

[7] Ibid., p. 69.

References

Combs, A. W., et al. *Florida Studies in the Helping Professions.* University of Florida Social Science Monograph, Number 37. Gainesville: University of Florida Press, 1969.

Combs, Arthur W. and Donald Snygg. *Individual Behavior: A Perceptual Approach to Behavior.* Rev. ed. New York: Harper & Brothers, 1959.

Fromm, Erich. *The Sane Society.* Greenwich, Conn.: Fawcett, 1955.

Gale, Raymond F. *Developmental Behavior: A Humanistic Approach.* Toronto, Ontario: Macmillan, 1969.

Goble, Frank. *The Third Force.* New York: Pocket Books, 1971.

Maslow, Abraham. *Motivation and Personality.* New York: Harper & Row, 1954.

_____ *Toward a Psychology of Being.* New York: Van Nostrand, 1962.

May, Rollo. *Man's Search for Himself.* New York: New American Library, 1953.

Morris, Van Cleve. *Existentialism in Education.* New York: Harper & Row, 1966.

Skinner, B. F. *Beyond Freedom and Dignity.* New York: Knopf, 1971.

Watson, John B. *Behaviorism.* Chicago: University of Chicago Press, 1930.

STUDY HELPS AND CLASS ACTIVITIES

Annotated Bibliography

In addition to the books referred to in this introductory section, the following are recommended reading:

Bach, Richard. *Jonathan Livingston Seagull.* New York: Avon Books, 1970.

The real Jonathan Seagull lives within us all. A beautiful allegoric rendition of the process of "becoming."

Barrett, William. *Irrational Man.* Garden City, N.Y.: Doubleday & Co., Inc., 1962.

A very readable account of the history of existential thought. Good introduction to a study of existential philosophy.

Combs, Arthur W., ed. *Perceiving, Behaving, Becoming.* Washington, D.C.: Yearbook of the Association for Supervision and Curriculum Development, 1962.

A very readable and helpful source to the classroom teacher on the phenomenological point of view as applied to education. The yearbook contains chapters by Carl Rogers, Arthur Combs, Abraham Maslow and Earl Kelley.

Fromm, Erich. *Man for Himself.* Greenwich, Conn.: Fawcett Publishing, Inc., 1947.

Fromm discusses the problem of ethics, of norms and values leading to the realization of man's self and of his potentialities.

Glass, John F., and John R. Staude, eds. *Humanistic Society: Today's Challenge to Sociology.* Pacific Palisades, Calif.: Goodyear Publishing Co., Inc., 1972.

A book of readings containing some of the best from the humanistic writers as applied to sociology.

Greene, Maxine, ed. *Existential Encounters for Teachers.* New York: Random House, 1967.

Contains short selections from some of the most noted existential thinkers; the editor adds her own perceptive insights on the meanings for education.

Hall, Calvin S. *A Primer of Freudian Psychology.* New York: The New American Library, 1954.

An easy book for those who wish to know more about Freudian psychology.

Hesse, Hermann. *Siddhartha.* New York: James Laughlin, 1957.

An absorbing novel containing the story of a soul's long quest in search of the ultimate answer to the enigma of man's role on earth.

Jourard, S. M. *The Transparent Self: Self-disclosure and Well-being.* Princeton, N. J.: Van Nostrand, 1964.

Jourard explores the premise that man can attain health and fullest personal development only insofar as he gains courage to be himself with others and only as he finds goals that have meaning for him.

Krishnamurti, J. *Education and the Significance of Life.* New York: Harper & Row, Publishers, 1953.

A beautifully written philosophical discourse of an Eastern thinker, addressed to the problems of conformity and loss of personal values that are plaguing the Western world.

May, Rollo. *Existential Psychology.* New York: Random House, 1961.

A series of provocative essays by writers in the field of existential psychology, including May, Allport, Feifel, Maslow and Rogers.

Moustakas, Clark. *Personal Growth.* Cambridge, Mass.: Howard A. Doyle Publishing Co., 1969.

The struggle for identity and human values as related to education is the theme of this book. Authenticity of self and learning is emphasized.

Rogers, Carl R. *On Becoming a Person.* Boston: Houghton Mifflin Co., 1961.

One of Rogers' best-known works, this book deals with the meaning of personal growth and the potential of man.

Things to Do

1. Read widely in the area of "third force" psychology and keep a diary of your thoughts as you reflect on what you read. After a period of time, reread your diary. Has your thinking and outlook on life changed? How?

2. Make a chart comparing the major precepts of Freudian, behavioristic and humanistic thought. Discuss the implications of each school of thought for educational practice.

3. Make a chart comparing the major concepts of several of the humanistic psychologists.

4. Develop a "dictionary" of concepts introduced by the humanistic thinkers.

5. Use creative media (for example, art, creative writing, audio visual media) to illustrate the major concepts or generalizations you have gained from your study of humanistic psychology. Share these productions in class.

6. Attend a series of lectures or listen to TV programs that point up social problems. Write a critique of these lectures, relate them to your reading and point up implications for education.

7. Compile a set of thought-provoking questions raised by the ideas presented in books on humanistic thought. Divide the class into small groups, with about six people to a group. Share your thinking on each question in these small groups. Reconstruct your groups frequently enough so that people in the class can have an opportunity to interact with nearly everyone. Have a timekeeper tap a bell at the end of every seven minutes as a signal to rotate and form new discussion groups.

PART I

The Face of Relationship

THE TEACHER GAME
Fill in the Blanks

A teacher stands in front of the class.
A teacher takes attendance.
A teacher _____ .
A teacher speaks more than students do.
A teacher uses a teacher's lounge.
A teacher _____ .
A teacher grades students.
A teacher gets paid for teaching.
A teacher sends students to the principal's office.
A teacher makes assignments.
A teacher _____ .
A teacher has yard duty, bus duty, and hall duty.
A teacher _____ .
A teacher uses the blackboard more than the
*   students do.*
A teacher is called Miss, Mrs., Dr., or Professor.
A teacher dismisses the class.
A teacher _____ .

Mary Greer and Bonnie Rubinstein,
Will the real teacher please stand up?*

*Mary Greer and Bonnie Rubinstein, *Will the real teacher please stand up?* (Pacific Palisades, Calif.: Goodyear Publishing Company, Inc., 1972), p. 61. Reprinted by permission of the publisher.

Chapter **3**

The Political Environment of the Classroom

Classroom environments are social and interpersonal; but they are "political," too. It is the quality of the political environment that determines whether or not the school will be humane.

In schools, the social climate is fostered by all the interpersonal relationships of teacher-to-pupil, pupil-to-pupil and pupil-to-group. However, it is an oversimplification to view the classroom only as an arena of interpersonal relationships, for it is an arena of authority relationships as well. Many controlling transactions and interactions occur; policies and decisions are made and rules are enforced, adding a "politicizing" dimension. It is within this complicated network of authority relationships that the child develops his abilities to relate to others, to value, to choose. Here he gains his sense of self, and he vies with others for status and power in his struggle to belong and to be—he learns who he is or what his labels are. The political influences may serve to constrict the child, or they may free him and open him to growth. As social attitudes and behaviors are learned, the syntality, or group personality, is formed, and the child finds his place in it.

In the political environment, the teacher establishes either an open or closed system through his mode of relating to children. He controls them through reinforcing acceptable conforming behavior, or he opens them to personal growth and the expression of their individuality through supportive relationships. In the humanistic classroom, the teacher's role becomes that of a "relator" who helps the child respect and accept himself. The child in turn accepts and respects others, and he shares in making decisions and in solving problems that pertain both to himself and to the group.

In Chapter 3, quasi-democratic forces in the classroom and their effects on the child are examined, followed by a counter-description of the way things are, or could be, in a political environment that serves humane ends. This chapter serves as a prelude to Chapters 4 and 5, which depict teaching as "relating."

THE MICROSOCIETY OF THE CLASSROOM AND DEMOCRATIC IDEALS

The school is really a microsociety that reflects the values and attitudes of the larger macrosociety— the home, community and nation—that forms the real world of the child. Society has vested authority in the teacher, who is charged with the duty of educating the young. The young are required to belong to the group. (Children do not usually choose their classroom social groups, nor do teachers control the membership.) Except in cases where the district has open enrollment or where children are deliberately bused for the purposes of integration, children are thrown together because their parents reside in a given community, either by choice or happenstance. In any case, they bring their own selves and the values they absorb from their culture with them.

American children live in a political democracy and are circumscribed by the values that are held by its people, as well as by the justices and injustices the system has imposed on them, either directly or indirectly. The school has its own structures, rules and authority, which may be a mocking contradiction to the mores of the world the child knows. The school says: "You must be clean. You must use standard American English. You must not fight." On the other hand, the community subculture may condone physical combat, rather than "put-downs" or verbal "shoot-outs," for settling disputes. The language of the people who live in the area may differ greatly from standard American English. Because schools have their own structures and authoritative relationships, children are indeed involved in an environment that is not only social or interpersonal but that may be more accurately termed *political.*

Classroom groups are pockets of society organized to prepare the growing young to fit eventually into the maelstrom of productive economic life. These microsocieties ought to promote basic human values and develop human potentials—the goals of the democratic society. But the furthering of human values is not always compatible with the expectations of the macrosociety, which demands that individuals be adjusted to the society, that they fit in socially and economically. Herein lies a dilemma: Concern with basic human values and concern for getting the individual ready for society are not necessarily compatible expectations—at least when viewed through traditional school practice. The demands placed upon the school by the macrosociety inheres in an organization involving a power structure. To get the job done, control of individuals and groups of individuals takes place through the influence of the teacher, who, in turn, must fit into the bureaucratic structure of the school.

Analysis of Political Factors in Classrooms

What are the political arrangements in the classroom, or the means through which teachers influence, control and make decisions? How are these arrangements related to the ideals of a political democracy—freedom, justice, equality and respect for the dignity and worth of the individual? How do they relate to pragmatic practice and the real values of the American macrosociety?

Let us look first at the concept of freedom. Compulsory attendance laws require that children attend school. In traditional classrooms, the curriculum is set before children, and the role of the teacher is first that of a presenter or displayer of materials, and then that of an evaluator or judge who determines how well the child is doing in relationship to school expectations, which place high value on verbal performance, extrinsically motivated through grades. In the classroom as in the macrosociety, a tremendous sorting process takes place, so that certain talents and attainments (such as learning to read) are rewarded, but other talents are ignored. Children acquire their sense of self-worth through these evaluations made by the school. They become competitors for rewards and seek to raise their self-esteem through outdoing others. The "turned off" (and children drop out of school psychically long before the legal age) seek other avenues for status, which may force them into the role of hostile troublemaker or compliant do-gooder.

Dreikurs, an Adlerian psychoanalyst, classified children by life styles (1968). He referred to them as the "active-constructives" (those, for example, who wish to be first in their class); "active-destructives" (the clowns, bullies or defiant rebels); the "passive-constructives" (the charmers who succeed in receiving special attention and favor without doing anything themselves); and the "passive-destructives" (the lazy and stubborn). The role the child selects to play is determined by his orientation to life. The school, although it probably did not begin the orientation, is certainly responsible for perpetuating it.

Freedom to rise, or social mobility—a value permeating the macrosociety—has also led to an emphasis on performance in the educational sector. Standardized tests have been used to sort children out on a continuum of superior to inferior achievement, and there is a trend to hold the school accountable for educational performance as judged by achievement tests. The success syndrome, especially prevalent in middle-class homes, hangs heavy over the heads of many children. Schools have used a single criterion—academic achievement—to let children know whether or not they are valued in the school culture. Although assigning grades to academic achievement has served as a spur to some children, it has also led to superficiality in meeting the overall goals of education. The grading system usually gives great status to the aggressive or the competitive, but penalizes children of passive temperaments, those of lesser verbal intelligence, and those who may bloom late but do very well when given time to mature. (Often these last children are among the gifted but are labeled early in life as slow learners or underachievers.)

Most schools emphasize competition rather than cooperation, and children are even told they are cheating if they help each other. I recall one classroom where the student teacher was so distrustful of her second graders that she barricaded the children's vision with books so they would not "cheat." Competition is used to spur children onward, and there is room at the top for only a few. Even the gifted have few alternatives in which to excel or simply enjoy. The middle grade child is caught in the press for the kind of individual performance that is valued by teachers and parents, while the social mores of his age group may devalue grades or school industry, and the child may forfeit his production in order to be accepted by the group.

"Justice" and "equality" (or "injustice" and "inequality") in the classroom are usually meted out by the teacher through his judgments. To gain favor with the judge, children may learn to apple-polish or may become compliant. Research into creativity has shown that the creative—the non-conforming, divergent thinkers who insist on head-

ing their papers their own way, or coloring the grass yellow instead of green, or drawing their own umbrella instead of coloring the ones on the page, or being on cloud nine while the rest of the class is on page fifty-seven—are usually not very well liked by their teachers. A friend recently confessed to me that her daughter, an excellent seamstress, had done very poorly in sewing class, because she had machine-stitched the band around a skirt, foregoing the hand-done whipping stitch. Through observation, the girl knew that the band of a store-bought garment is stitched by machine, but her nonconformance to classroom standards brought her a low grade.

The school often stresses achievement to the detriment of childhood. Most Americans worship success that is measured in limited, economic terms. In existential terms, success and achievement are the by-products of self-expression and using one's potentialities. It is a matter of where we place the emphasis.

Some unfortunate children come from homes where parents live vicariously through them; the child is valued not for himself, but as a means of realizing the competitive ambitions of Mother or Dad. Instead of receiving the foundations for self-esteem, such children are used to fulfill the parents' status needs. In a competitive school situation, these children often become the "I-can't-ers" or the "attention getters,"—"active-destructives" or the "passive-destructives" in Dreikurs' classification. They have little chance of finding their true selves or of being appreciated for what they are innately.

Coopersmith (1967), in his study of the antecedents of self-esteem, has shown that parents who give children warmth, clearly defined limits, and acceptance for their feelings and views successfully communicate a concern for the child's welfare. These are the kinds of emotional supports young children need for a sense of being valued and loved, for building a positive self-image. Children who come to school with a head start toward an adequate self have some basis upon which to counteract the negative devaluing effect that the school may have. A child without home support has a chance to see himself differently at school, if the teacher is warm, is respectful and provides defining limits—but the child who gets support from neither home nor school has little chance of ever viewing himself with real esteem. Happy is the child who is supported in both home and school!

Combs, drawing from the yearbook *Perceiving, Behaving, Becoming,* has listed factors that hinder an atmosphere for growth and creativity in the classroom. Viewed from the orientation presented in this chapter, these factors are largely political:

1. *Preoccupation with order, categorization, and classifying.*
2. *Overvaluing authority, support, evidence, and the "scientific method"—all the good answers are someone else's.*
3. *Exclusive emphasis upon the historical view, implying that all the good things have been discovered already.*
4. *Cookbook approaches, filling in the blanks.*
5. *Solitary learning, discouraging communication.*
6. *The elimination of self from the classroom— only what the book says is important, not what I think.*
7. *Emphasis upon force, threat, or coercion. What diminishes the self diminishes creativity.*
8. *The idea that mistakes are sinful.*
9. *The idea that students are not be trusted.*
10. *Lock-step organization.*[1]

Power Structure of the Classroom

In comparing the microsociety of the classroom with the socio-political macrosociety, it becomes obvious that the classroom contains an organization of individuals that inherently involves a power structure, too. In this environment, actions take place and limits are set that control individuals and groups. It is inherent in any social structure that there be authority of a sort, to cement the organization together and to keep it moving toward its goals. But the question is, *Whose* authority? The teacher, through ascribed leadership, is the authority figure of the classroom. Sometimes teachers reign with very tight control, but if children do not meet their own status needs, they will vie for power within the socio-dynamics of the classroom, either with the teacher or with other children. In

the class social structure some influential key figures are accorded prestige, while others are sifted hierarchically into a social continuum from top to bottom. Human relationships become politicized as they are transformed into power relationships. Bad feelings result, as children see that some members have more worth than others.

The alienation and apathy of powerless groups plague society at large. Apathy is also prevalent in many classrooms, especially among groups that have been sorted into the lower echelons of society or the classroom social structure. For this reason, sociologist Dan Dodson maintains that classrooms should be laboratories where children learn how to take power, while the group is shielded from power that is abused. Teachers should give children experience in shared decision making and should help them examine the responsibilities that go with the power to decide and to choose. In order to overcome apathy and make it safe for children to examine issues confronting the group, it is incumbent upon the teacher to build an emotional climate where status needs of all children are met, where each child has opportunities to lead as well as to follow and where every child can be noticed and appreciated for his human qualities.

As teachers exert their authority in the classroom, three influences impinge upon them—some operating from within the teacher himself, some operating within the class as a decision-making body, and some operating from outside the teacher or the group. Certain decisions may be handed down by administrative fiat to the teacher— acceptable behavior in the halls, playground and cafeteria is prescribed; a certain grading system is used; curriculum guides must be followed. These decisions may be influenced by outside forces such as community pressure. Teachers, in turn hand these decisions down to the group. Other decisions the teacher makes because of his knowledge of the class and the responsibility he inwardly feels toward his pupils. But if he is to establish a climate for learning that is humanizing, he must allow children to participate in areas of decision making where they perceive themselves as able doers assuming responsibility for their actions. In classrooms where most of the curriculum is imposed from above or outside, these decisions may be as simple as resolving conflicts within the group, deciding what to do in free time, determining equitable access to interest centers, or using committees for a class party.

Teachers are circumscribed with political forces, which often hinder them in their work. They need to recognize these forces for what they are, even if they cannot change them; at least, they can try to bring counteracting forces into the classroom to balance the negative effects that may be brought in from the outside. Jackson has pointed out in *Life in Classrooms* (1968) that the bureaucratic structure of the school has a hidden agenda, which is antagonistic to and more real than many of the experiences introduced into the curriculum to promote "social learning." Teachers often have no control over these outside forces; they are usually required, for example, to "grade" and to enforce school rules and regulations, such as lining up in the halls, even though they may not believe in the established policies.

Sarason made a study of "constitutional issues," to find out whether teachers shared with children the responsibility and opportunity to set the rules, or *modus operandi*, of the classroom. He discovered that children are usually not involved at all:

We did an informal observational study of six classrooms, two each in grades 3, 4, and 5 in a suburban school system. In each of these six classrooms we had an observer who sat in the classroom for the first month of school beginning on the first day. The task of the observer was to record any statement by teacher and child that was relevant to "constitutional issues." The results were quite clear:

1. *The constitution was invariably determined by the teacher. No teacher ever discussed why a constitution was necessary.*

2. *The teacher never solicited the opinions and feelings of any pupil about a constitutional question.*

3. *In three of the classrooms the rules of the game were verbalized by the end of the first week of school. In two others the rules were clear by the end of the month. In one it was never clear what the constitution was.*

4. *Except for the one chaotic classroom neither children nor teachers evidenced any discomfort with the content of constitutions–it was as if everyone agreed that this is the way things are and should be.*

5. *In all instances constitutional issues involved what children could or could not, should or should not, do. The issue of what a teacher could or could not, should or should not do, never arose.*[2]

In the course of this study, Sarason worked quite intensively with the teachers and reported that after extended discussion the teachers were finally able to verbalize the following assumptions that related to their "constitutional" behavior:

1. *Teacher knows best.*

2. *Children cannot participate constructively in the development of a classroom constitution.*

3. *Children want and expect the teacher to determine the rules of the game.*

4. *Children are not interested in constitutional issues.*

5. *Children should be governed by what a teacher thinks is right or wrong, but a teacher should not be governed by what children think is right or wrong.*

6. *The ethics of adults are obviously different from and superior to the ethics of children.*

7. *Children should not be given responsibility for something they cannot handle or for which they are not accountable.*

8. *If constitutional issues were handled differently, chaos might result.*[3]

Sarason goes on to say:

If one does not make these assumptions, which is to say that one thinks differently about what children are and can do, one is very likely to think differently about what the role of the teacher might be. In this connection it is instructive to note that as I pursued the issues with the groups of teachers, and the assumptions could be clearly verbalized, many of the teachers found themselves disagreeing with assumptions they themselves recognized as underlying their classroom behavior.

Equally as instructive was the awareness on the part of a few that if one changed one's assumptions one would have to change the character of one's role, and this was strange and upsetting, as indeed it should be because they realized that life in the classroom for them and the children would become different.[4]

As Sarason worked with these teachers he was overwhelmed to discover that several teachers in the group were adamant in their view, saying, in effect, that young children must have their lives structured for them by adults "because they were too immature to participate in and take responsibility for important decisions governing classroom life." "What I became aware of," says Sarason, "was that these teachers thought about children in precisely the same way that teachers say that school administrators think about teachers; that is, administrators do not discuss matters with teachers, they do not act as if the opinions of teachers were important, they treat teachers like a bunch of children. . . "[5]

Dreikurs, noting the inconsistencies in American society, pointed out that the adult population—and especially teachers in schools—tends to hold social values that are not compatible with democratic values. In order to develop the "good" student, teachers frequently reinforce "the desire for self-elevation, the idea of perfectionism, the idea of masculinity and femininity, the fear of mistakes, the desire for personal success, and the idea that reason and objectivity are always preferable to emotion and subjectivity." Probably, because teachers succeeded with these values in their own school experience in authoritarian classrooms, they now enjoy their status and power in acting out the same values in their own classrooms. However, if schools are to be humanistic, teachers should be valuing "unique usefulness, cooperation, and relationships as equals rather than self-elevation or personal success . . . humanness rather than masculinity or femininity as such . . . the courage to be imperfect rather than perfectionism and the ensuing fear of mistakes; and valuing and trusting emotions and subjectivity as complementary modes of reason and objectivity."[6] Teachers would do well to rethink the values that are promoting their own classroom behavior.

THE POLITICAL ENVIRONMENT OF THE HUMANISTIC CLASSROOM

Let us look now at an idealized classroom environment that evolves from humanistic concerns. In this environment, mutual trust and respect exist between teacher and pupil and among pupils, and there is a climate of freedom that permits children to pursue individual goals. Absorbed in work that has personal meaning for him, each child sees himself as a creature of value—as having a unique contribution to make. All types of abilities and contributions are recognized and appreciated: Susan draws well and is the key person in designing scenery for the play that will be presented in the auditorium. Peter, newly immigrated from Germany, cannot yet speak English but designs the queen's crown with diligent aplomb. Bill, although mediocre in academic ability, brings his hammer and nails to school, constructing a library corner and display table out of plywood and orange crates. Ken, two books "below grade level" in reading, is good in sports and is frequently a team leader on the playground. Jack, a science wizard, stimulates the class by bringing in his outside projects. Shy Penny is in charge of refreshments at the Valentine party. Judy, Barbara and David are good readers, organize well, and frequently lend their talents as leaders in interest groups. Gary has a sense of humor and breaks the tension when the atmosphere is "up tight." Joe is always reliable and follows through in organizing the class to clean up the "messes." On and on it goes—each child discovers he has a talent that is appreciated by the teacher and in turn by other children. The teacher uncovers talents and works these into class activities in the ongoing stream of events. Children become aware of the unique contributions each can make, and they gain respect for one another. They develop pride in the group esprit de corps and become mutually supportive.

Decisions regarding the choice and nature of classroom work are shared among teacher and children, increasing the probability that each child will give his fullest endeavor. Teachers encourage children to suggest and help plan topics of study. These may range from snakes, to weather, to astronauts, to bird houses, to cooking, to any other demonstrated interest of a child or the group.

Mini-groups are formed, with the teacher serving as a resource person and guide rather than as a foreman overseeing the job. Interests are contagious, and topics are repeated for children who have caught the excitement of their peers. Children may be caught up in publishing a class paper, running a school store, following the development of the current astronaut flight, or trying to reach a goal they have set for themselves. Children are engaged in meaningful work for their own reasons, not merely those of the teacher. The demands of the situation impose a discipline that is needed to get the job done. Cooperation is usually needed, and often there is a differentiation in task.

At other times, "learning and living together" problems arise, which require group problem solving. For example, following the Kent State incident and upheavals on the local college campus, a group of fourth-grade boys decided to stage a fight with the girls on the playground. Although both the principal and classroom teacher were aware of the brewing problem, they did not head off the plot but allowed the crisis to develop; then they dealt with it in a talk-out discussion in the classroom, where the children, using their own common sense, realized where and why things had gone wrong and the folly of their actions. There was no recurrence of the problem; the children learned a greater sense of responsibility for their actions.

LEADERSHIP OF THE TEACHER

It can be seen from the foregoing discussion that much revolves around the leadership of the teacher and that his leadership may work to either free the child or close him off. In the humanistic classroom, the role of the teacher in creating the environment of social climate and structure is primarily that of a helpful "relator" who facilitates growth, rather than that of a "benevolent dictator" who seeks power as a means of compensating for his own deprivation or of overcoming his own low estimate of self. The major function of teaching in the humanistic classroom is, in fact, "relating"; the mode of relating developed within the classroom affects the perceptions of the pupil regarding himself and his world, and is highly significant in determining, in turn, the mode through which the child learns to relate.

However, it should not be construed that teacher authority in itself is bad; it is only the misuse of authority that has been decried by critics of the autocratic classroom. Lest confusion arise, it should be remembered that the teacher has the ascribed status of classroom leader. In his attempt to be a democratic leader, the teacher should view himself as the senior partner but should not abdicate his leadership role, even though he encourages leadership to shift temporarily to various class members.

Children need the security of a responsible adult who is always there. Removing adult authority does not create a climate of freedom for children. In fact, the tyranny of a peer power takeover will likely ensue if a responsible adult is not present to guide (even though it may be from backstage). Dennison has aptly pointed out, in *Lives of Children*, that teachers have a responsibility to pupils: they must provide an environment where children can learn. He refers to a "natural authority" possessed by adults, because they have lived longer and have experienced more. This is legitimate authority:

When [the teacher's authority] takes on a positive instead of a merely negative character, the children see the adults as protectors and as sources of certitude, approval, novelty, skills. In the fact that adults have entered into prior agreements, children intuit a seriousness and a web of relations in the life that surrounds them. If it is a bit mysterious, it is also impressive and somewhat attractive; they see it quite correctly as the way of the world, and they are not indifferent to its benefits and demands. These two things, taken together— the natural authority of adults and the needs of children—are the great reservoir of the organic structuring that comes into being when arbitrary rules of order are dispensed with. The child is always finding himself, moving toward himself, as it were, in the near distance. The adult is his ally, his model—and his obstacle (for there are natural conflicts, too, and they must be given their due).[7]

The question, then, is not an "either-or" one of teacher authority *vs.* pupil self-determination. Rather, it is a question of the *style* of authority the teacher employs. Authoritative relationships revolve deeply around the personality structure of the teacher, causing teachers to be controlling and withholding—or freeing and open—in their relationships with children. The teacher needs a clear sense of identity, if he is to be a leader who is open, expansive and always vigilant in seeing opportunities to bring out the best in children. He needs to be free from psychological defenses that may befog his own perceptions. His visibility and respect in the classroom are brought about by his own authenticity as a person who respects and believes in others as well as in himself. His relationship to the child, as suggested by Fromm, should be that of a rational authority who is leading the child to expanding levels of independence and freedom, rather than that of an irrational authority who reinforces a relationship resembling that of master and slave, in which the child is kept in a continuing state of dependence and self-degradation.

How does a teacher establish an environment in which pupils can become involved in meaningful work, can make decisions cooperatively and can enter into helpful interpersonal relationships? Such an egalitarian environment is established primarily through the teacher's own mode of relating. From the Frommian view, the mode may be described as one of "unconditional love" or "unconditional acceptance" of the worth of each child. From a political view, it may be thought of as the democratic mode. In this milieu, all the children are viewed with respect and worth, because they are they. Respect and love of the teacher is not purchased by behavior conforming to the teacher's wishes; rather, the behavior of the pupil becomes constructive as he finds his place as a person of worth within the classroom group. The pupil is not dependent on the teacher for a sense of self through praise given for conforming. Rather, the teacher helps the child to discover and trust his uniqueness, and to express himself in the ongoing activities of the classroom. The teacher's way of relating becomes contagious (albeit by small degrees, at times), so that a special kind of communication system develops. The teacher relates to each child on the child's own wavelength, so that children begin to recognize and value their own special qualities and their own individuality.

The teacher moves in and helps disturbed children before they reach their frustration levels; he reassures shy children until they begin to trust their own judgments; he makes suggestions to puzzled children to help them on their way; he gives a smile or a nod to the children who are absorbed and working diligently on their own. He takes note of children's out-of-school activities and remembers to inquire about them. He kids the jovial children but talks seriously with the sensitive ones. A nonverbal esprit de corps develops, which enables the children to become active in discovering their own goals.

Children who are made to feel adequate and comfortable with themselves—just the way they are—have a basis for confidence that will enable them to become independent as well as interdependent beings, who trust their own judgments and are able to proceed in their unique ways while also valuing their neighbors. The kind of political environment the teacher is seeking makes possible, in Jasper's words, "the interlinkage of independent human beings." In this environment, children become "aware of their duty to discover one another, to help one another onward wherever they encounter one another, and to be ever ready for communication, on the watch, but without importunacy. Though they have entered into no formal agreement, they hold together with loyalty which is stronger than any formal agreement could give."[8] Growth occurs when there is interdependence or reciprocal dependence, when goals are determined jointly, when there is mutual trust and real communication.

It is a tall order to create an environment that frees people to grow. The teacher must be a leader *par excellence* to do so, because success depends upon relating individually to pupils and helping them identify personal goals, while at the same time helping them work as a unit toward group goals or within group structure. Both individual and group confrontation are sometimes necessary.

In the two chapters that follow, the person of the teacher and his relationship to individuals and the classroom group will be amplified, and models of "helping behavior" and group problem solving will be reported. An inventory of the behavior of the teacher as a "relator" will conclude the next chapter in "The Face of Relationship," Part I of the book. Teaching procedures that contribute to the concept of meaningful work in the classroom will be dealt with in Part II, "The Face of Mediation." Classroom organization for group interdependent living will be discussed in Part IV, "The Face of Choreography."

Notes

[1] Arthur W. Combs, *The Professional Education of Teachers* (Boston: Allyn and Bacon, Inc., 1965), p. 36.

[2] Seymour B. Sarason, *The Culture of the School and the Problem of Change* (Boston: Allyn and Bacon, 1971), p. 175.

[3] Ibid., p. 176.

[4] Ibid., p. 177.

[5] Ibid., p. 177.

[6] Arthur W. Combs, ed., *Perceiving, Behaving, Becoming* (Washington, D.C.: Association for Supervision and Curriculum Development Yearbook, 1962), p. 204.

[7] George Dennison, *The Lives of Children* (New York: Random House, 1969), pp. 24, 25.

[8] Karl Jaspers, "Man in the Modern Age," in *Existential Encounters for Teachers,* ed. Maxine Greene (New York: Random House, 1967), pp. 46, 47. Reprinted by permission of Farrar, Straus & Giroux, Inc.

References

Combs, Arthur W. *The Professional Education of Teachers.* Boston: Allyn and Bacon, Inc., 1965.

Coopersmith, Stanley. *The Antecedents of Self-Esteem.* San Francisco: W. H. Freeman, 1967.

Dennison, George. *The Lives of Children.* New York: Random House, Inc., 1969.

Dodson, Dan. "Education and the Powerless." In *Education of the Disadvantaged,* edited by Harry A. Passow et al. New York: Holt, Rinehart and Winston, Inc., 1967.

Dreikurs, Rudolph. *Psychology in the Classroom.* New York: Harper & Row, 1968.

Fromm, Erich. *The Art of Loving.* New York: Bantam Books, Harper & Row, Publishers, 1956.

Gardner, John W. *Excellence: Can We Be Equal and Excellent Too?* New York: Harper Colophon Books, Harper & Row, Publishers, 1961.

Greene, Maxine, ed. *Existential Encounters for Teachers.* New York: Random House, 1967.

Jackson, Philip W. *Life in Classrooms.* New York: Holt, Rinehart and Winston, Inc., 1968.

Lasswell, Harold D. *Power and Personality.* New York: The Viking Press, 1962.

Sarason, Seymour B. *The Culture of the School and the Problem of Change.* Boston: Allyn and Bacon, 1971.

Sorauf, Francis J. *Political Science.* The Charles E. Merrill Social Science Seminar Series, edited by Raymond H. Muessig and Vincent R. Rogers, Columbus, Ohio: Charles E. Merrill Books, Inc., 1965.

Thelen, Herbert A. "Group Interactional Factors in Learning." In *Behavioral Science Frontiers in Education,* edited by Eli M. Bower and G. Hollister. New York: John Wiley and Sons, Inc., 1967.

Chapter 4

Teaching Is Relating

Teaching is relating. A teacher relates to his subject matter, and he relates to the pupil. If he does not, he is not a teacher. He will not inspire and he will not promote personal growth. Knowledge is not enough and a dynamic personality is not enough, if the teacher uses his erudition and dynamism only as a means of enhancing himself. The teacher must be fundamentally concerned about the person he is teaching, and he must see his role as a facilitator of growth. His joy is in watching pupils unfold. He gets his greatest pleasure, in fact, when he sees independence released, creativity flower, individuality emerge—when he sees self-actualization in process.

The teacher has two resources at his disposal. He has his own person. Being a facilitator of growth depends, first of all, upon what the teacher *is*—he must be a special kind of person, for he uses himself as an "instrument"[1] to help others. Second, the knowledgeable "relator" exercises growth-facilitating skills that can become built-in dispositions to act in freeing ways. The teacher must learn to (1) impart trust, (2) understand the child accurately and unambiguously, (3) influence and help the child, and (4) constructively resolve problems and conflicts with the child or the group.[2] If the teacher is to maintain his authenticity, these skills must become a natural part of his behavioral repertoire.

In this chapter we will look at the teacher as an authentic person, at his skills in interpersonal relationships and at models or technologies for facilitating the "helping" process. These models illustrate and elaborate on relating and helping skills described in the earlier part of the chapter.

THE AUTHENTIC TEACHER

If the teacher is an authentic person, then he can be an authentic teacher. What a teacher is as a human being is probably the greatest determiner in establishing effective relationships.[3] If he knows himself, accepts himself and is open to his experience, then he can relate naturally and authentically to those he teaches without feeling threatened; he can grow toward his own becoming, in a mutual interchange with the children whom he, in turn, is influencing. If the teacher has thought through the values he lives by, he will develop a consistency that others can count on and can trust. If he is emotionally secure and independent as a human being, acting out of his own sense of values, and if he can maintain his separateness from others and value their differences without requiring that the others conform to his values, then he can help the child grow in self-trust and independence. If he knows his own strengths and limitations, and can accept them and still like himself, then he is free to express warmth, caring, liking, and respect for other people. The teacher needs the courage of imperfection, the ability to fail. He must free himself from unresolved conflicts over his own relationships to authority, which may compel him to dominate and control. Probably most important, the teacher needs to be a spontaneous person who has entered fully into the joy of living, who is interested in people and who is aware of the world about him and the possibilities of life.

Moustakas has pointed out that "freedom, love, beauty, justice and truth" are values that separate superficiality and trivia from meaning and depth in a relationship. "If there is love and honesty in the individual and in his relationships, then the person is genuinely present . . . in such a way that his freedom is used responsibly."[4] When the teacher fails to see the child, first of all as a human being, and then fails to enfold the child's presence as a *person*, there is no reality between them, no mutuality and no relationship. "The significant adult must exist for the growing [child] as someone there, to be met, related to and affected by, as a real person whose very presence helps to evolve awareness and beauty, stimulates and challenges potentialities, and provides an opportunity for expansion of self in the aesthetic and spiritual realm as well as in intellectual pursuits."[5]

Moustakas, in his book *The Authentic Teacher*, describes an experience revealing the negative effects of a teacher's relationship on a child:

Recently, I visited a second-grade classroom during a reading lesson. When the children saw the principal and me enter the room, they were eager to read to us. The teacher asked for volunteers. A child, with a smiling face and shining eyes, sitting next to me, is called to read. She sighs with joy as she begins, "Casey joins the Circus." Apparently, she has learned that a good reader varies her tone of voice, reads loud enough for others to hear and

reads fluently. Wanting to make an impression, wanting to get the praise of her teacher and class-mates, she hurries through the paragraph assigned to her. But something is wrong, Mrs. Bell interrupts the child. She pushes the book away from the child's face and says in a slow deliberate voice, hovering over the child, "You are reading carelessly. That's not showing respect for what is printed on the page. It's not showing respect for our visitors or the other boys and girls. You are making sense but you simply are not reading the words in the book. I've told you about this before, Betsy. Now you go back and read what's printed there so we can all follow you." The child returns to the beginning of the paragraph but something has happened. She has no direct, open way of responding. The staring, judging faces of the other children frighten her. She reads in a reluctant manner, pronounces words haltingly. There is a weak, muffled quality in her voice. She has been hurt. She is no longer certain. She completes the reading and slumps wearily into her chair.

The real tragedy is not in the critical words of the teacher or in the subdued, minimized child, but in the fact that no relationship exists. There is the teacher as law-giver and statement-giver, as the one in authority. There is the adult voice, belittling, shaming, minimizing, humiliating the child into exact reading. The teacher uses the visitors, the other children, herself, to prove her point and impress the child. She does not keep the issue between herself and the child, where it belongs. And it is all done matter-of-factly, as professional duty. It is all so impersonal and feelingless.[6]

INTERPERSONAL SKILLS OF THE AUTHENTIC TEACHER

Imparting Trust

Little happens in a relationship, until people learn to trust each other. Forming a climate of trust is one of the most important tasks of the teacher. His own empathy helps, and if the teacher can reduce the child's fear of rejection, failure and betrayal, a reciprocal trust and acceptance will result. Empathy is essential in a relationship that has meaning and depth. The teacher needs the ability to see the world through the child's eyes and to enter into the legitimacy of the child's feelings. He remembers his own feelings of ecstasy when he successfully read the first page in the primer all by himself, or when he swished the gooey paints around with his fingertips and made a picture of his own house. He also feels the anger and despair of the child who is thwarted by unmet wants or needs.

Authentic teachers are open with children. The open teacher is interested in the child and in what he is saying or doing—and he also shows the child that it is important for him to know what the child feels and thinks about what he, the teacher, is saying and doing. The teacher discloses his own feelings to the child, and if he is successful in developing a climate of trust, the child will become self-disclosing also. When a child expresses his feelings of anxiety or inability to perform a task, it is important that the teacher accept and support him: "Long division is really hard. I remember what a rough time I had when I was in the fourth grade. Let's see if we can figure out what is troubling you," says the teacher. Judging statements, on the other hand, cut off communication: "You have not been trying very hard. . . . This is easy and if you would pay attention when I explain the work, you would know how to do this."

Honesty, consistency, empathy, acceptance, openness and being genuine about one's feelings are the pathways leading to trust. These qualities are consciously developed by the humanistic teacher.

Accurately and Unambiguously Understanding the Child

By listening accurately and carefully observing the child's behavior with an eye to seeing how things are from his point of view, the teacher picks up many clues that help him understand the child. The humanistic teacher does not try to press his own thinking and feeling on the child. Rather, he paraphrases the child's thoughts, or he reflects back statements of feeling to let the child know he is heard and understood.

The following account, written by a student observer in a fifth grade classroom, illustrates the value of empathy and attentive listening. She reports:

This incident took place in the afternoon around one o'clock. I wanted to get to know the students on an individual basis. Several times I would just go and sit next to a child and start talking to him, not relating as a teacher to student, but just as a friend. By doing this I learned a lot about the children. One day in particular I noticed a girl, Karen, just sitting at her desk, with her head on her hands just staring away. I went over and sat by her.

ME: Karen, what's up, what are you doing?

KAREN: Oh, nothing, just sitting here.

ME: It seems as though you don't feel like doing anything. I get that way a lot, too. Sometimes I don't feel like doing anything at all.

KAREN: (Pausing and thinking awhile) . . . Well, maybe that's true, I don't know.
(A little conversation went back and forth, then Karen came out with a remark that shocked me.)

KAREN: (Stuttering) I think . . . (pause) . . . I think I don't like myself.

ME: You don't like yourself. . . . I wonder why (musing).

KAREN: I'm ugly and I probably will never get married. Oh maybe, when I'm 80, but that's too late!

ME: You're worried already about getting married. . . . (pause) . . . You know, I think you're very cute.

KAREN: No, I'm not cute!

ME: Karen, looks are not everything. They're nice, but it really matters more if people are nice to each other. Just as long as everyone is happy and you help make other people happy.

KAREN: Well, I'm not always nice to other people and they're not always nice to me.

ME: Well, everyone does have good and bad days and their ups and downs.

KAREN: I think I'm just not happy with myself. (I was surprised but did not show it. There was a pause without a response from me.)

KAREN: You know what I see when I look in the mirror at myself? I see nothing, just nothing! I don't like myself when I look at myself so now when I have to look at myself I see nothing. (She said this very strongly.)

ME: You don't like yourself so when you look at yourself you see nothing. . . . Karen, you seem to have really thought a lot about this.

KAREN: I have, but now, I don't like to think of myself at all.

(By some stroke of luck I was saved by a switch of classes. I was shocked to hear this from a ten-year-old and didn't know what to do. I told Mrs. C. She was surprised but not as much as I was. She feels Karen is insecure because recently her parents opened a store and have had to be there almost all day until 11:00 at night. She thinks it's been hard for Karen to adjust to being on her own and alone so much.)

Although this illustration does not show a solution to a problem, the door has been opened to further communication. Karen has been listened to and knows that someone cares about her and understands. A basis of trust has been established.

The manner of listening and responding to the child is crucial in building a meaningful relationship where the teacher can enter, psychologically, for a moment into the world of the child and can accurately and unambiguously understand him. When the teacher really hears what the child is saying and responds relevantly, he lets the child know that he cares about him and really wants to understand. But if the teacher fails to listen and responds irrelevantly, he says in effect, "I don't care about what you are saying, and I don't want to understand it."[7]

The Carkhuff and Gordon models presented later in this chapter emphasize tuning in on clues that indicate the meaning of the child's behavior.

Influencing and Helping the Child

"Accentuate the positive" is a good slogan for teachers to follow. Nothing succeeds like success. Otto (1968) proved this point in experimental classes conducted for the purpose of developing human potential. His most successful techniques emphasized positive experiences and concentrated on strengths. He also showed through psychological tests that tired children gain new energy when they are commended and that their energies diminish

markedly when they are either discouraged or criticized.

When a climate of warmth and acceptance is present in a relationship, the teacher can confront the child and help him build a realistic view of himself. The child knows he's "okay," even though he may have some academic weaknesses. Constructive comments pay off, when children know the teacher is on their side. Feedback is important in a learning situation and can be received with profit when the focus is kept off the person and directed instead toward specific situations or behaviors in the "here and now," when it concentrates on accomplishments rather than on the person's self. Even praise can be harmful, if it focuses on the person's self rather than on what he has done: "You are being very helpful in straightening up the library table," is more constructive than saying, "You are a good boy." Johnny may seriously doubt that he is a good boy, but knowing he has been helpful makes him feel good (Ginott, 1969).

Constructive feedback and honest confrontation are important steps in opening the child to growth. Glasser's model of Reality Therapy (reviewed in the last section of this chapter) is instructive here. Gordon and Carkhuff have also shown how confrontations may be used successfully.

Constructively Resolving Problems and Conflicts
with the Child or the Group

Resolving conflicts and interpersonal problems is probably the most difficult of the teacher's tasks. He needs to allow for the separateness of the child and to enter into his "feeling world" empathically. If the teacher recognizes the legitimacy of the child's experience, he allows the child to be himself and to be in disagreement with him (the teacher) if need be. Even when the child behaves in ways that are offensive or disruptive, the teacher can express acceptance of the child's person.

Ginott, in his bestseller *Between Parent and Child,* has called attention to the importance of handling feelings separately from acts; he believes the cornerstone to discipline is the "distinction between wishes and acts." We may need to set limits on acts, but we should not restrict wishes or eliminate feelings. Sometimes dealing with feelings takes care of the problem, as exemplified in the following dialogue:

MOTHER: It looks as if you are angry today.

SON: I sure am!

MOTHER: You feel kind of mean inside.

SON: You said it!

MOTHER: You are angry at someone.

SON: Yes, you.

MOTHER: Tell me about it.

SON: You didn't take me to the Little League game, but you took Steve.

MOTHER: That made you angry. I bet you said to yourself, "She loves him more than she loves me."

SON: Yes.

MOTHER: Sometimes you really feel that way.

SON: I sure do.

MOTHER: You know, dear, when you feel that way, come and tell me.

At other times, limits must be set. When mother found Ted, age five, doodling on her living-room wall, her first reaction was to pummel him. But he looked so scared that she could not bring herself to hit him. Instead she said, "No, Ted, walls are not for drawing. Paper is. Here are three sheets of paper." And mother started cleaning up the wall. Ted was so overwhelmed that he said, "I love you, mommy."[8]

When children are caught up in disputes, the teacher draws each one out and discovers that facts have different and special meanings to everyone involved. His sphere of perception is wide enough to see them all. The following accounts of student observers illustrate the point. The first account describes the intervention of the student with an angry, disgruntled child who was "turned off" by the teacher:

Friday, Nov. 12, 1:30:

We were in another room for a music class. I was sitting there watching the children when I became involved with one student. The music teacher brought in several new instruments to explain and teach the children how to play. A group of boys were causing trouble.

MUSIC TEACHER: Boys, if you can't listen, then you can leave, you're not disrupting *my* class!

Roy, one of the boys, mimicked her. The music teacher ignored his behavior. During the whole class there was a constant battle between Roy and the teacher. When it was time to dismiss for P.E., the teacher said the girls could go first because they knew how to behave.

ROY: I don't have to wait. (He pushed a few girls, knocked down a chair and ran out.)

(The music teacher, in dismay and disgust, just let him go, saying nothing. I ran after Roy and made him walk back.)

ME: Roy, you don't seem to be very happy. What's troubling you?

ROY: Nothing's the matter.

ME: You seemed to be upset in music, but nothing is the matter.

ROY: I hate music! and besides she steals those instruments. (Pauses a few minutes.) I don't know. I just said that because I hate the teacher and music.

ME: Do you think anyone else in that class enjoys music?

ROY: Yes.

ME: Should they get the chance to enjoy it?

ROY: (After thinking awhile) I guess just because I hate music I shouldn't stop them from enjoying it.

ME: If you think so, I guess so. Do you think you disrupted anyone else besides the students?

ROY: I guess I bothered the teacher, but she deserved it.

ME: (Trying to relate to Roy so he could understand better) Roy, what would you do or how would you feel if you put a certain model airplane together, looked up information about it to explain to the class, had everything planned to do and when you got up there, the kids decided they weren't interested and ruined your whole plan?

ROY: I'd beat them up!

ME: You'd feel that angry at them.

ROY: Well, yes, they ruined all my stuff.

ME: Roy, what do you think you just did in that classroom?

ROY: (After a few minutes he said with his head down and never once looking at me) I guess just because I didn't want to learn I shouldn't stop someone else. I could just sit there and not disrupt the music teacher's lesson.

ME: (Not knowing exactly what to say) I think we've just solved your problem. (Then I let him go on to his P.E. class.)

Perhaps not totally on target, the above incident does show constructive resolution of conflict. Although Roy did feel guilty and ashamed at one point (his head was hanging down, showing the possibility of self-devaluation), he became aware of how other people felt, and he did experience contact with a student teacher who cared enough about him to help him understand the point of view of other people and the consequences of his actions. A great deal of pent-up emotion was released.

The second account illustrates the common failure of teachers to let children air their grievances and to permit each one to express his point of view. The children did not feel heard, and in this case, as the reader will note, Terri felt unjustly treated and was probably left with bottled-up feelings of anger and revenge. This incident took place in the halls when the children were passing to the music class. They were asked to line up in an orderly manner and be quiet. The student observer was in the back and watched what happened between two boys and how a teacher took over. She writes:

Jeff pushed Terri. "Move," he said.

TERRI: Get out of here. (Terri pushed back at Jeff.)

(The two boys started a big commotion among the whole group of children. Mrs. C. saw this and came over.)

MRS. C.:   (Yelling at Terri and a boy named Mark) Terri and Mark, step out of line. The rest of you may go.

MARK: (Looking puzzled) What did I do? I was just standing in line. (I observed that he had been quiet and standing in line.)

TERRI: It's Jeff's fault, I didn't do anything. Why don't you go get him?

MRS. C.:   I saw that it was *you* causing the trouble.

(She continued to talk to both boys, but I was not able to stay there to see what happened. Both boys came into music class late. Mark sat down and participated with the class.)

TERRI: Jeff, you're going to get it. It's your fault. I'm going to beat you up for this.

JEFF: Oh, no, you're not. (They started fighting again.)

MUSIC TEACHER: Terri, leave the room and sit outside.

(Terri clenched his fist at Jeff and walked out. The music teacher went outside to talk to Terri. They both came back in, and Terri was quiet and sullen for the rest of the period.)

Listening to the child, resolving conflicts, getting problems aired and solved requires deft handling. Note the special techniques in the Gordon and Glasser models that follow.

MODELS OF RELATIONSHIPS

Those in the helping professions of psychotherapy, counseling and guidance have developed some specific models that may be used by anyone who wishes to be a helper—that is, in the sense of helping people to clarify their perceptions and feelings about self and others, and to resolve conflicts between and among people—including parents and teachers. In fact, many new books written by these professionals are addressed specifically to parents and teachers. In this section we will review three of these models: Robert Carkhuff's "Art of Helping," Thomas Gordon's "Effectiveness Training," and William Glasser's "Reality Therapy."

Carkhuff Model: Art of Helping[9]

Robert R. Carkhuff, noted authority on human and community resource development, has created a model for the guidance profession that is based upon the concepts of "responsive" and "initiative" behavior on the part of the counselor or helper. He found that two dimensions are present in true helping processes: (1) the ability to respond accurately to another person's experience, and (2) the ability to initiate effectively from one's own experience. Helpers who offered high levels of responsive and initiative dimensions had helpees who demonstrated constructive change or gain. Teachers who offered high levels of responsive and initiative dimensions had students who learned more and better. The goals of the Carkhuff model are (1) self-exploration, (2) self-understanding, and (3) constructive action. Carkhuff says:

In order for an individual to change his behavior he must first explore himself in those areas where he is not living effectively. Responding to the individual elicits self-exploration. . . . In exploring himself, the person seeking help is attempting to understand his different feelings about himself. The only purpose for exploration is understanding. . . . A helper has to filter the helpee's experience through his own and enable the helpee to understand his experience at deeper and fuller

levels. . . . When the helper moves beyond simply responding to the individual's experience to initiating from his own experience, he facilitates self-understanding. Self-understanding is not real until the individual has acted upon it. The only purpose for understanding behavior is to be able to act to change the behavior. The more accurately a person understands himself, the more constructively he can act—for himself and others. . . . A fully alive communication process makes possible constructive action.

Three of the tasks of the helper are outlined in Table 1: (1) attending to the helpee, (2) responding to the helpee, and (3) initiating confrontation. If these tasks are carried out constructively, the way is opened for full communication to take place.

TABLE 1. TASKS OF THE HELPER

Task I: Attending

Tasks	Commentary	Illustrations
ATTENDING PHYSICALLY	Basically, attending involves a physical act on the part of the helper, which communicates his interest.	(To the student: Go back and read the anecdote written about Karen by the student observer. We will be dubbing in responses from that situation in this column to illustrate.)
(1) Symbolically nourishing or holding	Symbolically, we may offer the helpee a moment of brief respite from a world that is closing in on him. The helper offers a glass of milk or a cup of tea; he may hold the helpee's hands through a difficult moment.	Karen is sitting listlessly at her desk, head on her hands, just staring away. (The student observer places her hand on Karen's shoulder in an affectionate way.) She says: "Karen, what's up? What are you doing?"
(2) Posturing	Our posture communicates our readiness to respond to the helpee's needs. One way is to face him fully. When sitting, we incline our bodies toward the helpee. When standing, we attend most fully when we move closer to the helpee.	The student observer crouches by Karen's desk, leaning forward and looking intently into Karen's eyes in a concerned way.
ATTENDING PSYCHOLOGICALLY	We attend psychologically to the helpee when we communicate a "hovering attentiveness."	
(1) Maintaining eye contact	The helpee is aware of our efforts to make contact psychologically through making visual contact.	The student observer maintains eye contact throughout the conversation.

(2)	Observing cues	The helper observes the helpee fully, taking in all of his appearance and behavior. The helpee may also observe the helper's attentiveness.	She observes these cues: Karen is listless. She is lost in her own world. She stutters and pauses when she tries to express herself. She gives emphatic negative responses about herself.
(3)	Communicating interest	When the helper is intense but relaxed, he communicates attentiveness. When he consistently attends, he communicates his interest.	

ATTENDING THROUGH LISTENING		The more we attend to the helpee, the better we can listen to the cues of his inner experience. The more we view the helpee, the more we prepare ourselves for listening to him.	
(1)	Have a reason for listening	The helper should be listening for the important things that the helpee is revealing about himself.	
(2)	Be non-judgmental	We must suspend temporarily the things that we say to ourselves. Just let the helpee's message sink in without trying to make decisions about it.	
(3)	Wait to respond	Wait at least a full 30 seconds before responding in any way to the helpee's expressions. The helpee will see that the helper is struggling to understand fully what he is saying.	
(4)	Recall content and repeat it verbatim	Use the second-person pronoun and restate what the helpee has said.	The student observer might respond: "You say you're ugly and you're afraid you'll never get married."
(5)	Look for themes	The helpee will probably make the same points over and over in different ways. The themes will tell us what he is really trying to say about himself in relation to his world.	The dominant theme is self-negation: "I'm ugly." "I'm not always nice to people and they're not always nice to me."
(6)	Reflect on content	We can easily listen at a rate two or three times that at which people speak. We can take advantage by reflecting upon what the helpee has said.	
(7)	Hear	Hearing means understanding what it is the helpee is trying to express in his behavior and his speech.	The student observer understands that Karen feels rejected and lonely.

Task II: Responding

Tasks	Commentary	Illustrations
RESPOND TO BEHAVIOR		
(1) Respond to physical behavior	When all other clues to the helpee's experience confuse us, we must return to the most basic evidence of all—the helpee's behavior.	The student observer made these observations: Karen's head was on her hands. She was staring away.
(2) Observe physical energy and activity	When an individual's energy level is low, he functions poorly. Many helpees often function at low levels of physical activity. Because of inner conflicts, their energies are drained.	Karen's energy was at a low ebb. Karen was inert.
(3) Observe stereotyped behavior	A low-functioning person tends to pose his body in a very stereotyped way. When he hangs his head forward and speaks lifelessly, he communicates a depressive mood. When he stands rigidly and is tense in his verbal and physical behavior, he communicates a state of tension.	Karen had a slumped-over posture. She appeared to be depressed.
(4) Observe incongruent behavior	Being incongruent simply means that the person is not consistent in different aspects of his behavior. There may be a discrepancy between what a person says and what he does, or between how he thinks he behaves and how he actually behaves in real life.	Karen says she's ugly. The student observer sees that she's really "very cute."
RESPOND TO FEELINGS	The first goal is responding to the helpee's feelings. The helpee must get his feelings out in the open if he is going to deal with them.	
(1) Listen to helpee's words	The tone of the helpee's voice and his facial expressions will be valuable clues to his inner feelings. When we listen to the helpee's words, we must ask ourselves how he feels about the experience that he is relating.	Karen gives sad negative responses. Karen really does feel sad; life seems pretty hopeless.
(2) Empathize	The helpee will check out the "feeling words" of the helper. These are simply the words that we use to communicate our understanding of the helpee's feelings.	The student observer empathizes: "You don't feel like doing anything. I get that way a lot, too. Sometimes I don't feel like doing a thing."
(3) Suspend one's own frame of reference	We communicate respect for the helpee's frame of reference by suspending our own. The helpee then has the feeling that he is free to explore himself without fear of retaliation. While suspending our own frame of reference, we must continue to communicate in a genuine manner.	The student observer said: "Looks are nice, but the most important thing is if you're nice to people and they're nice to you. Just as long as everyone is happy and you help make other people happy." Instead, she might have said: "You feel sad because you think you are ugly."

(4) Respond with feeling words; develop interchangeable responses	A response is interchangeable if both the helper and the helpee express the same feeling. This means the helper could have said what the helpee said, and the helpee could have said what the helper said.	
	The helper's response should focus initially upon the helpee's feelings about himself; we may do this by using a simple, "You feel . . . " formulation.	The student observer might have said: "You feel sad." "You feel discouraged." "You feel lonely." "You feel blue."
RESPOND TO MEANINGS	As a helper, you must express the personal meaning for the helpee. Meaning is not possible without understanding both the feeling and the content expressed by the helpee.	
(1) Supply the content	Look at these feeling states and the related content areas: *Feeling* *Content* Happy. . . . . . about being promoted. Angry . . . . . toward my teacher for giving me a low grade. Sad . . . . when my kitten died.	The student observer might have said: "You feel sad when you look in the mirror." The student observer might have said: "You really feel discouraged with yourself when you look in the mirror."
(2) Provide a reason	Meaning puts the feeling in context. "You feel . . . because . . . " captures both the feeling and the meaning: "You feel sad because your kitten was like a person to you and now she is gone."	The student observer might have said: "You feel sad because you think no one likes you—that you won't ever get married."

Task III: Initiating

Tasks	Commentary	Illustrations
INITIATING ADDITIVE UNDERSTANDING AND CONFRONTATION	When the helpee comes to understand himself at levels interchangeable with those he has expressed, then he signals us of his readiness for movement to the next stage of helping—the initiative phase.	
(1) Lay a base for initiating additive understanding and confrontation, by giving interchangeable responses, and then extend the base.	The more interchangeable responses that we make to the helpee's experience, the higher is the probability that we will be accurate when we attempt to add to his understanding of himself. We must respond to helpee expressions in an extended exchange in a way that captures the helpee's expressions at the level that he is presenting them: "You're really unsure of what you're doing there." "Somehow you just feel smothered by your parents."	"You really do feel sad . . . your loneliness is unbearable."
(2) Initiate additive understanding	When we go beyond the helpee, we say that we are being additive. When we are additive, the helpee will come to experience himself more accurately in the area of his concern. We do this by drawing increasingly upon our own experience.	"You feel sad when you look in the mirror. You feel sad most of the time."

Additive responses are always formulated from the helpee's frame of reference: "Certain feelings about yourself keep coming up."

"You are sad when you look in the mirror so you see nothing."

Look for dominant themes

When one common theme stands out above the others, we call it a dominant theme. "One feeling about yourself in relation to your world keeps coming up over and over . . . "

The student observer might have said: "Feelings about yourself keep coming up—you don't like yourself and you say no one else likes you, either."

When we formulate an additive response, we call upon our own experience to interpret the helpee's experience. Expressions such as, "What I really hear you say is . . . " or "What it all adds up to for me is . . . " are effective formulations for us as helpers.

(3) Initiate con-frontations

When we make responses that go beyond what the helpee has said but come clearly from an external frame of reference, we are confronting.

Mild con-frontations

Mild confrontations often take the form of opening up for consideration discrepancies in the helpee's behavior. "On the one hand you say . . . but on the other hand you do . . ." "You say you're feeling pretty good, but you feel that some things aren't going so well."

Direct con-frontation

Sometimes a direct confrontation made exclusively from the helper's own frame of reference may be essential. Direct confrontations should be made as constructive as possible.

The student observer might have said: "You say you're ugly, but the important thing is that you're nice to people and they're nice to you."

"You say you're feeling pretty good, but you look to me like you're dragging your tail."

The student observer might have said: "You say you're ugly, but I can see you're really cute."

Another kind of discrepancy in behavior is between how the helpee really is and how he wants to be. We may confront people with strengths as well as weaknesses. Good helpers are ever alert to the helpee who may be better than he thinks he is.

"You say you're ugly and no one likes you, but I saw you were chosen first on the team for the softball game."

In the context of an understanding relationship, you may find that confrontation facilitates breaking through the defensive barriers that the helpee has thrown up. On these occasions, you may tell the helpee directly how you feel about what you see: "I feel that you are . . . " Effective confrontations are productive of new exploration on the part of the helpee. The confrontation, then, is effective in opening up new areas for exploration and in recycling the helping process at deeper levels in critical areas.

"I feel you are fooling yourself— you say you are ugly when you really feel lonely."

Gordon Model:

Effectiveness Training.[10]

Thomas Gordon's "Teacher Effectiveness Training" program is a spin-off from P.E.T. (Parent Effectiveness Training).[11] A short resume is presented here to help the teacher visualize how Gordon's principles of "active-listening," "I-messages" (confrontation), and "conflict resolution" work.

Example: Teacher-Student Conflict Resolution. Let us note an example of conflict resolution between a teacher and a second grader:

Situation: *Gilbert has been disrupting his second-grade class for some time by refusing to remain at his seat or in a reading group. The class is busy and Miss Stein has time to talk to Gilbert, who is looking out the window.*

MISS STEIN: Gilbert, I think we have a problem that I'd like to solve. I'm really tired of yelling at you to stay in your seat or to come to the reading group. Sometimes you've even left the reading group, and I've had to go get you and leave all the other kids just sitting there.

GILBERT: I don't like reading.

MISS STEIN: I see. You just hate to read.

GILBERT: Uh-huh.

MISS STEIN: I think I understand, but I still hate to keep yelling at you and chasing you around to get you to sit in your seat.

GILBERT: I don't want to sit in my seat all day. All I do is just sit in my seat all day.

MISS STEIN: You really get tired of that.

GILBERT: Yes, I like to walk around and stand over here.

MISS STEIN: You would rather move around and be near the window than sit in your seat.

GILBERT: Yes. I don't like to sit over there. It's too crowded.

MISS STEIN: If I understand, Gilbert, the thing you don't like about your seat is that it is too crowded there.

GILBERT: Uh-huh. I can't get out.

MISS STEIN: You feel hemmed in.

GILBERT: Huh?

MISS STEIN: You feel like you can't get away.

GILBERT: Yes, I can't get away. When I'm in my seat I can't get away and when the bell rings I have to stay there.

MISS STEIN: When everyone goes out you have to stay behind.

GILBERT: When recess comes everyone lines up and I'm always last.

MISS STEIN: You hate to be the last one in the line all the time.

GILBERT: Yes.

MISS STEIN: You would like to be the first one in the line sometimes.

GILBERT: When I stand over here and the bell rings I can be in front.

MISS STEIN: I see. (Pause) I have an idea, Gilbert. Do you think you would mind sitting in your seat if we moved your chair over by this window?

GILBERT: Right here (pointing to where he is standing)?

MISS STEIN: Yes. Right here. Then you could be first in line sometimes instead of always being the last one.

GILBERT: Okay. And I'll sit here and do my work.

MISS STEIN: And you will stay in the reading groups, too, because you know you will have your chair by the window?

GILBERT: (No response)

MISS STEIN: You don't seem to like that idea, staying in the reading group.

GILBERT: No, when the bell rings when I'm in the reading group it's too crowded, too.

MISS STEIN: You're afraid that if the bell rings and you're in the reading group you'll be left behind again.

GILBERT: Yes. It's way up there. [pointing to the front of the room where the reading groups meet] I can't get out.

MISS STEIN: It's too far from where you line up.

GILBERT: To go out.

MISS STEIN: You would like to be closer to the door.

GILBERT: (Smiling) Yes, and if we have a fire drill I can be by the door.

MISS STEIN: I see, you would like to be by the door in case we have a fire drill, or maybe if we have a real fire.

GILBERT: Yes. If we have a fire I can be by the door.

MISS STEIN: That's what would make you feel good, to be by the door if there is a fire. Then you could get out.

GILBERT: Yes.

MISS STEIN: Well, I have been thinking of moving the reading groups to that table in the back of the room by the door. If I did that, do you think you would be able to stay in the group?

GILBERT: Yes, I'll stay in the group.

MISS STEIN: Well, it looks like we have solved our problems, Gilbert. We'll move your seat over here right now, and tomorrow we will have our reading groups in the back of the room at that table. Then you will be able to stay in your seat instead of wandering around the room, and you'll stay in the reading group.

GILBERT: Okay.[12]

The above account is a problem-solving episode in which the teacher's major role was listening actively. She tuned in on what was troubling Gilbert, and by decoding his messages she was able to reflect back to him what he was really saying. They were able to arrive at a mutually agreeable solution to a problem.

Active Listening

Gordon's model is designed to effect communication among people. Communication breaks down when there is a lack of understanding and a lack of acceptance of the other person's point of view. As we saw in the Carkhuff model, active listening is an effective way of understanding the other person and of entering into his feelings. It supplies feedback to the child and lets him know that you understand and feel with him. It keeps the door open for the child to explore his problem. The parent or teacher feeds back only what he feels the sender's message meant—nothing more, nothing less. Active listening leads to insight; sometimes the child is able to solve his own problem, or the parent or teacher can solve the problem with the child.

In their brief encounter, Miss Stein put aside her own thoughts and feelings, and instead listened and tried to understand Gilbert's thoughts and feelings. Her feedbacks generally began with "you." Through consistently listening and reflecting to Gilbert what she heard, Miss Stein showed understanding and empathy for Gilbert's feelings—but she put the responsibility on him to stay with the problem until it was solved.

Sending "I-messages"

When the teacher cannot accept the behavior of a child and must confront him to work out a better solution, the "I-message" is a way of communicating honestly to a child the effect his behavior is having on you, the teacher. This approach is less threatening to the child than suggesting there is something "bad" about *him*. Notice the difference in the following two messages sent by a parent after a child kicks him in the shins:

1. "Ouch! That really hurt me—I don't like to be kicked."

2. "That's being a very bad boy. Don't you ever kick anybody like that!"

"I-messages" (example 1 above) are more effective than saying "You . . . " because they give the child the responsibility for modifying his own behavior.

Note the negative effects of the following series of "You-messages" in a confrontation between parent and child:

PARENT: *You're* getting awfully irresponsible about doing *your* dishes after breakfast. ("You-message")

CHILD: *You* don't always do *yours* every morning. ("You-message")

PARENT: That's different—Mother has lots of other things to do around the house, picking up after a bunch of messy children. (You-message")

CHILD: I haven't been messy. (Defensive message)

PARENT: *You're* just as bad as the others, and *you* know it. ("You-message")

CHILD: *You* expect everyone to be perfect. ("You-message")

PARENT: Well, *you* certainly have a long way to go to reach that when it comes to picking up. ("You-message")

CHILD: *You're* so darned fussy about the house. ("You-message")

Contrast these "you-messages" with the possibilities that lie within the following "I-messages" of a teacher who needs to confront:

When you erase the material I *leave on the boards labeled SAVE,* I *have to take time from other things to rewrite it the next day, and* I'm *feeling helpless to prevent that happening to* me. *(The teacher then shifts gears to "active listening," if the children protest or become angry.)*

When you are so loud and active, my class shifts its attention to you, which prevents me *from teaching them the skills* I *want to and* I *get to feeling terribly frustrated. (The teacher then shifts to "active listening.")*

When our class makes a lot of noise on the way to the cafeteria, it disturbs teachers whose classes are still in session. Since I'm *supposed to be in charge of you,* I'm *afraid they will think* I'm *a poor teacher. (Shifts gears to "active listening.")*

When the cart is returned in this condition, I *have to take time to clean it up, put the lids on the right jars and locate the missing clay-boards, which are jobs* I *dislike and which interfere with other jobs* I *was planning to do, so* I *feel hurried and resentful.*[13]

Conflict Resolution through Problem Solving

The Dewey problem-solving method has been used by Gordon as a way of resolving either conflicts between two individuals or conflicts within a group. The method is democratic and works, if all the members' needs are considered and if everyone can accept the proposed solution without sacrificing some felt need. This method is especially suitable for class meetings dealing with problems affecting the entire group. The following six steps are involved:

STEP I: Define the Problem in Terms of Needs (not competing solutions).

First, the problem should be stated in a way that does not communicate blame or judgment. Sending "I-messages" is the most effective way for stating a problem. ("I get disturbed when . . . because . . . ")

Second, verbalize the other person's side of the conflict. If you don't know his side, ask him to state it for himself. The process of "active listening" may be necessary in order to clarify problems. Frequently, problems will get redefined as they are discussed. Before moving on, be sure everyone accepts the definition of the problem.

STEP II: Generate Possible Solutions (no evaluation allowed in this step).

The group should brain-storm and come up with all possible solutions. Refrain from evaluation and criticism of solutions. Use active listening and treat everyone's ideas with respect. If things bog down, state the problem again.

STEP III: Evaluate and Test the Various Solutions.

Everyone must be honest for this to succeed. Are there flaws in any of the possible solutions? Any reason why a solution might not work? Will it be too hard to implement or carry out? Is it fair to everyone? Use active listening in this step.

STEP IV: Decide on a Mutually Acceptable Solution.

A mutual commitment to one solution must be made. Usually when all the facts have been exposed, one clearly superior solution stands out. State the solution to make certain everyone understands what is about to be decided. Sometimes writing it down is necessary.

STEP V: Implement the Solution.

After a solution has been agreed upon, it is generally necessary to talk about implementation: WHO does WHAT by WHEN? Trust is important, but if a member fails to carry out his end of an agreement, confront him with "I-messages."

STEP VI: Evaluate the Solution.

Sometimes weaknesses in the solution will show up, and the problem will need to be returned for more problem solving. Decisions should always be open for revision, but no one should unilaterally modify a decision.

Your best tools for effective problem solving will always be:

ACTIVE LISTENING

CLEAR AND HONEST SENDING OF "I-MESSAGES"

RESPECT FOR THE NEEDS OF THE OTHER

TRUST

BEING OPEN TO NEW DATA

PERSISTENCE

FIRMNESS IN YOUR UNWILLINGNESS TO HAVE IT FAIL

Glasser Model: Reality Therapy[14]

William Glasser, in *Schools Without Failure,* presents a "Reality Therapy" model that is purported to improve relationships in the classroom and to solve social problems.

Glasser believes there are two kinds of failure—failure to love and failure to achieve self-worth. These failures, which are caused by the unfulfilled needs of "loving" and achieving "self-worth," account for failure to cope with academic or other tasks that concern teachers. If a person can give and receive love with some consistency throughout life, he is to some degree a success. According to Glasser, love and self-worth are so intertwined that they may properly be related through the use of the term *identity.*

Identity is Glasser's theme throughout his writings. Love and self-worth are the two pathways mankind has discovered to a successful identity. It is the school's business, therefore, to deal with both of these basic needs. By developing knowledge and an ability to think, children will feel worthwhile. By learning social responsibility, children can experience love. If children are responsible for each other, care for each other and help each other—not only for the sake of others but for their own sake—love, in the social sense, becomes a reality. If people do not develop an identity of love and self-worth—a "success identity"—they will develop a "failure identity" leading to delinquency or withdrawal; if they withdraw, they will be uninvolved and will feel lonely.

In reality therapy, children are considered responsible for fulfilling their own needs *and* for their own behavior. Deviant behavior is the result of bad choices. In order to make better choices, children need to be strongly and emotionally involved with others who have success identities

and who can make wise choices. Involvement with people and with the curriculum, through thinking and problem solving, prepares children to live successfully in their world. Warm, positive teachers can help children through modeling "caring" and "problem-solving" behavior.

Glasser contends that in order to break a cycle of failure, teachers must work *in the present* and deal with immediate behavior that needs to be changed. (Delving into past history is not necessary and may even serve to prejudice the teacher.) Better behavior leads to good feelings, which in turn lead to still better behavior. It is an upward, progressive cycle, which will eventually perpetuate itself. The steps in the process of turning a failure identity into a successful one are as follows:

1. *Get the child to make a value judgment about what he is now doing that is contributing to his failure.* If a child misbehaves in class, the teacher must ask: "What are you doing?" (Never ask, "Why?" Children are rarely able to handle "why" questions regarding their own behavior.) When the child tells the teacher what he is doing, the teacher then asks: "Is your behavior helping you? (Helping the class?) (Helping the school?) If the child says, "No, my behavior is not helping," the teacher says: "What can you do that is different?"

2. *Ask the child to choose a better course of action.* If the child cannot come up with some plausible changes he can make in his behavior, the teacher should suggest some alternatives and help the child plan a better course of action.

3. *Get the child to make a commitment to a plan.* For example, a teacher might work with a child who talks continually and interrupts the class. Together they could work out a new seating arrangement, in which the child is away from children who excite him so that he loses control. This simple plan carried out in cooperation with the child helps him to be quiet. He learns responsibility when he evaluates the situation and commits himself to a plan that he thinks will be more helpful to himself and to others.

4. *Do not allow the child to make any excuses.* After the child makes a value judgment and a commitment to change his behavior, he is held to the commitment. The teacher must not

accept any excuses from the child who fails to keep his commitments. This is self-discipline, and it teaches responsibility.

Classroom Meetings

A classroom meeting, in Glasser's frame of reference, is a non-judgmental discussion about problems that are important and relevant to the children. Used from kindergarten onward, meetings can serve to siphon off steam in the class by providing a better alternative. Glasser classifies three types of meetings: social problem solving, open-ended and educational-diagnostic. Here we will confine our discussion to the social problem-solving meeting, in which three major principles are involved:

1. *All problems relative to the class as a group and to any individual in the class are eligible for discussion.* A problem can be brought up by an individual student about himself or someone else, or by the teacher as he sees a problem occur. In addition to school problems, problems that a child has at home are also eligible for discussion if the child or his parents wish to bring them up.

2. *The discussion itself should always be directed toward solving the problem; the solution should never include punishment or fault finding.* From the beginning, the children should be oriented toward the idea that the purpose of the meetings is not to assign fault nor to punish people who have problems or are doing wrong; rather, the purpose is to help those who have problems to find better ways to behave. When meetings are conducted in this way, the children learn to think in terms of a solution. It should also be understood that many problems are not readily solvable or have no single right answer, and that their best solution might be not-so-bad alternatives.

   It is important in class meetings for the teacher, but not the class, to be non-judgmental. The class makes judgments and from these judgments works toward positive solutions. The teacher may reflect the class attitude, but he should give opinions sparingly and make sure the class understands that his opinions are not law.

3. *Meetings should always be conducted with the teacher and all the students seated in a tight circle.* This seating arrangement is necessary if meetings are to be productive. Communication cannot take place when people talk to the backs of heads.

SUMMARY

Children's emotional needs are met within the context of interpersonal relationships in the classroom. One of the problems of the beginning teacher is that he, too, often feels insecure and is anxious about being liked. However, if he shifts his focus to liking the children and providing an involving environment for them, his own need to be liked will be met in the process.

In this chapter the importance of being a "real" teacher-person has been pointed out. The way to authenticity is through self-understanding, and this is the place where the neophyte should begin. Every teacher, new or experienced, should have interests outside the classroom; everyone needs a significant person—friend, husband, wife—with whom he can share himself in depth, so that he need not bring his personal problems into the classroom.

Every sincere teacher can build upon his own uniqueness and can develop interpersonal behaviors that lead to trust and empathic understanding. He can learn to help and influence the child, constructively resolving conflicts in the classroom. The teacher is influencing responsibly when he frees the child to be himself, to examine his own behavior and to act responsibly.

The chapter closes with a summary of behaviors of a teacher functioning in a "helping relationship." As you read through these statements, think of them as broad principles of action and check your behavior against them. Do you find any clues about things you do or do not do that are interfering with your classroom relationships? Do you find evidence to confirm what you are already doing? Reflection on one's behavior can open one to growth, provided that reflection also leads to new action.

THE TEACHER AS "RELATOR"
IN THE POLITICAL ENVIRONMENT OF THE CLASSROOM

I.   **As a relator, the teacher expresses himself spontaneously as the person he genuinely is; therefore, he:**

   1.   communicates a warm, relaxed, open and receptive attitude in his transactions with children.

   2.   manages his negative feelings in a responsible way and lets children know what his real feelings are.

   3.   displays honesty and fairness in his transactions with children.

   4.   lets the children know what his expectations are and behaves consistently with them.

   5.   levels with the child and/or group, taking the blame when he himself makes a mistake.

   6.   approaches his work with confidence, optimism and buoyancy.

II. **As a relator, the teacher cares about, supports, empathizes with and encourages each child; therefore, he:**

   1.   makes himself available to each child in the group and personalizes his attention to the physical, psychological and academic needs of each child.

   2.   talks to each child as a person and draws him out in conversation.

   3.   really listens, hears and shows an interest in what each child is saying.

   4.   responds with honest consideration to the ideas of each child.

   5.   expresses confidence in each child's ability to progress.

   6.   makes realistic, positive statements of recognition regarding each child's accomplishments.

III. **As a relator, the teacher helps the child clarify perceptions about himself and his behavior, and helps him with his peer relationships; therefore, he:**

   1.   lets the child know he considers him a worthy individual who can do things.

   2.   gives the child non-verbal cues of acceptance.

   3.   sees situations through the eyes of the child and looks for the goals of each child's actions.

   4.   responds non-judgmentally when the child shares his feelings or attitudes.

   5.   asks the child for his point of view in troublesome situations.

   6.   puts in words the feelings he thinks the child is expressing.

   7.   acts and responds in ways that add deeper feeling and meaning to what the child has said; confronts the child with the contradictions between verbalized perceptions and behavior.

   8.   when necessary, confronts the child with his "problem" behavior privately, asks the child what he is doing and if he thinks his behavior is helping him.

   9.   encourages feedback from peers to the child or from the child to peers in specific situations.

   10. helps the child set limits on his behavior, so that he does not interfere with the rights of other people.

   11. suggests some new outlets or alternatives for the child.

12. separates the child's feelings from his behavior when redirecting behavior; shows through actions and/or words: "We like you, we know how you feel, but we cannot accept this behavior."

13. recognizes the power and status roles each person in the group is playing and tries to free the child from a role that is destructive to him or to the group.

14. provides opportunities for each child to experience a leadership role.

IV. **As a relator, the teacher facilitates individual and group decision making, trying to free children rather than control them; therefore, he:**

1. sizes up the developmental growth and past experience of the child and/or group to determine what decisions may be shared.

2. provides opportunities for the child and/or group to make decisions and to choose from alternatives.

3. makes use of situations in which children must make choices in relationship to their values.

4. helps children become aware of the values they have acted upon; helps them think through principles of action to try out in new situations.

5. helps the group identify problems that are common to the group and helps them work toward solutions that allow everyone to pursue a meaningful course of action.

6. supports the right of each child to express his point of view during the problem-solving process.

7. lets individuals and/or the group live with the decisions they make.

8. helps the group evaluate the effectiveness of group decisions and make new decisions if appropriate.

Notes

[1] Arthur W. Combs, *The Professional Education of Teachers* (Boston: Allyn and Bacon, Inc., 1965), p. 8.

[2] David W. Johnson, *Reaching Out* (Englewood Cliffs: Prentice-Hall, 1972), p. 3.

[3] See the account of "The Florida Studies in the Helping Professions" described in Arthur W. Combs, et al., *Helping Relationships: Basic Concepts for the Helping Professions* (Boston: Allyn and Bacon, Inc., 1971).

[4] Clark Moustakas, *The Authentic Teacher* (Cambridge, Mass.: Howard A. Doyle Publishing Co., 1966), p. 2.

[5] Ibid., pp. 14, 15.

[6] Ibid., p. 3.

[7] Johnson, op. cit., p. 74.

[8] Haim G. Ginott, *Between Parent and Child* (New York: Macmillan Company, 1965), p. 95. Dr. Ginott is also the author of *Between Parent and Teenager* (1969) and *Teacher and Child* (1972).

[9] Digested by permission of the publisher from Robert R. Carkhuff, *The Art of Helping* (Amherst, Mass., Box 222: Human Resource Development Press, 1972).

We recognize that concepts from the Carkhuff model cannot be absorbed from such a brief introduction, but the student or in-service teacher is encouraged to study Carkhuff's writings, try his ideas on for size in the classroom and if possible participate in a workshop offered by Dr. Carkhuff when the opportunity presents itself.

[10] Digested by permission of the publisher from Dr. Thomas Gordon's *Parent Effectiveness Training: The "No-Lose" Program for Raising Responsible Children* (New York: Peter H. Wyden, Inc., 1970).

We recommend that you study Dr. Gordon's entire book, *Parent Effectiveness Training*, role-play situations with your peers or colleagues, and test the behaviors out in the classroom.

[11] Many "Parent Effectiveness Training" and "Teacher Effectiveness Training" classes are springing up across the country. If this method seems plausible to you, explore the possibility of enrolling in one of these workshops. Write to Effectiveness Training Associates, 110 South Euclid Avenue, Pasadena, California 91101.

[12] Reprinted by permission of the publisher from Thomas Gordon's *Teacher Effectiveness Training Notebook* (Pasadena, Calif.: Effectiveness Training Associates, 1972), pp. 51, 52.

[13]Reprinted by permission of the publisher from Thomas Gordon's *Teacher Effectiveness Training Notebook* (Pasadena, Calif.: Effectiveness Training Associates, 1972), p. 41.

[14]Digested from *Schools Without Failure* by William Glasser. Copyright © 1969 by William Glasser; reprinted by permission of Harper & Row, Publishers, Inc.

References

Carkhuff, Robert R. *The Art of Helping.* Amherst, Mass.: Human Resource Development Press, Box 222, 1972.

Combs, Arthur W., et al. *Helping Relationships: Basic Concepts for the Helping Professions.* Boston: Allyn and Bacon, Inc., 1971.

_____. *The Professional Education of Teachers.* Boston: Allyn and Bacon, Inc., 1965.

Ginott, Haim G. *Between Parent & Child.* New York: Avon Books, A Division of Hearst Corporation, 1969.

Glasser, William. *Schools Without Failure.* New York: Harper & Row, Publishers, 1969.

Goble, Frank. *The Third Force.* New York: Pocket Books, 1971.

Gordon, Thomas. *Parent Effectiveness Training.* New York: Peter H. Wydon, Inc., 1970.

_____. *Teacher Effectiveness Training.* Teacher Notebook. Pasadena, Calif.: Effectiveness Training Associates, 1972.

Johnson, David W. *Reaching Out.* Englewood Cliffs, N. J.: Prentice-Hall, Inc., 1972.

Moustakas, Clark. *The Authentic Teacher.* Cambridge, Mass.: Howard A. Doyle Publishing Co., 1966.

Otto, Herbert. "Motivation and Human Potentialities," in *Humanitas,* III, 3, Winter 1968.

Rogers, Carl R. "Characteristics of a Helping Relationship," in *The Personnel and Guidance Journal* (September 1958), pp. 6-15.

Chapter 5

Relationships
in the
Classroom

Anecdotal accounts of student teachers functioning in the role of relator are highlighted in this
chapter. Both negative and positive influences are
analyzed, showing (1) how barriers to communication are created; (2) how children reveal themselves
in open communication; and (3) how teachers help

children resolve problems by responding relevantly
to their concerns.

CREATING BARRIERS IN COMMUNICATION

The "Put-down" Message

"Put-down" messages belittle children and cause
them to be defensive. In the first illustration,
Sherry bids for attention by playing the "helpless"
role. The teacher, trying to enforce responsibility,
ends up reinforcing a feeling of inadequacy. She
does not get through the impasse of the child's
real concern.

Situation 1. 9:30 A.M. It was time for Sherry and me to start
her reading lesson. However, she convinced me to start on the
math, because she disliked reading so much. I went along with
her, since her work for the week had been most satisfactory.

Analysis of Behavior

SHERRY: I don't understand how to do this.

ME: You haven't even looked at the problems, so how
do you know you can't do them?

The teacher's tone is accusing. She
reflects her doubt.

SHERRY: They look hard to me, and I can't get the hard ones.

ME: These are just like the ones you did yesterday.

Now she belittles the problem.

SHERRY: No, they're not. Look at this one—that's too hard
for me to do. Come on, you've gotta help me.

ME: Sherry, wait a minute. Debbie needs my help. You already know how to do those problems; now get to work.

Lecturing and criticizing follow.

Sherry suddenly threw her book on the floor and hollered, "I'm not gonna do them then. I'm going to the learning center. You won't help me."

Then Sherry's behavior breaks down.

ME: You know how to do those problems, Sherry. I know it and so do you. It doesn't make sense to get angry with me because I know you can do them.

Now the teacher admonishes and blames.

Sherry stood there for a couple of minutes with her arms folded and her mouth protruding, as if to let me know that she was really upset with me. After a while she discovered I wasn't paying her much attention, so she picked up the book.

"Is this right?" she said, after completing one of the problems.

The teacher "wins" at the expense of the child's feelings.

Sherry tries a new tack for getting attention, but her basic problem has not been helped.

In the following situation, a senior student teacher and an assistant are working together. The assistant tries to be helpful but doesn't hear the child's real message—which may be "I need attention" or "I'm bored." She creates interpersonal problems between herself, Tommy and Nancy by commanding, lecturing, blaming, imploring, threatening and interrogating. She controls in the end, but no doubt there is unresolved resentment in the children.

Situation 2. Tuesday, March 22, First Grade. Miss L ___ , the senior student teacher, was telling a story to the class seated in a group around her. I was sitting behind the children, trying to watch the few rowdy ones and listen to the story, too. Tommy and Nancy began fussing, so I moved next to them. Nancy had been playing with a broken eraser, scheming to get other children interested enough to try taking it away from her. During the whole story period she complained to me that she didn't want to hear the story.

Analysis of Behavior

ME: Nancy, if you don't want to hear the story please sit still. There are others who want to hear it.

The assistant student teacher confronts Nancy by pointing out the needs of others.

(Nancy was teasing Tommy with an eraser that had been pulled off one of the pencils they wrote with. In order to justify her playing and teasing, she claimed it as her brother's eraser.)

TOMMY: That eraser isn't her brother's.

(Tommy tried to take the eraser from Nancy several times. They both started fooling around the blackboard and the play clock with the movable hands.)

ME: All right, you two. I want you to sit down right now!

The assistant student teacher makes a demand.

(They sat down. Tommy began to whistle quite loudly.)

ME:	Tommy, do you know you're disturbing the class? Others want to hear the story.	Now she lectures.
TOMMY:	No, I'm not!	
ME:	Every time you whistle someone turns around.	She continues with criticism.
TOMMY:	So what?	
ME:	(Placing my index finger on his mouth) Tommy, please keep quiet.	Next she implores.

(Tommy whistled again.)

ME:	You can't seem to listen too well. One more time and we'll move over to the corner and have a talk about your behavior, away from the rest of the group.	She criticizes and moves in with a threat . . .

(I was prepared to get up and take his arm. He whistled again but started crying when I took his arm.)

ME:	Are you going to whistle again and misbehave?	. . . and follows with interrogation. The teacher wins—the child submits. He is probably frightened.
TOMMY:	I won't do it again.	

(I could tell Tommy was sincere. He didn't want to talk with me in the corner, and he listened to the rest of the story. He didn't whistle the rest of the afternoon. Nancy was playing with the eraser by herself while I was busy with Tommy. She rolled it on the floor. I got to it before she did and picked it up.)

NANCY:	Give me back my eraser. It's mine, it belongs to my brother. You can't have it.	
ME:	What have you been doing with it that I took it away?	The student teacher confronts with a question.

(No answer.)

ME:	You weren't listening to the story and you were disturbing the class.	Now she passes judgment.
NANCY:	(Making a face) Give me my eraser.	
ME:	If you can sit quietly till story time is over, then and only then you'll get it back.	She threatens and sets a condition.

(Story time was only another couple minutes and she sat quietly. I gave back her eraser when it ended.)	The student teacher keeps her promise. This is a redeeming feature.

Interrogation

Many teachers assume that if they approach the child with the "why" question, the child will be able to analyze his own behavior and respond in more acceptable ways. "Why?" is a good question in developing thought processes, but children under duress usually can't explain their behavior; they feel guilty and confused when asked to do so.

Situations 3 and 4 show the inadequacy of interrogation in the helping relationship.

In Situation 3, the student teacher attempts to use active listening but turns the encounter into a probing exercise. She ends up "making a deal" with Mike to get him to feel okay about doing his work. She does tune in with active listening at times; but, although she provides a solution, she does not necessarily get at Mike's real problem.

Situation 3. Ricky lost his *Think and Do Book,* so he could not work in his book as the rest of the children in his group were doing. I sent him to work in another group. Mike became restless and would not do his work. He was upset. I asked him if he wanted to talk about it, and we began to talk.

Analysis of Behavior

MIKE:	Ricky doesn't like me.
ME:	You feel Ricky doesn't like you.

The student teacher reflects what Mike is saying.

MIKE:	Yes.
ME:	Do you know why?

She begins to question.

MIKE:	No.
ME:	Do you think Ricky feels he is accomplishing all he wants to do?

Now she probes.

MIKE:	No.
ME:	Do you think he feels you might be stopping him from doing his work?

She asks other questions, hinting at criticism and suggesting solutions.

MIKE:	No.
ME:	Do you think you might be able to help him?

MIKE:	No. (Pause) How come he gets to work in the other group? I want to work in the other group, too.

Mike finally comes out with his real concern.

ME:	You want to work in the other group.

The teacher tunes in with active listening.

MIKE: Yes.

(I noticed it was too late to have Mike join the other group, so I decided to see if he would like to do something special with me.)

ME: You seem to want to do something special, too.

She makes another active listening try.

MIKE:	Yes.
ME:	Would you like to do something special with me?

Then she suggests a solution.

MIKE:	Yes.
ME:	Let's make a deal. If you will do some work in your workbook, I'll do something special with you.

She arranges an alternative solution for Mike's problem. Is she bribing?

MIKE: Okay.

(Mike went to his desk and began to work. Later he and I did something special.)

She keeps her promise, helping to establish trust.

In the following incident, Lucy presents a problem: She doesn't like multiplication and division worksheets. The student teacher comes close to bringing out the real problem—general feeling of rejection—but shuts Lucy off with probing questions that the girl cannot handle.

Situation 4. Tuesday, March 20, 1:05 P.M. It was independent math study. I helped kids that either asked or looked lost. They were working on multiplication and division worksheets, fourth and fifth grades.

Analysis of Behavior

ME: Can I help you with anything?

> The student teacher opens with a helpful question.

LUCY: No, I don't like doing these.

ME: Why not?

> Then she probes.

LUCY: It's too hard . . . I can't do them. There's too many papers. . . . Nobody likes me.

ME: Why do you feel that nobody likes you?

> She probes again.

LUCY: I don't know. They just don't. (Another girl snickers.)

ME: So you feel that they laugh at you and make fun of you?

> She reflects Lucy's feeling through active listening.

LUCY: Yes.

ME: Why? Do you make faces so that they laugh?

> But she comes back with another "why" question and then suggests a reason.

LUCY: Sometimes. But they just don't like me.

ME: But there must be a reason. What do you think?

> She probes again.

LUCY: I don't know why. . . . (She half-heartedly tried to continue her problems.)

> Lucy is frustrated, because she doesn't feel understood and she has gained no real insight.

Exhorting, Preaching, Moralizing, Lecturing

Pep talks don't help. In this example, the student teacher thinks she is getting through to Anne by giving her the "you-know-you-can-do-it-if-you-try" routine. Anne finally uses the "sour grapes" out. She lacks self-confidence, needs to become independent but begs for attention. She might be helped if she could be heard first.

Situation 5. Thursday, March 22, 11:00 A.M. in the library area. Every day the children have a question known as "brain food." They find the answer to the question in their spare time.

Analysis of Behavior

ANNE: Help me find the answer to the brain food question.

ME: Okay, I'll help you find the answer if you help me look.

> The teacher secures cooperation at the outset.

ANNE: Okay, I will. (Pages through encyclopedia)

ANNE: I don't know how to find it. It's too hard.

ME: It's not hard if you know your alphabet. Do you know it?

> But she denies the child's stated feeling here.

ANNE:	Yes, but I can't do it.	
ME:	You think you can't do it?	
ANNE:	No, I don't know how. You find it.	
ME:	Anne, you know you can do it. You found the answer yesterday. You just have to keep trying. (She finds the page she is looking for in the encyclopedia.)	She exhorts and preaches. She does not accept Anne at face value.
ANNE:	These words are too hard. Read it to me and find the answer.	
ME:	Anne, if you practice reading, you won't find it hard any more. When you first learned how to tie your shoes, it was hard too. But now, don't you think it's easy?	Now she belittles.
ANNE:	Yes.	
ME:	Then keep trying and it won't be hard any more. (I started to get up to leave.)	She keeps on exhorting.
ANNE:	Oh, I don't want to know the answer anyway.	Anne gives up. She wasn't really heard.

Moralizing and lecturing don't help. In the following episode, Denise is reinforcing a standard coping mechanism—pouting.

Situation 6. The students that Mrs. M ___ thinks are ready to be drilled on the multiplication tables are equipped with headphones and a recorded tape—not as a formal test, but mainly to find the children's level. On the second set of activities, Denise becomes confused.	*Analysis of Behavior*
DENISE: This tape is going too fast. This is stupid and I don't get it. I give up, I'm not doing this!	Denise is an "I-can't-er" when her abilities are threatened.
ME: If you don't understand that one problem, skip it and go on to the next one. One does not learn by simply giving up. Anyone can do that. Just try.	Lecturing and moralizing are not meeting the need.

But Denise simply stared at the paper and pouted.

Reassuring and consoling don't help. The student teacher in the following instance is probably shutting off what could have been an invitation to talk. Reassurance does not get at Margie's problem, and she does not accept the teacher's point of view.

Situation 7. The students at Tyler have received their school pictures and have been told how much each package costs. They are to return the pictures they do not want.

Margie took a beautiful picture, but she said to me: "These pictures are horrible and my Mom will return all of them, I know."

"You took a very nice picture," I said. I'm sure your Mom would like one to keep and to show to others."

"No," Margie replied. "They're ugly!"

Analysis of Behavior

Margie's real message may be: "Mom doesn't value me enough to spend money on my pictures."

Although intended to be reassuring, this response is off target.

Is "being ugly" a disguise for "Mom doesn't care?"

CHILDREN REVEAL THEMSELVES IN OPEN COMMUNICATION

The following series of vignettes reveal insights into children's problems and motivations. Here the children were helped simply because they were heard, and they usually revealed a deeper, more pervasive problem than the surface one exhibited. With new insight, the humanistic teacher can look for ways to help the child in other encounters, or perhaps he can make changes in the environment that will help.

Situation 8. In this episode the student teacher realizes that Petra, a little girl who is apparently gifted, actually feels frustrated because she cannot always come up to the expectations that she sets for herself. She perhaps at times feels inferior when she sees less-gifted peers sail easily along using simpler techniques, and maybe she feels that her own painstaking work is unappreciated. The following conversation helps Petra gain awareness of herself.

Time: Christmas season, 10:00 A.M. The children were working with their pictures on the floor near the wide vista of windows. The following dialogue ensued between Petra and me as I stooped down on the floor and met her eyes.

PETRA: (While concentrating on her own painting) I hate my picture.

ME: You hate your painting?

PETRA: Yes, I just hate this old painting.

ME: Sometimes you hate the pictures you paint. You are not always satisfied with your work.

PETRA: (Pause) I hate my Christmas tree but I *like* hers. (Petra pointed her brush toward her neighbor's painting.)

ME: You like Sally's Christmas tree better than the one you painted. (There was a long pause while Petra kept painting. Then she looked over her work carefully. She turned and made eye contact with me.)

PETRA: I made my Christmas tree the hard way. She made hers the easy way! (I noticed for the first time that Petra was attempting to make branches on her tree. Her painting was more elaborately designed than the one Sally was making. Sally's painting was based on a triangle. I think Petra must feel frustrated, occasionally, because she cannot paint the detailed and artistic things she conceives in her mind. Maybe she was hoping I would notice that the work she was doing was more complicated than her neighbor's and was looking for praise.)

Situation 9. By listening reflectively, this student teacher gains information that will help him work more knowledgeably with Rick in the future.

It was Halloween, and everyone was in his costume getting ready for the parade and party. One little boy was dressed up as a drunk and held an empty beer bottle in his hand. Everyone was admiring his costume except Rick, who appeared to be busy doing something else.

ME: Hi, Rick. All the costumes are so funny. Which ones do you like best?

RICK: I like almost all of them except Mark's.

ME: Mark is the drunk.

RICK: Yeh, that's a stupid costume.

ME: That's a stupid costume?

RICK: My father used to drink all the time.

ME: All fathers do that sometimes.

RICK: Yeh, but he used to do it all the time and he was real mean. He used to come home and holler. He scared me and I used to get stomach aches.

Situation 10. Here is an incident in which a child seeks out a student teacher because she wants to share a problem. (Miss J __ must have previously established a good relationship, to make Karen feel so safe.) But the bell rings before she can lead Karen to examine her real problem—the reason she is not being accepted. (After being made aware of the difficulty, Miss J __ observed Karen more carefully and noticed that she tended to be bossy. Miss J __ knew she needed to make Karen aware of her own behavior so she began to look for ways to do this.)

Time: 2:30 P.M. I was sitting in the room while some of the children were doing their work and others were walking around. Karen, a fifth grader, walked over to me.

KAREN: Debbie, can I talk to you privately?

ME: Sure, Karen, let's go over here. (I pointed to a corner of the room where it would be more quiet.)

KAREN: I have sort of a problem.

ME: Do you want to talk about it?

KAREN: Yes. It's about Nancy and my best friend, Laurie. You see, Nancy is trying to take Laurie away from me.

ME: You think Nancy is trying to become good friends with Laurie.

KAREN: Yes, and she doesn't want me and Laurie together.

ME: You feel that Nancy is trying to break up your friendship with Laurie.

KAREN: Nancy hates me and is trying to get Laurie to hate me too.

ME: You think that Nancy dislikes you.

KAREN: Nancy hates me and I don't know why. All Nancy's friends hate me and now she's trying to get Laurie against me. Laurie is my only friend!

ME: You think maybe Laurie will start ignoring you.

KAREN: I'm afraid she will. Lately she's been with Nancy a lot more. See, they're together now!

(As we talked, Laurie and Nancy were across the room playing cards.)

KAREN: The only time I can be with Laurie is on the way home from school. We live near each other.

(The bell rang and the children began to leave the room.)

Situation 11. In this situation, Michael appears to be two different little boys, because of the two different ways in which he is handled. The regular teacher makes Michael into a stubborn, pouty child; the student teacher enables him to unleash his pent-up anguish. The student moves in with empathic understanding, not with pity, and reflects Michael's feeling. (This must have helped, for Michael was able to move on to "business as usual" in just a few minutes. He knew he was understood.)

The whole class was sitting in a semicircle around the teacher, who was taking attendance. When she called Michael's name, the following occurred:

TEACHER: Michael.

(No answer)

TEACHER: Michael, are you here?

(He sits with a pout on his face and does not answer.)

TEACHER: Michael! Answer me! Are you here today?

(Still no answer)

TEACHER: All right, Michael. You can just sit there in that seat until you decide to tell me if you are here.

(The rest of the class began to snicker and laugh, and those sitting next to Michael teased him. After the lesson, the rest of the class moved into small groups for individual work, and I went to talk to Michael.)

ME: You don't seem very happy today, Michael.

MICHAEL: No.

ME: Something must have gone wrong for you this morning.

(Michael was silent for a few seconds, then he burst into tears.)

MICHAEL: My dog died! He got killed! He's all squished in the street.

ME: Oh, Michael! Your pet died, and that's why you are so unhappy. You must have really loved him!

MICHAEL: Yeah, I did.

(I wanted to give him a little hug, just to show that I understood how he was feeling, but he suddenly walked off and joined another group of children.)

Situation 12. By being empathic, Miss B ___ learns a great deal about Pam in the following situation. At times she gives solutions—but in ways that show she is human and that she identifies with Pam's problem. The questions she asks are not the probing kind, but ones Pam can answer without deep searching. (Knowing about the problem, Miss B ___ will no doubt look for ways to give Pam a more prominent and accepted place in the group. Pam knows that the teacher is a friend who cares. This helps.)

Thursday morning, during reading, I was asked to give individual instruction to Pam. She is considered a slow learner and is known to have emotional problems. I decided to take her out into the hall to work, so that there would be less distraction.

ME: Hi Pam! How are you doing in your workbook?

PAM: I'm not going to work. I'm going to the Learning Center.

ME: There is a class in the Learning Center, so no one is allowed to go in there right now.

PAM: I'm not doing any work. I hate it!

ME: Oh, you hate reading? Even your workbook with the stories and pictures?

PAM: It's too hard!

ME: Sometimes it is hard. It takes a lot of work. Let's go out in the hall, and we will work on it.

PAM: No!

ME: I want to help you, and I think I can. Will you let me try?

PAM: I'll go in the hall. (We sat in a quiet place in the hall, but she did not seem willing to work.)

ME: Do you feel like working?

PAM: No, I hate it. I still want to go to the Learning Center.

ME: I tell you what, let's forget about your workbook and just talk for a while.

(No reply)

ME: You said you wanted to go to the Learning Center. You go there often. Do you feel better in there because you can work by yourself?

PAM: Yes, I don't like to be with everyone else.

ME: Don't you like the other children?

PAM: Yes. . . (hesitating) I mean not always.

ME: You feel bad when you are around them?

PAM: (Beginning to cry) They hate me.

ME: You feel bad because you feel that you don't have any friends?

PAM: They hate me. They call me names all the time. They push me and won't ever let me play with them anytime. No one will sit next to me. I'm always alone. No one likes me.

ME: You really feel miserable. Do you ever play with anyone?

PAM: I tried to play jump-rope with Natalie and Jackie, but they always say the game is closed.

ME: Sometimes people aren't always considerate of others. How about the other girls?

(No response, but Pam stopped crying.)

ME: You know, there are a lot of other girls in your class . . .

PAM: I'm too dumb. They all know it. They just ignore me or call me a liar or stinky.

ME: I don't think you are dumb. I know for a fact that Mrs. H __ and all your student teachers like you. You know, if you aren't doing anything at all to make the other children mad, they shouldn't act that way. I think if you are extra nice and feel

	better about yourself, you might feel better. What type of things do you like to do that you could invite your classmates to do with you?
PAM:	Just about anything.
ME:	Do you ever see any of the children when you aren't in school?
PAM:	No, I don't live near anyone.
ME:	Who do you play with at home?
PAM:	Some Mexican boys who live in my building.
ME:	Do you have any sisters or brothers?
PAM:	Two sisters. I play with Diana sometimes. My older sister is 15. She is married. She takes care of me when my mother isn't home.
ME:	Do you ever talk with her about this problem?
PAM:	No. Sometimes I tell my mom. She says to ignore them, but I can't ignore them.
ME:	I can't solve your problem for you. But I think you should know that the teachers do like you, and that you are not dumb. Sometimes I have trouble making friends, especially if I try to make myself noticed by being loud or borrowing things without asking. It sometimes helps to be extra nice and really try hard to make yourself happy.
PAM:	I feel better. Maybe tomorrow I will come to school happy and not always run to the Learning Center. (She picked up her workbook and finished the assignment by herself.)

RESPONDING RELEVANTLY TO CHILDREN

In the next series of episodes, student teachers listened attentively and fed back relevant responses. The results are evident.

Situation 13. Because the teacher takes time to listen without advising or lecturing, Nadine (a fifth-grader) seems to conclude that it's okay to be working with a fourth-grade math book and that through persistence she will soon be ready for the next book.

Tuesday, April 10, 10:15 A.M., in the classroom. Nadine was taking out her math book to begin her assignment. I was standing near her desk. Nadine showed little interest as she looked for the page of her assignment.

NADINE:	I'm in fifth grade and I'm still in a fourth-grade math book.
ME:	You don't like being in a fourth-grade book?

NADINE: No, it's too easy. Look! (She opened her book to simple addition problems and began to recite the answers confidently.)

ME: You think being in a fourth-grade math book is too easy.

NADINE: Yes, I know all of this stuff.

ME: You think you know it all?

NADINE: Yes, I should be in the sixth-grade book. (She looked for a page with simple division problems.) See, I know this. It's sixth-grade level. This one's sixth, too.

ME: You know these problems well, but are the rest of the problems just as easy?

NADINE: No, I don't know a lot of the pages in the fifth-grade book.

ME: You don't?

NADINE: No, I haven't gotten that far yet. But I'm almost finished with the grade-four book, and then I'll be able to do the fifth-grade book.

(She turned around and began to do her problems.)

Situation 14. The student teacher is astounded at the outcome in the following situation and finds out it pays to trust.

Thursday, April 5, 10:45 A.M., in the classroom. I was helping Chris with his math, practicing problems on the blackboard. I wrote out the problems and he followed me, writing the answers.

CHRIS: Don't go so fast! I can't write the answers down as fast as you can write the problem.

ME: That's okay. Take your time. (After he wrote some of the answers down I erased the problems and put up a new one. He was obviously having difficulty with some of the problems.)

CHRIS: I can't go this fast!

ME: You don't think you can write the answers as fast as I write the problems?

CHRIS: No! You're going too fast. I don't want to do this anymore.

ME: You don't *want* to do it?

CHRIS: No, I can't. You make me nervous.

ME: Maybe we could do the problems at your desk. Okay?

(We went to his desk, where he seemed more relaxed, and he finished the problems with little difficulty.)

(If I had stopped with believing that he really didn't know the answer, I couldn't have seen his real problem. I think I've also learned how important trust can be.)

Situation 15. Miss E ___ and Ronny mutually agree to an alternate solution when Ronny announces he doesn't like worksheets. The solution is found through active listening.

Time: 2:10 P.M., during a science unit I was teaching on insects.

RONNY: Miss E ___ , I don't want to do these stupid papers.

ME: Oh, you're not interested in studying insects.

RONNY: I like learning about insects. I just don't want to do these worksheets.

ME: You don't like worksheets. You'd rather learn about insects in some other way.

RONNY: Yes, but no worksheets!

ME: Okay, Ronny. If you will look in your insect book from the Learning Center and then draw a picture about something you learn, that will satisfy me.

RONNY: Me, too.

Situation 16. Here a student teacher facilitates in the solution of Liane's interpersonal problem. At one point she attempts to give a solution which is rejected in favor of one that Liane thinks of herself. This makes the outcome doubly satisfying.

Oct. 26. Liane was sitting at her desk with a face two miles long. I walked over to her.

ME: How ya doing Liane?

(No reply)

ME: You look kinda mad.

LIANE: I'm not mad.

ME: Are you sad?

LIANE: (With tears brimming at the edges of her eyes) Yes, but I can't tell no one about it.

ME: You can't tell anyone—not even me?

LIANE: Well, Jackie moved her seat—she changed with Dean and now she doesn't sit at our table anymore.

ME: You're sad because she changed and you think you lost a friend?

LIANE: (Nodding) Yes.

ME: What about Elaine? She is still at your table and she is your friend.

LIANE: Yes, but not like Jackie.

ME: No, Jackie seems special.

LIANE: (Nodding again) Yes.

ME: You wish she would move back here.

LIANE: Yep!

ME: I wonder how you could get her to move back. Maybe you could go over and talk to her.

LIANE: No!! I'm not good at saying how I feel to people. I'm embarrassed.

(I was silent for a while because I know how she feels—I'm the same way.)

ME: Maybe there's *some* way we could get Jackie to understand how you feel.

LIANE: I know. (Her face brightened.) I could write her a letter—I'm good at that.

ME: Great idea! Writing always helps me say things better. If you want maybe we could go to the Learning Center while Jackie reads your letter.

LIANE: O.K. (Smiling)

(Liane wrote her letter and put it on Jackie's desk, and we went to the Learning Center. When we came back, Jackie was back in her desk at Liane's table. Liane was ecstatic. The two played together for the rest of the day!)

SUMMARY

In this chapter, situations depicting the results of pupil-teacher encounters were chronicled. Examples showed that lecturing, belittling, criticizing, demanding, threatening, interrogating, and moralizing shut off communication and resulted in defeat for either teacher or child, sometimes for both. In contrast, when teachers listened empathically and fed back non-judgmental, relevant responses, children tended to open up and share their anxieties and concerns. Both teachers and children became more aware of the real problems involved and sometimes children found their own solutions. Thus when teachers function as helpful "relators" they often discover that potential discipline problems fade away and the atmosphere is cleared for productive work.

STUDY HELPS AND CLASS ACTIVITIES

Annotated Bibliography

In addition to references at the ends of the chapters in this unit, the following books are recommended reading:

Avila, Donald L., Arthur W. Combs and William W. Purkey. *The Helping Relationship Sourcebook.* Boston: Allyn and Bacon, Inc., 1971.

A book of readings directed to essential aspects of a helping relationship—the process, the persons doing the helping and the helped.

———, Donald L. Avila and William W. Purkey. *Helping Relationships: Basic Concepts for the Helping Professions.* Boston: Allyn and Bacon, Inc., 1971.

The authors detail the major concepts related to the person of the helper and the act of helping. They draw from research into the helping professions.

Axline, Virginia M. *Dibs: In Search of Self.* New York: Ballantine Books, 1964.

A portrait of a little boy achieving a successful struggle for identity through therapy.

Bany, Mary A., and Lois V. Johnson. *Classroom Group Behavior: Group Dynamics in Education.* New York: The Macmillan Company, 1964.

Class group interaction has an important influence upon individual learning and behavior. The authors discuss both theory and techniques.

Combs, Arthur W. *Educational Accountability: Beyond Behavioral Objectives.* Washington, D.C.: Association for Supervision and Curriculum Development, 1972.

Assessment for learning and accountability for education are related to the concept of humanistic goals of education.

Dinkmeyer, Don, and Rudolf Dreikurs. *Encouraging Children to Learn: The Encouragement Process.* Englewood Cliffs, N. J.: Prentice-Hall, 1963.

The authors develop the concept that all behavior has social meaning, is purposive and is goal-directed. The encouragement process is basic to all developmental and corrective efforts. Both techniques and theory are described.

Fromm, Erich. *The Art of Loving.* New York: Bantam Books, 1956.

This is one of Fromm's most widely read books, in which he gives a daring prescription for love, showing the need for "unconditional" love in the development of the human psyche.

_____. *Escape From Freedom.* New York: Avon Books, 1965.

This classic explains why freedom can be frightening and totalitarianism can be tempting.

Fuchs, Estelle. *Teachers Talk.* New York: Anchor Books, 1969.

As interpreted from an anthropological view, Teachers Talk was written to provide insights into the concerns and needs of neophyte teachers in inner-city schools.

Gardner, John W. *Self-Renewal; the Individual and the Innovative Society.* New York: Harper Colophon Books, Harper & Row, Publishers, 1963.

If a society hopes to achieve renewal, it will have to be a hospitable environment for creative men and women. It will also have to produce men and women who have the capacity for self-renewal. This book is companion to Gardner's Excellence.

Ginott, Haim. *Teacher & Child.* New York: The Macmillan Company, 1972.

Much anecdotal material makes this a vibrant book, as the author addresses the teacher's question: How can I improve life in the classroom today?

Greer, Mary, and Bonnie Rubinstein. *Will the real teacher please stand up? A Primer in Humanistic Education.* Pacific Palisades, Calif.: Goodyear Publishing Company, Inc., 1972.

Far more than a book of readings, the selections, pictures and warm-up exercises add up to a truly affective experience for those who spend time with this book.

Gross, Ronald, and Beatrice Gross (eds.). *Radical School Reform.* New York: Simon and Schuster, Inc., 1969.

Read this book if you would like a sampling of the thinking of Herndon, Kozol, Holt, Goodman, McLuhan, Clark, Ashton-Warner, Dennison, Kohl and several other writers who have contributed to the radical school reform movement. Excellent for a survey of this topic.

Harris, Thomas A. *I'm Okay–You're Okay: A Practical Guide to Transactional Analysis.* New York: Harper & Row, Publishers; 1969.

The goal of transactional analysis is to strengthen and emancipate the Adult from the Parent and the Child (the three active elements in each person's make-up), making possible the freedom of choice and the creation of new options.

Hentoff, Nat. *The Way It Spozed to Be.* New York: Bantam Books, 1965.

Certain things are "spozed" to happen in school—children should sit still, be quiet, read textbooks, do workbooks and pass exams. Nat Hentoff tried something else. His kind of order worked–but it didn't match the system, he was a threat, and out he went.

Hess, R. D., and J. V. Torney. *The Development of Political Attitudes in Children.* New York: Doubleday & Co., Inc., 1967.

Political attitudes begin early. The authors of this research report show how and why.

Holt, John. *Freedom and Beyond.* New York: E. P. Dutton & Co., Inc., 1972.

A provocative book, in which the author argues for change in the classroom. Holt shows how we might better meet the needs of children and calls for alternatives and choice.

_____. *The Underachieving School.* New York: Dell Publishing Co., 1969.

Holt turns to an examination of specific problems of American education—the tyranny of testing, the rat race for college, the failure of ghetto school programs, compulsory attendance, reading failures and teachers who talk too much.

Illich, Ivan. *Deschooling Society.* New York: Harrow Books, Harper & Row, Publishers, 1970.

Illich is brilliant and visionary, if not radical, as he speaks to the harmful effects of "schooling" and proposes the disestablishment of the school.

Kozol, Jonathan. *Death at an Early Age.* New York: A Bantam Book, 1968.

A shocking and heart-breaking story of life in a Boston ghetto school.

Lederman, Janet. *Anger and the Rocking Chair: Gestalt Awareness with Children.* New York: The Viking Press, 1969.

The author describes methods derived from Gestalt therapy used in teaching children who don't fit the "system." Beautifully written.

May, Rollo. *The Art of Counseling.* Nashville, Tenn.: Abingdon Press, 1967.

Written for the church worker, this book gives principles of counseling that are understandable to the teacher.

Meil, Alice. *The Shortchanged Children of Suburbia.* New York: Institute of Human Relations Press, 1967.

The author of this paperback pamphlet points out that suburban children are shortchanged in their opportunities to associate with culturally different children.

Neill, A. S. *Summerhill.* London: Oxford University Press, Inc., 1962.

A much-read story of an experimental school where the principles of freedom and non-repression were tried.

Pfeiffer, J. William, and John E. Jones. *Structured Experiences for Human Relations Training.* Iowa City: University Associates Press, Box 615, 1969.
A spirally bound book in which many experiences that have been used for human relations training are detailed. Simple to follow, and there are no restrictions on the duplication of material.

Postman, Neil, and Charles Weingartner. *The School Book: For People Who Want to Know What All the Hollering Is About.* New York: Delacorte Press, 1973.

The authors emerge from the ferment in education and answer the question: What Is a Good School? from a humanistic outlook.

Renfield, Richard. *If Teachers Were Free.* Washington, D.C.: Acropolis Books, 1969.

Free teachers lead to a freer educational system. The author's proposals have profound, revolutionary implications not just for education, but for American society as a whole.

Things to Do

1. Develop a creative project, such as making cartoons or symbolic drawings depicting "political" factors in the school environment. Draw upon your readings and experience for ideas.

2. What school practices have you experienced, observed, or engaged in that are defeating to humanistic goals of education? For example, what school practices contribute to a feeling of alienation or a "not okay" identity, lack of success, inability to create or think through problems? Which of these negative practices are imposed on teachers? Which of these practices could be changed by teachers working in traditional classrooms?

   Put your ideas in a chart similar to the following:

School Practices Defeating to Humanistic Educational Goals

Practices that can be changed in traditional classrooms	Practices that can't be changed, because of the bureaucratic structure of the school

3. Select a controversial issue in education. Interview a wide spectrum of people at different age levels to discover their beliefs and attitudes toward the issue. Summarize your findings and report to the class.

4. Form book study groups. Get together on a weekly basis to discuss the books you are reading or set aside a portion of class time on a regular basis for this purpose. Many of the books in the annotated bibliography are available in paperback for a nominal price. Pool your resources and purchase a number of books you most want to read. Set up a class circulating library.

5. Organize a field trip into a culturally different school-community. Spend a half-day visiting in the school and a half-day interviewing people in the community—be sure to interview a good cross-section. Look for the life-

style of the community and notice the effects of community attitudes in the school and its curriculum. It will be important to have a committee do planning at the school site with the principal of the school you visit.

(See the article by Arthur T. Allen and Dorothy I. Seaberg, "The Community Survey: A Neglected Tool," in the November 1967 issue of the Teachers College *Record.)*

6. Organize the class into small groups and have each group become an "authority" on the ideas presented by one of the following psychologists:

   Carkhuff, *The Art of Helping*

   Dreikurs, *Psychology in the Classroom*

   Ginott, *Between Parent and Child/Teacher and Child*

   Glasser, *Schools Without Failure*

   Gordon, *Parent Effectiveness Training*

   Harris, *I'm Okay – You're Okay*

   Moustakas, *Authentic Teacher*

   Role-play incidents of encounter and confrontation between teacher and child or teacher and groups, making use of the strategies suggested by your particular psychologist. Base the incidents on your own experience in a classroom as a teacher or an observer, if possible.

7. After reading what several authors have to say about interpersonal relationships, think of incidents that could be used to role-play the situations below. Replay each situation, using a variety of interpersonal behavior to show both "helpful" and "damaging" practices a teacher may use. Draw from personal experience as much as possible. Discuss each situation from the point of view of what is happening to the child and how he sees the situation.

   a. Role-play a situation where a primary child comes to the teacher and tattles on another child.

   b. Role-play a situation in which a child becomes emotionally upset.

   c. Role-play a situation in which a child accomplishes something that required his best efforts.

   d. Role-play a situation that makes the teacher angry.

   e. Role-play a situation in which a child has misbehaved and gone beyond the classroom limits, infringing upon the rights of other people.

   f. Role-play a situation in which a middle-grade child solicits approval from the teacher on things he does. (Assume he does this repeatedly.)

   g. Role-play a situation in which the child says, "I can't."

8. For pre-service teachers: Write a descriptive vignette about your favorite teacher. Share these vignettes in small groups. What seem to be the "hallmarks" of these teachers? What qualities, if any, do they share in common?

9. Have a small group study Johnson's *Reaching Out* and/or Pfeiffer and Jones' *Structured Experiences for Human Relations Training;* then plan one or two class periods, using some of the suggestions given to increase sensitivity, awareness and better communication.

10. Action Project—Improving Relationships in the Classroom: Over a period of time keep anecdotal records that involve interactions between yourself and the children in the classroom. (See Part III, "The Face of Diagnosis," for the technique; also see the examples in Chapter 5, "Relationships in the Classroom.") Use the format below as a way of recording and analyzing these interpersonal relationships:

Anecdotal Record	*Analysis*
Write the anecdotal record in this column. At the conclusion of the anecdote, hypothesize what you think may have been the cause of the child's behavior. (Keep in mind how you think *the child* is *perceiving* the situation.)	Analyze the record in this column in terms of the behaviors you were using. Note the place where a breakdown in communication occurred, if any. If you wish your behavior had been different, state here what you wish you had said or done.
Example:	
Every day after I drill some children with their math flash cards, I walk around the class helping students with their problems for the rest of the period.	

At the end of the period, I was collecting all the math folders of the children in the class. Randy threw his math folder right at me. I quickly put his folder back on his desk and said, "You hand that folder to me properly, young man." Randy proceeded to do as he was told and said, "You old bag, you." At this point I was simply stunned and just stood there—Randy walked away.

Hypotheses concerning the cause of behavior:

(1) Randy feels inadequate about his ability to do math.

(2) This is misplaced hostility; Randy is taking his aggression out on me because he is angry about what is happening to him at home.

(3) Randy rebels against authority because he is always told what to do and never reasoned with.

(4) Randy feels down-graded because of the manner in which I treated him.

A breakdown occurred when I *commanded* Randy to hand his folder in properly.

Alternate teacher behavior:
"Having to do math really makes you feel mad, doesn't it, Randy?"

At the conclusion of your project, write an evaluative summary, pointing out the progress you have made in relating to the children and the discoveries you have made about things that improve relationships. Compare what you have done with the behaviors stated in "The Teacher's Role as Relator," at the end of Chapter 4.

PART II

The Face of Mediation

A real teacher is on my side.
A real teacher lets me be me and tries to
understand what it's like to be me.
A real teacher accepts me whether he likes me or
not.
A real teacher doesn't have expectations of me
because of what I've been or what he's been.
A real teacher is more interested in how I learn
than what I learn.
A real teacher doesn't make me feel anxious or
afraid.
A real teacher provides many choices.
A real teacher lets me teach myself even if it takes
longer.
A real teacher talks so I can understand what he
means to say.
A real teacher can make mistakes and admit it.
A real teacher can show his feelings and let me
show mine.
A real teacher wants me to evaluate my own work.
                          *Mary Greer and Bonnie Rubinstein**

*Reprinted by permission of Goodyear Publishing Company, from *Will the real teacher please stand up?* by Mary Greer and Bonnie Rubinstein, copyright 1972.

Chapter 6

The Teacher and the Technological Environment of the Classroom

The teacher confronts the child with a contrived environment in order to bring about intellectual and creative growth. Either he intervenes directly in the child's experience or he interposes something within the life space of the classroom to stimulate the child to action. In doing so, he creates an environment that is technological in nature, and he functions as a mediator within it. In a humanizing classroom, the style and mode of the teacher's interventions facilitate learning, enabling the pupil to find meaning in his work. Part II, "The Face of Mediation," explores the nature of the technological environment and the teacher's role in translating what he knows about the learner and the nature of learning into viable classroom practice.

THE SIGNIFICANCE OF INTELLECTUAL AND CREATIVE POWER IN HUMANISTIC EDUCATION

The two goals previously discussed in "The Face of Relationship"—helping individuals to become self-aware, find identity and follow their unique patterns of individuation, and helping individuals to become related to self and others—are co-requisites to the release of creative potential and the development of independent thought processes.

In creating the technological environment, the teacher is concerned with the processes that develop the many facets of "selfhood." Just as the quality of relationships the teacher develops helps to determine the *kind of person* the child will become, so also the manner in which the teacher mediates helps to determine the *kind of thinker and creator* the child will become. Until man is free as a confident and independent self, his creative and intellectual powers will remain subdued and stunted. Conversely, if man does not develop intellectually and creatively, he will be stunted in becoming self-aware and in relating to others. The technological environment must, therefore, enable the child to be in touch with himself and his feelings as he explores his world creatively and intellectually.

Rogers (1969) asserts that in the modern world of rapid change, the most socially useful learning is found in developing the process of learning, becoming increasingly open to experience, and incorporating the process of change into the self. Precise knowledge is less important to the growing person than the ability to think, communicate, relate to others, solve problems, inquire, discover and create.

Technology in Education
and the Function of Mediation

In this model, "technology" is used in its generic sense, meaning an application of an underlying science. Teaching technology is to education as engineering is to the science of physics, or as medical practice is to biology (Hilgard, 1964). Technology, therefore, refers to the "theory into practice" dimension of any science or art. Teaching technology derives its form out of what we know about people, how they learn and how behavioral change is effected, as well as through using what is known about the characteristics of given subject matter and the skills to be taught. Humanistic purposes in education imply the design of teaching technologies that use humanistic means to achieve humanistic ends.

Mediation means intervening or interposing. The teacher interposes something within the environment with which the child interacts—it may be questions, materials or multi-sensory experience. The problem for the teacher, then, is to make appropriate stimuli available for the child's inter-action and to help the child select and organize these stimuli in ways that develop his thought processes. In essence, what the teacher does is to provide the learner with opportunities for various kinds of experiences suitable to his level of development. The teacher cannot predict exactly the effects of these experiences, but by providing a wide variety of stimulating things to do, he enhances opportunities for broader learning.

THEORY INTO PRACTICE:
DEVELOPING CREATIVE
AND INTELLECTUAL PROCESSES

Providing a Climate
for Creative Expression

Man's tendency to actualize himself or to realize his potential is the wellspring of creativity. According to Rogers (1959), safety and freedom are the two most essential environmental conditions for releasing creative power. The teacher induces psychological safety into the environment, through accepting and understanding the child and by keeping the child's creative products relatively free from external evaluation. The teacher prizes the child, accepts him as an individual of unconditional worth and has faith in him and in his ability to create. He respects the child's creative efforts without reference to external standards and gives reassurance and encouragement along the way. In such a climate, the child is free to create.

Freedom does not, however, connote a lack of structure or imply planlessness. In the environment, the teacher provides frameworks and guidelines to protect the child's freedom as well as his psychological safety. The learner has the freedom to select and develop ideas of his own within the framework. Guidelines are flexible, not rigid. The child feels free to be himself and to create in a fashion unique to him. Thus, an atmosphere of freedom, understanding and stimulation permits the child to launch out and express himself as a creative person.

Mediating Knowledge Through Inquiry
and Problem Solving

The individual's intellectual "window to the world" depends upon the development of his reason and knowledge. Rational power develops when the mind is freed or opened, so that many ideas can be examined without threatening the "self"—the individual's perceptual field is broadened, he perceives more clearly. He is able to examine new ideas and integrate them into his thought processes, if they appear to be valid and congruent with his life experience.

Problem solving requires creative and critical thinking, and leads to insight. If rational and creative power is the goal, then the educative process must be concerned with solving problems and making discoveries. Humanistic teachers confront children with problems related to their real concerns on their own level of development, so that they may begin to weigh alternatives and make decisions on the basis of reason, rather than pure emotion. Knowledge and skills are needed, but they are used within a broader context of solving problems in order that the individual may realize rational power.

The process of inquiry involved in problem solving has the potential for developing the individual's thinking processes to the fullest capacity. The humanistic teacher mediates in ways that develop these processes. Traditional roles of teachers and pupils are transformed. Instead of absorbing knowledge from authoritative sources, the child functions as experimenter, hunter, investigator, discoverer and decision maker, while the teacher reverses his traditional role of "fount of knowledge" and becomes a confronter, catalyst, facilitator and guide. The child inquires into his own questions, delves into primary sources of information, generalizes on the basis of data and comes to his own conclusions.

The following account of a problem-solving experience shows how even young children can identify problem areas, raise questions, seek information, and formulate and test hypotheses. They can come to reasoned conclusions when they are trusted and given support.

Solving Our Problems

I would like to tell you about a problem that faced my 35 first graders. This problem was close to their hearts for it concerned the class dog.

Early in the term I was given a small, black, many-breeded, long eared, brown-eyed puppy. With the permission of the principal, I took the dog, soon christened "So Good" by the children, to school. Through discussion we planned the best way to take care of our pet. There were continual problems to solve concerning So Good's home, food, and training.

Our discussion on "What is good for our dog to eat?" involved us all for we were eager to get all the information we could. Through reading and looking at simple books, talking to dog owners and asking the local pet shop owner to come to our class, we gathered all the facts. The food committee, different each week, voted on by the children, provided for So Good's needs. We also learned that crayons were not in a dog's diet and so were very motivated to keep them off the floor.

The children had made her a comfortable home out of a large box. It was provided with windows and a door. Of course, under the children's care, So Good was growing and growing. One day she jumped out of her box right into the middle of a child's painting on the floor. "We better build higher walls," said the children and went to work on it that afternoon. But So Good went over these,

too, and it looked as though our dog just didn't want to be housed in. And so the problem, "What shall we do with our little puppy that has gotten so big?" arose. Thirty-five serious little ones faced this problem and these were some of the suggestions:

"Let her run around outside. She will come when we call because she loves us."

"Tie her up."

"Tie her to a tree in the yard."

"Let her walk around the room and do what she wants."

All the suggestions were discussed and negated because of their unrealistic nature. The children were quick to see that none of these would work.

We called for help; this time from an upper-grade boy who is known for "how good he takes care of his dog." He came and suggested that it was time to leave the dog at home where she would have more freedom. My first graders accepted this and a farewell party for So Good was planned. There were some tearful good-byes but we were sure that this would be best for the dog. So Good became the receiver of the children's letters and a few weeks later we got a turtle who was christened "So Good II."

In this situation, these young children were faced with a problem, and after gathering and considering the facts they were able to answer it realistically. They were taken out of their make-believe world to the realities of life, which they faced without any traumatic experience. I can honestly say that none suffered loss of "So Good" but instead had grown from this experience.

The security and ability to make decisions carried over into other situations. Their alertness for all possible answers to a problem led them to consider what could be done to make a happy Christmas for all children. They decided to collect toys throughout the school. They did a creative job of solving their repair and wrapping problems. What was most significant to me was that my leadership was needed less and less as the children got better organized and had clearly defined their goals.

From letting children solve their own problems, under adult guidance, comes all good things. It is in this way that we help children develop their own unique personalities and to see their relationship to others in society. It can and does work with young children. [1]

In the inquiry process, the teacher is not concerned so much with actual facts or a select body of knowledge sequenced for learning at given grade levels as he is with the process of how knowledge is generated and how big ideas can be uncovered and used as organizing concepts for making sense out of the world. In the inquiry process, children discover knowledge, but they also come to understand the *tools* used by scholars in uncovering knowledge. Children can delve into an historical study of their own town, for example, by interviewing old-timers, investigating old newspapers in the library, and studying the genealogy and contributions of founding families; these activities give them a sense of history. Or they can carry out experiments such as planting seeds in various kinds of soil and watching them grow under controlled conditions. They can experiment with the effects of temperature on air and water, and make hypotheses. They can keep charts of temperature, barometric pressure, wind velocity and cloud conditions when studying the weather. Thus, they begin to identify with the process of discovery that the scientist uses. As "geographers," children can make comparative studies of population centers and sparsely settled areas in their own state, using these studies as the bases for hypotheses that relate to physical and cultural geography. They can compare regions of the world having similar geographic conditions and note how topography and climate affect life. In order to experience the work of the social scientist, children can design and carry out questionnaire and survey studies that relate to problems in their school or their town.

The teacher mediates with open-ended questions during the process of search: Why do you think this happened? What solutions haven't you tried? Are there other materials you can test? How can you prove your point? What other sources of information can you find? How will you record your observations?

THEORY INTO PRACTICE: DEVELOPING CONCEPTS AND SKILLS

Learning Skills

Because children have their own inner rhythms, aptitudes, prior experiences and psychical states, it is important that they be allowed to develop skills in a manner and pace natural to them. This development involves communication skills—reading, writing, speaking, listening—computational skills, and any kind of psycho-motor skill involving physical dexterity. It is beyond the scope of this book to discuss the teaching of the language arts, mathematics and other subject-matter disciplines. However, there are some overarching principles that teachers need to build into their mediational behavior when helping children acquire any kind of skill. Most fundamental is the fact that children need situations that require the use of skills naturally. There are countless out-of-school activities that attract children—buying things in the store, cooking and baking, constructing models or realia, playing games, looking at or listening to the media, going on trips and excursions, and observing people at work. An activity-oriented curriculum, therefore, provides for the *natural* use of skills and concepts. Publishing a class newspaper, setting up a play store, writing books, composing TV programs, participating in dramatic activities and carrying out experiments illustrate this principle.

When children must learn specific psycho-motor skills, such as handwriting, it is important that teachers provide good models by demonstrating and showing concrete examples. Illustrating good letter formation provides a model for children to emulate. Children need to understand something about the behaviors involved—left to right progression, or perhaps the way the pencil is held. In an activity like folk dancing, the pupil needs to understand the specific movements involved in the entire dance. Cues given by the teacher, such as pointing out the size of a letter or the direction of its movement, will help the child modify and perfect his own performance. Skill development—be it related to communications arts, computational ability or psycho-motor activity—requires that the skill and related fundamental knowledge be used in a variety of activities that have intrinsic meaning to the child. The teacher structures activities or arranges a provocative environment to provide for this practice. Sometimes children discover they need specific knowledge, or a skill such as setting up the format for writing a letter, in order to carry out an activity; then the teacher and individual children will take time out to concentrate on the skill, so they can use it to accomplish the ongoing activity.

In any practice activity—such as completing reading worksheets, working math algorisms, or practicing with writing—the teacher encourages the child to find his own mistakes. A child's question may be countered with a question from the teacher, which helps him refocus his attention and discover his own answer. When the child asks for help in a story problem, the teacher may draw out the essential elements needed to understand the problem through adroit questioning. When a child reads some of his own stories to the teacher in an individual conference or when the teacher reads back a composition to the child, he may discover many of his own errors.

In any area of skill development, the best learning situations provide for individualized work. In reading, for example, the child progresses at his own qualitative pace, using material geared to his abilities that he often selects himself. Feedback to the child in individual conferences or in small groups is important. The child notices the progress he is making, and he focuses on his own problems. On the basis of feedback, the child and teacher can make new plans. Sometimes the feedback indicates the need for reteaching. It is essential for the teacher and the child to keep records, so both will be aware of the pupil's progress and can use this information to make new plans.

Concept Development

Concepts evolve out of first hand sensory experience. The child must manipulate his world through the use of his senses—seeing, hearing, smelling, touching and tasting—in order to find personal meaning and develop his own conceptions. The teacher, as mediator, is aware of the nature of the child's background of experience and draws upon it, but also supplements with enriching first-hand experiences in cases where children have no basis for understanding the spoken or printed word. A teacher in an inner-city school, for example, discovered that the children had never heard of "applesauce," a term used in a story they were reading. She brought a hot plate and apples to school, and the children gleefully pared the apples and then cooked and ate them. Now they knew what applesauce was!

In school, the teacher, as mediator, provides a rich multi-sensory environment to enrich the child's experience. The activity-oriented curriculum we have already described provides a hub of experience that is natural to the child. The child can be taken into the real world—the world outside of school—for part of his learning, but the teacher must also bring the real world to him through films, books, manipulative materials, pictures, mock-ups and simulated experience. Through experimentation and manipulation of materials, the child makes discoveries and gains insights leading to the formulation of concepts. Rich conceptual understandings form the base for making generalizations that lead to principles governing bodies of thought.

THEORY INTO PRACTICE:
MEDIATING THROUGH THE PHYSICAL ENVIRONMENT

In creating a physical environment for learning, the teacher organizes "stations" where language, math, science, social studies and art activities may be carried out more or less independently. There is a bountiful supply of library books, magazines, games, charts and original storybooks, as well as multi-level texts in language, reading, science, social studies and math. Most of these materials are obtained from commercial sources, but some may be made by the teacher or children. Slide, filmstrip and film projectors, tape recorders, listening posts, typewriters, record players—all with accompanying software—may also be a part of the environment. Certain schools consolidate these media and library materials in a "learning center" serving all the children in the school. But if this is done, the teacher usually has some facsimiles of the equipment of the larger learning center within his own classroom.

In a setup like this, children may have many

options for learning a particular skill such as phonetic analysis, map reading or number facts. They may choose to learn, for example, from tape recordings, records, filmstrips, books, workbooks, games or charts, or they may join a skill group working with the teacher at the blackboard.

Space is freed by moving desks out of their traditional rows and into various groupings. Learning carrels and screens may be used to section off areas of the classroom. The latter serve a dual purpose by displaying children's work. Some classrooms are carpeted to absorb noise and enable children to sit on the floor for various kinds of activities.

THEORY INTO PRACTICE:
PROVIDING A SETTING FOR LEARNING

Humanistic education provides for open learning in which the child is free to learn in his best ways, through his own interests, in his own qualitative style and at his own pace in an environment of open interpersonal relationships. In the technological environment, the teacher creates a setting for learning that is in harmony with the nature of learning and the learner.

Since teachers cannot learn for children, they must help them to become self-initiating and actively involved in the learning process. As mediators, teachers stimulate children by tapping their motivations and interests. Humanistic teachers take into account at least three factors in setting the stage for learning: (1) they help children find purposes in school activities, (2) they involve children actively in the learning process, and (3) they select, or encourage children to select, topics and materials that are relevant to their real concerns. The following evaluation of a study of teeth mediated by a first grade teacher suggests some of the principles involved:

A Study of Teeth—Grade One

The entire experience of studying teeth was evidently very meaningful to all of us. Generally, we considered and possibly reached the goals for which I planned and then some. For instance, we altered some attitudes concerning the make-up of our bodies. Initially, the internal structure, especially blood, was extremely distasteful to us, but we soon became so enlightened because of our curiosity that we are much more realistic and scientific now. Also, in collecting ads concerning tooth paste, we discovered some pretty reasonable promises made in these ads. Critical consideration of the ads reinforced our understanding that dentrifices are aids in dental health.

Some children at the onset of the unit were quite frightened by the idea of visiting the dentist. However, the scientific knowledge and understandings derived have done much in altering and changing attitudes. Sharing dentist experiences with the class has become a prestige device of not so much "the hero meeting the enemy" but "a wise person knowing where to be helped."

To exemplify the penetrating curiosity of the children, a child absorbed with the discussion of germs once asked, "How do they eat the enamel, do they have teeth?"

My cooperating teacher told of a fellow teacher inquiring about our study. She visits the same dentist many of our children do and she spoke of the dentist's comments concerning the children's unexpected knowledge and attitude. Evidence of this sort is rewarding; however, hearing the children express things at various times gives much more evidence of the worthwhileness of the unit.

Even though the unit ended formally, weeks ago, a toothbrushing reminder chart I gave each child has been kept up-to-date by the majority, and without my urging, many have brought the charts to class to show. Also, they continue to bring their deciduous teeth to school and verbalize what happens and why. Some children relate incidents that have occurred at home in which they have enlightened their elders regarding care of the teeth.

I altered and revised much of my planning. For example, our bulletin board displays served as a culmination for each phase of study. That is, we drew pictures for the phases of dentist, brushing teeth, and foods. Our formal culminating activity, giving plays concerning a trip to the dentist, served as good summarization and evaluation. Thus children incorporated all the main points of the study. They made up their own plays, and their props included x-rays, pamphlets, nurse attire, first teeth, and so on. In evaluating each play, the children had good insight into the things they expressed that correlated with what we had discovered.

The strongest feature of the study was simply that it was of great interest, and without writing a book, I believe I have cited enough evidence. Perhaps I should also mention the great interest in the actual teeth the children were able to touch and view. Some of the teeth were cut in two and others showed cavities and drilling.

Considering the interest in the physical being, I can imagine that a similar class could undertake a study of the entire body to last a semester and not become bored. In fact, in gathering materials for this unit, I believe I have enough organization to launch just such a study in the future.[2]

Seeing Purposes for School Activities

For learning to be personally meaningful, children must feel that school activities are related to their own needs and goals. In the incident we have just read, the whole class was studying the same topic—which may be assumed to have posed special problems, for not everyone is necessarily interested in teeth.

However, from the general tone of the account, we can infer that the teacher herself was "turned on," and that her enthusiasm stimulated the children. The topic, although chosen by the teacher, was chosen with considerable care. Miss M ___ had first thought about using a unit on the beaver from the curriculum guide, but she decided that six-year-olds whose parents were blue-collar workers in a large city had few, if any, encounters with beavers. One day Miss M ___ , looking into the toothless grins of the children, realized that teeth was a topic of potential interest to all. She arranged displays with pictures and models of teeth and articles of dental care, and then one day said, "Wouldn't it be fun to study about teeth?" After eagerly discussing, planning and deciding together, the unit was launched. Teeth were indeed of very personal and real concern. What interest the children may have lacked in the beginning was soon overcome: "Some children at the onset of the unit were quite frightened by the idea of visiting the dentist. However, the scientific knowledge and understandings derived have done much in altering and changing attitudes," she reported. " . . . My cooperating teacher spoke of the dentist's comments concerning the children's unexpected knowledge and attitude." Later Miss M ___ said, "They continue to bring their deciduous teeth to school."

Active Involvement

The pupils in Miss M ___ 's class were involved actively in the learning process. Knowledge about teeth, dentists and dental care became a means of overcoming fear of the dentist. Children were placed in active roles of inquirers, expressers, discoverers and performers as they raised questions about dental care, made discoveries about teeth, talked about their experiences, drew pictures, kept charts and dramatized trips to the dentist. Complementing these roles, the teacher was a motivator, a guide, a sounding board, a resource person, a scrounger for materials, an appreciator and an encourager.

References made to evaluation show that Miss M ___ often involved the children in looking at their own learning, and together they determined what they had accomplished. The children tested their learning in daily living.

Providing Relevance

It is obvious that Miss M ___ 's selection of a topic was totally relevant to the children. It came right out of their basic developmental concerns—all first grade children lose baby teeth. Many of them are afraid to go to the dentist.

The children as well as the teacher became involved in bringing materials to school. Everyone had personal experiences to contribute—but simulation of their real experiences through dramatizations also gave them opportunity to identify with the physical changes of tooth-losing and the care of teeth. The variety and nature of the activities permitted all the children to experience success.

Nature of Learners
and the Setting for Learning

The teacher constantly keeps in mind the nature of the learner, as he creates a setting for learning that fosters personal, creative and intellectual growth in the life of the child. The following principles serve as reference points to the teacher:[3]

Nature of the Learner	The Setting for Learning
1. The learner, like all living organisms, is a unitary, integrating whole.	1. The desirable setting for functional learning provides for natural integration of feeling-doing-thinking.
2. The learner, like any other living organism, seeks always to maintain equilibrium or balance.	2. Desirable learning experiences provide opportunity for success in meeting needs and solving problems, but also give constant challenge to go beyond immediate situations.
3. The learner is a goal-seeking organism, pursuing aims to satisfy needs, thus to maintain equilibrium.	3. The desirable setting for learning is dominated by purposes and goals set up by the learner or learners, either by themselves or with appropriate guidance for the total group, including consultants.
4. The learner is an active, behaving, exploratory individual.	4. The setting for learning provides freedom to explore, to construct, to question, to differ, to make mistakes; freedom to develop creative contributions. The limits of freedom are democratic controls, rights of others and good taste.
5. The learner has a pattern and rhythm of growth peculiar to the individual. There are notable differences between individuals in speed of learning, energy output, depth of feeling, facility of insight.	5. The setting for learning provides a wide variety of learning experiences, adaptable to levels of maturity, to different rates, interests and abilities.
6. The learner brings with him a personality and a set of aims, values, social habits.	6. The purposes and experiences established in the environment arise out of and are continuous with the life of the learner, the family background and social-class status, as well as the individuality of the learner.
7. A learner may be quite immature in relation to one set of standards and experiences, and mature in relationship to another.	7. Learners need sympathetic guidance. They need protection from situations in which they cannot yet act intelligently; they need protection from fears and anxieties, plus challenges to grow, to conquer problems, to develop self-reliance. The learner needs guidance from consultants who know and understand the problems of a growing personality, who see learning as a developmental process. Guidance must be free from domination or coercion.
8. The learner is a social being, if normal, and naturally seeks activities involving other persons.	8. The setting provides varied opportunities to work in "we" relationships, which develop eventually into self-directed group activity.

9. The learner behaves according to his perceptions.

9. The setting for learning takes into account the child's beliefs, feelings, values, attitudes, goals. Significant learning takes place when the subject matter is perceived by the student as relating to his own purposes. Learning is then the discovery of personal meaning.

10. The learner seeks both security and freedom.

10. The setting for learning provides a climate of acceptance, in which the learner develops autonomy within a framework of limitations governed by the needs of others and the natural limitations imposed by the environmental setting. External threats are kept at a minimum, enabling the learner to perceive and assimilate new ideas.

11. The learner, a valuing organism, evaluates himself through his perceptions of the feedback he gets from his environment.

11. The setting for learning encourages self-criticism and self-evaluation, while evaluation by others takes a secondary place. The environment provides for positive feedback and psychological support.

12. The learner develops his intelligence through continuous adaptive interactions with his environment. He learns through concrete operations before he reaches a level of abstract thinking.

12. The setting for learning provides situations in which the child can manipulate, question, discover, solve problems and confer. The relationship of the learner to subject matter must be one in which the child discovers and creates, so that he develops his own thinking structures rather than absorbing information through rote learning.

SUMMARY

In Chapter 6, we have seen that the teacher designs a technological environment in which he takes into account the nature of the learner and how he learns while keeping in mind the goals of humanistic education, especially the development of creative and rational power. The processes of learning, inquiry, communication and creativity take priority over product, or the subject matter that the child acquires.

In Chapter 7, "The Teacher as Mediator," we will explore the teacher's functions in planning and designing learning experiences and in interacting with children in the learning process.

Notes

[1] Written by Florence Forman and distributed in an education class on "Problem Solving and Critical Thinking" taught by Ruth Ellsworth, Wayne State University, 1959. Mimeographed.

[2] Dorothy I. Seaberg, "Experiencing the Role of the Teacher: A Case Study of Pre-Service Elementary School Teachers Practicing Role-Function Behaviors." Unpublished Ed.D. dissertation, Wayne State University, Detroit, Michigan, 1961.

[3] Items 1 through 8 are paraphrased from William H. Burton, "Basic Principles in a Good Teaching-Learning Situation," in *Phi Delta Kappan* 39 (March 1958), pp. 242-48. Item 9 is suggested by Arthur W. Combs, *Educational Accountability: Beyond Behavioral Objectives* (Washington, D.C.: Association for Supervision and Curriculum Development, 1972). Items 10 and 11 are suggested by Carl R. Rogers, "Toward a Theory of Creativity," in *Creativity and Its Cultivation*, Harold H. Anderson (ed.) (New York: Harper & Row, Publishers, 1959) and Carl R. Rogers, *Freedom to Learn* (Columbus, Ohio: Charles E. Merrill Publishing Co., 1969). Item 12 is suggested by Bärbel Inhelder and Jean Piaget, *The Growth of Logical Thinking* (New York: Basic Books, Inc., 1958).

References

Burton, William H. "Basic Principles in a Good Teaching-Learning Situation," in *Phi Delta Kappan*, Vol. 39 (March 1958), pp. 242-48.

Combs, Arthur W. *Educational Accountability: Beyond Behavioral Objectives,* Washington, D.C.: Association for Supervision and Curriculum Development, 1972.

Darrow, Helen F. "Open-Structure: Toward a Description," in *Individualization of Instruction.* Virgil M. Howes (ed.). London: Macmillan, Co., Collier-Macmillan Lmtd., 1970.

Hilgard, Ernest R. (ed). *Theories of Learning and Instruction* (63rd Yearbook of the National Society for the Study of Education, Part I). Chicago: University of Chicago Press, 1964.

Imhoff, Myrtle M. *Piagetian Ontogenetic Theory of Intelligence: Student's Summary with Recommended Readings.* Mimeographed. Los Angeles: California State University, Los Angeles, n.d.

Inhelder, Bärbel and Jean Piaget. *The Growth of Logical Thinking.* New York: Basic Books, 1958.

Rogers, Carl R. *Freedom to Learn.* Columbus, Ohio: Charles E. Merrill Publishing Co., 1969.

Rogers, Carl R. "Toward a Theory of Creativity," in *Creativity and Its Cultivation,* Harold H. Anderson (ed.). New York: Harper & Row, Publishers, 1959.

Seaberg, Dorothy I. "Experiencing the Role of the Teacher: A Case Study of Pre-Service Elementary School Teachers Practicing Role-Function Behaviors." Unpublished Ed.D. dissertation, College of Education, Wayne State University, 1961.

Torkelson, Gerald M. "The Greeks Had a Word for It: Technologia." *Educational Horizons,* 49, 3 (Spring, 1971), pp. 65-71.

Chapter 7

The Teacher as Mediator

The classroom is different from the outside world, where situations impinge upon the child at random. In the classroom, the teacher deliberately serves as a "go-between" or an "intervener" who sets up situations and guides children through them toward intended learning outcomes. The teacher has a definite objective in mind, or he believes the experience will be productive for some worthwhile educational outcome. He develops a plan that involves the selection, combination and use of the most appropriate methods, materials, and pupil activities for meeting a learning goal. He structures learning experiences in either a stepped or an open-ended fashion and keeps things moving through his interactions with children. Chapter 7 examines various aspects of lesson design and instructional interaction as key mediating forces in the learning process.

LESSON DESIGN

Teaching plans fall into two broad types. *Convergent* (programed) plans culminate in a specified learning goal that is usually defined as a skill or concept. *Divergent* (open-ended) plans lead children into inquiry, problem solving and various creative activities. In divergent planning, learning outcomes are sometimes identified and sometimes not; if they are identified, it is done after the fact. Either convergent or divergent approaches may be utilized in carrying out a single lesson, or in planning an ongoing problematic or topical study of some depth.

Convergent Design

Convergent lessons may be compared to a program that breaks the elements of a concept into segments, which are sequenced so that the learner, through his responses, has gained a grasp of the total concept by the time he completes all the steps. He is given feedback at each move, which tells him if his answer is correct; thus, his responses are reinforced. It is assumed that if the student hasn't learned, it is because the program hasn't taught—and that the fault lies with the program.

When a teacher selects a prepared program to fulfill a learning need of a child, he is using convergent, or programed, strategy. Various kinds of workbook exercises and worksheets may be lumped in the convergent category. In individualizing instruction, most teachers use a great many commercial and teacher-prepared practice materials, permitting the child to learn at his own pace. The teacher spends much of his time as a consultant, a resource person, a record keeper or a diagnostician, rather than intervening directly himself.

However, the teacher is also working convergently when he plans a sequential lesson in which he carefully guides the pupil(s) toward an established purpose, accomplishing that purpose in terms of specific behavior or performance. Appropriate feedback and reinforcement are included during the process. The Socratic method, for example, has been classified as convergent learning, because the teacher leads with questions, drawing the pupil out until he arrives at the understanding the teacher had in mind (Morris, 1966). Careful attention is usually given to moving from the concrete to the abstract and from the simple to the complex. This is a logical sequence. (See the sample lesson on "Understanding Place Values," on this page.)

But in a study of the discovery and early exploration of the New World, for example, the teacher might use a psychological approach, looking first at today's events because they have more appeal and meaning for the pupils, and then moving into a logical development of events surrounding the period being studied. The topic might begin with a series of questions: "Who faced more danger, the astronauts in the Apollo space flights or Columbus when he set out to find India by sailing west?" "How is the modern exploration of space like or different from the early period of exploration in the days of Columbus and Magellan?" "Was the early period of discovery and exploration of the non-European world motivated by the same concerns as the exploration of outer space today?"

The teacher begins his plan with a behavioral objective, stating the concept, generalization or skill the child will learn and indicating what it is the child will do to show that he has learned. Then the teacher devises an organized way of helping the pupil reach the objective. A convergent plan is not necessarily mechanical; it may be designed so

that the child works from concrete firsthand experience, manipulates materials and symbols, and makes discoveries. The following lesson, designed to teach place value, illustrates how behavioral objectives are stated and gives an example of the stepped progression of the lesson. The evaluation technique is built in at the end, in the form of worksheet activities the child will do to demonstrate his learning.[1]

UNDERSTANDING PLACE VALUES (TWO PLACES)

Behavioral Objectives

When shown a two-place number, the child will be able to identify the "tens" digit and the "ones" digit; the child will be able to perform a variety of activities (oral or written) demonstrating his understanding of place value (see step 10).

Program

1. Teacher sets up the number, using squared material, toothpicks and bundles of toothpicks, etc.

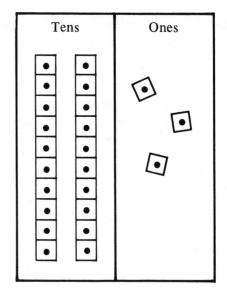

Teacher asks child how many squares there are. Child counts to determine answer. (Note: the child needs prior experience counting by tens as well as by ones.)

2. Elicit from the child and write down:

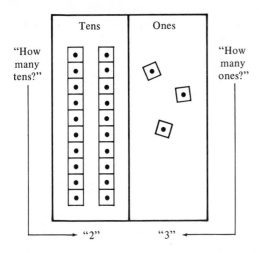

"How many tens?"

Tens	Ones

"How many ones?"

→ "2"   "3" ←

3. Point out that the answers to step 2 ("2" "3") look like 23! (This is a very important step, since often children recognize—i.e., can read and write— two-place numbers before they are aware of place value. Recognizing the familiar is reinforcing and motivating.)

4. Do steps 1, 2, 3 with other numbers (see step 7).

5. Teacher sets up a two-place number. Child reads and writes the number. (Drill cards, pre-arranged with pastings of square material helps.)

6. Teacher reads a number to the child; child sets it up. Teacher shows a written number to the child; child sets it up.

7. Increase in complexity:
    a. Two-digit numbers other than teens: e.g., 23, 31, 68.
    b. Teens: e.g., 14, 11, 17. The teens are difficult for the child to see vis-à-vis place value for two reasons: (1) The visual symbol *23* and the spoken *twenty-three* have the same left-right progression of tens and ones, whereas *16* and *sixteen* are reversed. If the spoken word for the number *16* were *ten-six*, it would be easier to read. (2) If shown a teen number set-up—e.g., one bundle of toothpicks and four single toothpicks, thus depicting 14—and asked

"How many tens?" the child is apt to reply, "Ten tens." The concept of *one ten* is more difficult to grasp than *three tens* or *five tens*.
    c. One-place numbers (e.g., 6, 8, 1) and multiples of ten (e.g., 20, 40, 50). These kinds of numbers are usually easier for children to manipulate than the other two-place numbers. On the other hand, because it has been emphasized that each column will have a set (or digit) in it, the child may have developed a tendency to look for a real number in each column. But the experience of dealing with one-place numbers and multiples of ten may focus on zero as a "place holder."

8. Use other materials: e.g., bundles of tongue depressors or wooden rods. Dimes and pennies may require special instruction to show the concept that only one coin—a dime—is worth ten pennies. (It is good to begin by using stacks of ten pennies held together with clear plastic tape; later, exchange one stack of pennies for a dime.)

9. Relate to sequence of numbers. Practice adding one more *one*, one more *ten*, two more *ones*, two more *tens*, etc. Note: Do not introduce the concept of exchange, other than activity 8 during this period, i.e., no more than 9 ones or 9 tens should be used.

10. Use a variety of relevant worksheet activities. For example:

Put a ring around the "biggest" number in each row		
6	16	61
30	8	19
41	42	43
36	9	10

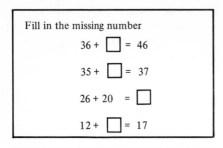

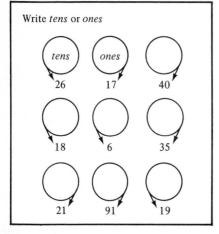

Divergent Design

Although convergent experiences are effective in teaching concepts and skills that the child needs for communicating, thinking and solving problems, they do not necessarily develop his ability as a critical thinker or creator. Learning processes such as critical thinking, problem solving and creative innovation are the heart of humanistic education and require divergent, or open-ended, approaches.

When the teacher is primarily concerned with the processes of reflective thinking and inquiry, leading the pupil to experience appreciation for a work of art, leading a class to examine values, or involving them in creative experience, the objective is set only to the degree that the teacher wishes the pupil "to have an experience with a process" or "to have an opportunity to appreciate" or "to create." The experience must be open-ended.

The many art films that have appeared in recent years exemplify the approach used by the teacher in divergent teaching. Although the film producer has a purpose in mind, the viewing participant is expected to beat his own drum. Each viewer takes from the film what he has sensed, that which has

spoken to his own experience—this is the reality of the message for him. Teachers working open-endedly take the same attitude in the classroom when providing moods and feelings as backdrops to creative expression. Closure, or converging on one "right" response, stunts growth and shuts the person off from awareness. Divergent experiences permit the participant to find his own closure, if he needs it, or to live with ambiguity as he rises to new levels of creative experience and expression.

In approaching an experience with an expressive objective in mind, the teacher does not know in advance what the outcome will be; his purpose is that the child will feel and respond to experience through the medium he is using—it may be his brush and paints, the story he is composing, the drama he is creating, or a topic or question he is investigating. The teacher does not force any particular response on the child but recognizes that each child is uniquely aware of his own experience. The product of his creation or problem-solving activity is less important than the fact that he has created and given expression to his own private experience.

Eisner has used the term "expressive objective" to differentiate between convergent instructional objectives and those that lead to divergent thinking and action. He says:

Expressive objectives differ considerably from those objectives called instructional. An expressive objective does not specify the behavior the student is to acquire after having engaged in one or more learning activities. The expressive objective describes an educational encounter: It identifies a situation in which children are to work, a problem with which they are to cope, a task they are to engage in—but it does not specify what from that encounter, situation, problem or task they are to learn. The expressive objective provides both the teacher and the student with an invitation to explore, defer, detour, or focus upon issues that are of peculiar interest or import to the inquirer.[2]

Kohl, in his book *The Open Classroom*, recounts an incident that illustrates the point:

One day Danny Caracco and I brought a hundred feet of blank film leader to class and showed it to the children. They picked up their magic markers and paints and inks and made film of colors and shapes. There was no need for instruction. Before we could say a word about how to make a film, the children were already making one. Before we had a chance to talk about the product of their work we were overwhelmed by their desire to see it—and to make a sound track of it, and to dance to their sound track, and to play the film of their bodies while they were dancing, and to flick the lights in the classroom on and off while all this was happening. In a few hours these kindergarten children had developed their own "mixed media" technology. We had just stepped aside and let them learn and teach us. [3]

Teachers, serving as models of creativity and inquisitiveness, are best able to help children develop their own creative and thinking powers when they allow and encourage children to express themselves freely without fear of censorship. In creative experiences such as writing a story, working with design, painting a picture, doing creative dramatics or creating a dance, the teacher allows the child to develop and live with his own experience. The teacher's role is simply to get the children into the mood and provide encouragement to keep them going. When sharing creative works or when discussing questions that have no right or final answers, teachers often make the mistake of bringing children to closure either by having them select the "best" answer or the "best" poem, or by having them decide what is "right" or "wrong" about a child's creation.

Koch, who achieved outstanding success in helping children write poetry, suggests that the teacher's role is one of being "playful, encouraging, and esthetic (rather than corrective)," so that children will be more willing to take risks. "One bar to free feeling and writing," says Koch, "is the fear of writing a bad poem and of being criticized or ridiculed for it. There is also the oppression of being known as not one of the 'best.' I didn't single out any poems as being best or worst. When I read poems aloud I didn't say whose they were, and I made sure that everyone's work was read every so often. If I praised a line or an image I put the stress on the kind of line or image it was and how excit-

ing it might be for others to try something like that too. That way, I felt, the talent in the room was being used for the benefit of everyone." [4]

Inquiry and Problem Solving

Problem solving and critical thinking, as well as creative expression, must be divergent. Children work randomly and in pursuing an idea may enter into whole new realms of ideas and questions. For example, the problem "Are magazine ads a reliable guide for selecting toothpaste?" may lead to many avenues of search—comparing advertisements to see what they promise, talking to different dentists to get their opinions, reading the labels on toothpaste containers and studying the properties of the materials from which various toothpastes are made, trying different kinds of toothpaste over a period of time and comparing results, or even manufacturing a toothpaste.

In the end, each child might choose his own toothpaste; and in addition to the objective data he has discovered, he would probably still be influenced somewhat by subjective feelings such as the taste or the package appeal of a product, or the things influential people have said about it. The teacher's role would first be that of a problem setter and then that of a helper and guide to children as they locate, select, evaluate, organize and use facts and knowledge while solving the problem.

Some teachers use dissonant questions with inherent contradictions as springboards for launching a new topic of study. These questions are open-ended and usually elicit many divergent ideas. The following examples are suggestive:

1. Big cities are usually located where trade routes, climate, natural resources are favorable. Brasilia is located where trade routes, climate, natural resources are unfavorable. Yet it is a big city. How come?

2. A lighted candle in a closed jar goes out after a minute or so for lack of oxygen. A live mouse in a closed jar is still lively after a minute or so. Yet mice breathe oxygen. How come?

3. Tom Sawyer, Huck Finn and Joe Harper, runaways on an island, become homesick and plan to go home—especially after they hear that they are believed dead and a funeral service is being

planned. Yet Tom persuades himself—and them—not to go home. How come?

When teachers are helping children identify and follow their own interests, planning is also crucial. This idea is illustrated by Cook in *The Headteacher's Role,* from the series *Informal Schools in Britain Today.* She says:

In our school, we use interest charts to help keep track of the work that is done. Although we feel that it is important to work from children's interests in a free way, it is also terribly important for the teacher to have a plan—a framework—upon which the work in class will be built. One way in which we do this is for the teacher to sit down, take an idea, and develop it on paper in all the directions it might go. For example, one group of children were interested in flight. The teacher thought of all the language she would expect from the idea of "flight"—all the words to do with planes, birds, space travel and so on. (This is valuable because, if the teacher has thought through these things, then, when the child is ready to use the words, they are at hand.) Cards were prepared, and so was material which would help the children. The teacher had also prepared some mathematical work on flight—about speed, about the height at which planes or birds fly. Later, when the children introduced the idea of kites, the teacher responded to this interest. Visits can be fitted into this plan and, as children feed in further ideas, or go in different directions, these too are added to the plan, with the children's names, so the teacher knows who has been involved in the work and can follow it up. [5]

INSTRUCTIONAL INTERACTION— THE TEACHER AS QUESTIONER

The Function of Questions in the Mediation Process

Although the question is the teacher's "Good Man Friday," the art of questioning has been understudied and in some cases ignored in teacher education. Most teachers ask questions that require only simple recall; few teachers are skilled in asking questions that really require students to *use* ideas (Sanders, 1966). Researchers have shown, in fact, that roughly 60 percent of the questions teachers

ask require only the recall of facts, that a mere 20 percent require students to think and that 20 percent are simply procedural in nature (Gall, 1971).

Sanders developed a framework for the study of classroom questions from Bloom's *Taxonomy of Educational Objectives* (1956) for the cognitive domain. Seven categories of thinking are proposed: (1) memory (recall); (2) translation (changing information into different symbolic form or language); (3) interpretation (seeing relationships); (4) application (solving a life-like problem by drawing on generalizations and skills); (5) analysis (solving a problem from conscious knowledge of the parts and forms of thinking); (6) synthesis (solving a problem requiring original, creative thinking); and (7) evaluation (making judgments according to standards). [6]

Gall and associates also used Bloom's taxonomy in developing a filmed mini-course for teachers and determined six main types of questions, each serving a different cognitive objective. Although it encompasses the same idea, their framework is perhaps easier for the teacher to keep in mind. Their categories of questions are shown in Table 2, p. 83. [7]

It is difficult for teachers to carry classifications of questions around in their heads, because they interact with children hundreds of times a day—sometimes individually, sometimes in small groups and sometimes with the total class. Teachers react spontaneously, and they do much of their thinking in response to situations as these develop. Borg (1970) has suggested that teachers might look at *question stems* as a way of checking up on the nature of the questions they are asking, for it is easier to keep "question words" in mind. Recall questions usually stem from *what, when,* and *name* openers, while questions aimed at developing concepts or thinking abilities often stem from openers such as *why, discuss, interpret, explain, evaluate, justify, compare* and *if* (Groisser, 1964).

Inductive approaches, in which pupils are asked to make observations or discoveries that they finally formulate into generalizations, provide more insight into learning than do *deductive* approaches, in which the teacher leads from a generalization and has pupils illustrate it with examples. In an inductive approach to teaching adjectives, the

TABLE 2. FRAMEWORK FOR CLASSIFYING QUESTIONS

Lower-order questions	Examples
1. *Knowledge:* Does the student remember what he has seen or read? Can he recall facts, observations, definitions?	If you were to pick out a non-pollutant detergent, what would you look for on the package label? What did you notice at the dairy yesterday?
2. *Comprehension:* Can the student organize what he knows? Can he give descriptions, state main ideas, make comparisons, and apply what he knows?	What is the main idea of this paragraph? Does everyone agree? Why? Compare the process of addition with the process of multiplication.
3. *Application:* Can the student apply techniques and rules to solve problems that have single correct answers?	Put an "e" on the end of "bit." Now what does the word say? ["Bite"] Regroup the tens into ones. Now how many ones do you have?

Higher-order questions	Examples
4. *Analysis:* Can the student identify motives and causes, see relationships, make inferences, and find examples to support generalizations?	Why was the school bond referendum defeated in our town? What examples can you find in this story to illustrate metaphors?
5. *Synthesis:* Can the student make predictions, solve problems or produce original communications, such as plays, stories and posters?	Can you design a container for an egg so that the egg will not break when it is dropped from the top story of the Atlas building? Let's test our ideas out. What do you think the outcome of this story will be? We have a problem in our science center—too many people want to work there at the same time. How can we solve this problem? Make a collage to show what you got out of this unit of study.
6. *Evaluation:* Can the student give opinions about issues, judge the validity of ideas, judge the merit of problem-solutions or judge the quality of art and other products?	What do you think was the most critical issue in the 1972 presidential campaign? Give your reasons. What makes a good story? (The teacher and class make a list.) Which of these qualities did our (your) story have? Go back over the stories in this unit and pick out your favorite one. Compare the characteristics of your story with the list. Does it have the same characteristics? Do you think the list should be changed? Why?

teacher might distribute a paragraph with all the adjectives underlined and ask the children to notice what these words have in common. Then the teacher may help the pupils formulate their own definition. In contrast, the teacher could give the pupils a definition and have them pick the adjectives out of the paragraph; this is a deductive approach. Actually, students need to use both approaches in order to firm up the concept, but it is better if discovery precedes application. Induction or discovery leads to insight, it develops problem-solving, thinking and creative powers, and it also aids memory. Deduction, on the other hand, provides practice in the application of principles, once they are understood, and helps learners use principles functionally when they apply them to the solution of problems.

INTERACTION PROCESS

As a mediator, the teacher interacts with children to help them develop their thinking powers: (1) he draws children out; (2) he probes to get at deeper levels of thinking; and (3) he maximizes participation and involvement of all children in discussion.

Drawing-out process

The child is not apt to volunteer very much if he feels unsafe or inadequate. In order to contribute, children need to feel accepted, to be understood and to feel that their ideas are important—that they count. The teacher can show the child that he is listening and attempting to understand without making corrective responses, which shut the child off. The teacher fosters a climate of acceptance through his interpersonal relationships (as was pointed out in Part I, "The Face of Relationship").

The teacher can also draw children out by employing several techniques. First, he can ask significant questions. If questions are phrased so that a "yes" or "no" will suffice, very likely that is all a teacher will receive for an answer. Tickling the child's imagination with provocative situations or posing open-ended questions, such as the dissonant question illustrated in the section on lesson design, not only develops creative thinking but makes it possible for children to contribute without thinking in terms of an arbitrary "right" or "wrong"

answer. Feeling and opinion questions tap a level of thinking beyond facts, and they also provide for a wider range of participation. Everyone has feelings and opinions, but they do not always feel safe to express them. The teacher can help by using his active listening skills.

Second, the teacher can attempt to understand what a child is saying—without agreeing or disagreeing. He can let the appropriateness of the response emerge as the discussion proceeds. "Do I hear you say that . . . ?" feeds back to the child the essence of what the teacher believes the child has said. The child can then make another try to make his point clearer.

Third, the teacher can salvage something useful from the child's response. He can put ideas in storage and retrieve them later if the class cannot profit from the contribution at the moment.

Fourth, the teacher can refrain from over-talking. Some teachers parrot children's answers needlessly, making it unnecessary for children to speak up. Many teachers are afraid of silence and rush in to answer their own questions, fearing that otherwise the discussion will collapse. Actually, pauses are facilitating; they give people time to collect their wits. Appropriate built-in pauses, then, may be considered part of good discussion technique.

Finally, the teacher can find a way to respond positively to all contributions, especially when children have given nonverbal cues indicating their insecurity. If the teacher does not react positively, the child may feel his contribution is stupid, and he is discouraged from volunteering the next time. All contributions deserve an accepting response, even though the response may be, "That's an interesting idea, I hadn't thought of that."

Probing

The vast majority of questions teachers ask stop at the factual or comprehension level. Comprehension questions serve several useful functions: they develop background for understanding and expanding a concept; they help the teacher know where the children are in their thinking; they make children feel successful when they can show command of pertinent information they know is "right." However, pupils are shortchanged if they are not guided into using higher processes of thought appropriate to their intellectual levels of development. Borg suggests that probing techniques help children expand on their ideas; thus, the teacher may: (1) prompt, or give a series of hints, to help a pupil who has given a weak or an incorrect answer; (2) further clarify, to help a pupil extend a partially acceptable answer; and (3) refocus the question and request the pupil to relate a completely acceptable answer to another topic.[8]

Maximizing Participation and Involvement

The humanistic teacher views discussions as times when children may interact freely with each other. The flow of communication is not from the teacher to the child and back again to the teacher, like a game of catch. The teacher asks questions—but he encourages children to ask questions, also. Each question is thrown into the discussion pot and stirred around by all the participants.

In order to facilitate more extensive participation, the teacher may do several things: First, he excites pupils in the learning process by being excited over the subject himself; ideas and creative responses that children contribute are rewarding to the teacher and his enthusiasm bubbles out naturally. Second, the teacher may elicit ideas from several people by inserting such statements as, "Who has another idea?" "Do you all agree with John?" "Can anyone else think of another reason?" "Are there other aspects of this problem that no one has thought about?" Third, the teacher adroitly asks more difficult questions of the child who needs to be challenged and easier questions of a child who is less far along, giving each a sense of involvement and success. The memory question or the comprehension question, although judged lower in Bloom's taxonomy of thinking, may not necessarily be the easier question, for some children

have a hard time with recall. Then, too, all children need experience with every level of thinking. Therefore, all types of questions should be spread around, but the teacher exercises judgment and does not call on a child if he is not sure the child is ready to respond. Last, the teacher postpones expressing his own opinions and ideas. Teachers, because they usually have high status in a group, can cut off thinking if they volunteer their own ideas too soon. Pupils will assume the teacher knows best and often will modify their thinking accordingly. However, the teacher does owe children a statement of his position after a topic has been explored thoroughly, and he may agree or disagree with a prevailing view after the pupils have had time to think it through, know what their own view is and feel that it is legitimate.

SUMMARY

In this chapter we have seen that the teacher mediates through designing both convergent and divergent learning experiences and through appropriate questioning. In a humanistic classroom, children will do a great deal of reflecting and creating; both teacher-initiated activities, oriented to interests and needs of pupils, and self-initiated activities provide pupils with meaningful work. This implies a responsive environment, or one that the pupil can manipulate. Some specific types of learning experience are illustrated in Chapter 8, "Making Learning Relevant." Chapter 14, "Choreography of Teaching," gives a global view of classes in action.

The teacher may wish to check his actions against the following inventory of mediating behavior. In doing so, he may discover factors he is overlooking in the teaching-learning process.

THE TEACHER AS "MEDIATOR" IN THE TECHNOLOGICAL ENVIRONMENT OF THE CLASSROOM

I.   **As a mediator, the teacher sets the stage for the learning process.**

   A. *The teacher helps children see purposes for school activities in relationship to their own needs and goals; therefore, he:*
   1.   shows through his own self that he is an interested learner.

2. values the feelings and self-concerns that children express and deals constructively with these in his teaching.

3. exposes children to many potentially interesting facets of the "here and now" world, building on and extending their interests and curiosity; helps children discover what their real interests are.

4. arranges a physical environment containing "learning centers" or "centers of interest" that provoke curiosity and "demand" exploration; encourages children to follow up on the interests stimulated by the environment.

5. helps children define problems and/or areas of study they consider interesting and of *real* concern.

6. uses teacher-pupil planning and elicits from children what they want to find out.

B. *The teacher involves children actively in the learning process; therefore, he:*

1. helps children use knowledge as a means of understanding and/or solving the problems of living, rather than as an end in itself.

2. places children in active, creative roles of explorers, hunters, researchers, inquirers, discoverers, communicators, expressers, designers, builders, directors, performers; lets them derive goals from their roles.

3. makes himself a counterpart to the pupil so that he becomes a sounding board; a motivator, a problem setter or bait setter; a guide; a facilitator or a catalyst; a consultant or resource person; an archivist; a scrounger for materials; an authentic admirer, appreciator or encourager; a fellow worker.

4. encourages children to find their own mistakes when they can; answers a child's question with a question, thus helping him to discover his own answer.

5. provides opportunities for individuals to test their learnings in new situations.

6. builds self-evaluation into the learning process and helps the child assess his own learning.

7. helps children use feedback to assess their progress relative to their own goals, standards and abilities, and to make changes in their plans.

8. keeps records and has children keep records of their progress toward fulfilling a goal or achieving competency.

C. *The teacher selects or helps children select topics and materials that are relevant to their concerns; therefore, he:*

1. selects content from basic human activities and makes these activities exciting and vivid; realizes that relevant content may be found in many places.

2. chooses and/or prepares materials that are consistent with the problem under study *and* the "here and now" world of the child.

3. invites children to bring in materials and to select from a wide variety of materials that the teacher provides.

4. adapts materials to suit the needs and abilities of children, the instructional tools available and the physical conditions prevailing.

5. provides opportunities for children to select topics of study for themselves.

II. **As a mediator, the teacher provides children with meaningful opportunities to acquire skills and concepts.**

A. *The teacher allows each child to develop skills in a manner and pace natural to him; therefore, he:*

1. sets up situations where the child acquires and uses his skills and understandings under circumstances that are similar to those he encounters outside of school.

2. provides good models for the performance of skills.

3. helps children understand the behaviors involved in performing a skill.
4. gives the child cues during practice periods to help him modify or perfect his skills.
5. spaces practice of skills and provides for periodic use of skills through meaningful activities.
6. picks out elements of a skill that a child cannot handle in ongoing activities and brings these elements into focus in practice periods.

B. *The teacher provides meaningful experiences for concept development; therefore, he:*
1. uses the children's background of experiences and provides a rich variety of new experiences.
2. involves children in many multi-sensory experiences that are natural to them.
3. provides experiences that are congruent with the child's life experiences; simulates real-life experiences.
4. uses community resources and direct experience whenever appropriate and feasible.
5. uses concrete materials, illustrations, manipulative objects and audio-visual aids to help children with their thought processes.
6. leads children to "self discovery" or insight in the formulation of concepts.
7. leads children to formulate generalizations based upon rich, conceptual understandings.

III. **As a mediator, the teacher makes open-ended plans to fulfill broad educational purposes or goals.**

A. *The teacher designs open-ended experiences with "expressive" outcomes; therefore, he:*
1. makes tentative, flexible plans for open-ended activities; plans in reference to the mood he wishes to create and looks for learning outcomes after the experience is over.
2. encourages the child to use his own ingenuity and to initiate his own experience in given situations, to let go and follow an idea where it leads him, to work randomly, to be original.
3. confronts children with provocative and dissonant situations; puts children in situations that call for their expressive or creative powers—to discover, to experiment, to invent, to improvise, to create.
4. asks open-ended questions designed to elicit divergent thinking.
5. lets the child know he values original and imaginative expression.
6. encourages children to use their senses in becoming aware of their surroundings.
7. appeals to different levels of awareness or insight; lets the child live with the insight he has, allowing him to grow into increased awareness.
8. allows the child to find his own temporary closure in an activity, or his own resolution of a concern, or to live with the ambiguity that an activity evokes until he works through his problem to a more mature level.

B. *The teacher helps children develop methods of attacking problems; therefore, he:*
1. gives the child freedom to approach problems in his own style and to arrive at his own personal meaning of an event.
2. leads children to locate, select, evaluate, organize and use facts and knowledge appropriate to the solution of a particular problem.
3. has children observe phenomena under study and encourages accurate observation.
4. provides children with books, hints, suggestions, references.
5. leads children to examine issues of controversy, to look at and weigh all sides of an issue, and to arrive at their own conclusions.
6. gives guidance to help the individual or group resolve conflicts or to change direction when working on problems or projects.

C. *The teacher designs and organizes materials and lessons to achieve pre-planned goals; therefore, he:*
1. gains sufficient knowledge and understanding to achieve a flexible mastery of the content or skill he is teaching.
2. identifies the particular concept, skill or generalization to be learned.

3.   states the learning objective in terms of the behavior or performance the child should demonstrate; knows the objectives of the commercially prepared materials he uses.

4.   gears the complexity (simplicity) of a lesson to the learning ability of the child.

5.   makes use of concrete sensory and manipulative materials, and builds opportunities for "self discovery" into a lesson or prepared material.

6.   gives clear directions and explanations and relates these to specific examples and illustrations.

7.   sequences ideas, experiences and materials in either a psychological order (for example, from present to past, from feelings to ideas, from global experiences to details) or a logical order (from the simple to the complex, from the known to the unknown, from the concrete to the abstract) depending on the nature of the material, and the interest and maturity of the child or group.

8.   keeps the lesson or material on focus in terms of the objective.

9.   develops procedures and constructs materials that move the child from one stage of development to another, using minimal steps of increasing difficulty with feedback at each step when a programed sequence is used.

10.   builds feedback into the lesson or program to help the child decide on the appropriateness of his responses.

11.   develops lessons or programed materials so that children will see relationships among facts and concepts, leading them to generalize and formulate principles in keeping with their stage of development.

12.   provides opportunities for children to write materials to teach each other.

IV.   **As a mediator, the teacher interacts with children to help them develop their thinking powers.**[9]

A. *The teacher listens thoughtfully and draws children out in the interactive process; therefore, he:*

1.   phrases questions that require more than a "yes or no" answer.

2.   asks thought-provoking questions and confronts children with contradictions, paradoxes, and problematic situations.

3.   pauses after asking a question before asking anyone to answer, and refrains from repeating himself.

4.   avoids repeating a child's response automatically.

5.   shows the child he is attempting to understand the ideas and feelings the child is expressing, neither agreeing nor disagreeing.

6.   is sensitive to the feelings conveyed by the child's voice or gestures and tries to meet the needs indicated by these cues.

7.   makes "yes" and "no" judgments only about facts, never about ideas.

8.   asks questions to elicit feelings and opinions as well as facts and ideas.

9.   accepts and makes use of good answers, even though they do not correspond with what he (the teacher) has in mind.

10.   Commends children on their good thinking; indicates to the child that he accepts his ideas and finds his contributions useful, worthwhile, pertinent, interesting or sincere.

B. *The teacher helps children develop, examine, elaborate, expand and clarify their ideas and beliefs; therefore, he:*

1.   asks questions to find out what the child knows relative to a given concept.

2.   listens for the central idea the child is expressing, notices what the child leaves out and asks him questions to bring out these aspects (that is, omissions of feeling, facts, ideas, or related points).

3.   keeps in mind the critical elements in or relationships among concepts that he is helping the child examine, and phrases questions to bring out these points.

4. asks children to apply or relate statements, ideas or opinions to specific illustrations, examples or evidence.

5. gives the child a series of hints to help him develop an idea.

6. moves from children's responses elicited from knowledge and comprehension questions to questions involving analysis, synthesis and evaluation.

7. frequently asks questions of the "why," "interpret," "explain," "evaluate," "justify," "compare," "differentiate," "contrast" and "if" nature.

8. asks the child to expand on a partially adequate answer, on overbrief statements or on responses that show faulty thinking.

9. raises questions about faulty assumptions or incorrect facts without assigning a value to what the child has said; commends the elements of the child's thinking that are sound.

10. helps the child examine his values or beliefs in relationship to the topic under discussion.

11. asks children to substantiate opinions and to question the reliability of sources.

12. encourages children to contribute divergent points of view.

13. has children note similarities and differences in making comparisons and leads them to synthesize a given set of ideas.

14. asks questions to help the child interrelate the various points he has made.

15. helps the child see his ideas and feelings in the context of ideas he has stated previously or in comparison with the ideas of others.

16. asks the child to relate an adequate answer to another topic or issue.

C. *The teacher guides discussions in ways that maximize participation and involvement of the class; therefore, he:*

1. encourages children to ask questions and to interact with each other.

2. gets excited over learning; shows enthusiasm for ideas and creative responses.

3. elicits responses from several different people on a given thought-question without repeating the original question.

4. gears the level of a question to the capability of the child; poses more difficult questions to the capable and easier questions to the less capable.

5. expresses agreement or disagreement or offers other ideas only after he has helped the child or group explore and feel comfortable with their own ideas.

Notes

[1] Reprinted by permission of Educational Activities, Inc., from *Teaching One Child—A Strategy for Developing Teaching Excellence,* copyright 1972 by Ernest Siegel.

[2] Elliot W. Eisner, "Instructional and Expressive Educational Objectives: Their Formulation and Use in Curriculum," in *Instructional Objectives,* American Educational Research Association Monograph Series on Curriculum Evaluation, No. 3 (Chicago: Rand McNally, 1969).

[3] Herbert R. Kohl, *The Open Classroom,* (New York: Vintage Books, 1969), pp. 61–62. Reprinted with permission from *The New York Review of Books.* Copyright © 1969 Herbert R. Kohl.

[4] Kenneth Koch, *Wishes, Lies, and Dreams: Teaching Children to Write Poetry* (New York: Chelsea House, 1970).

[5] Ann Cook and Herb Mack, *Informal Schools in Britain Today: The Headteacher's Role* (New York: Citation Press, 1971), p. 43.

[6] Norris M. Sanders, *Classroom Questions: What Kinds?* (New York: Harper & Row, 1966), p. 3.

[7] Meredith D. Gall, Barbara Dunning and Rita Weathersby for Far West Regional Laboratory, *Higher Cognitive Questioning, Teachers Handbook* (Beverly Hills, Calif.: Macmillan Educational Services, 1971) p. 29.

[8] Walter R. Borg, Marjorie L. Kelley and Philip Langer for Far West Laboratory for Educational Research and Development, *Effective Questioning, Teachers Handbook* (Beverly Hills, Calif.: Macmillan Educational Services, 1970), p. 71.

[9] Many of the items in this part of the inventory are suggested by Borg et al. and Gall et al., op. cit.

References

Bloom, Benjamin S. (ed.). *Taxonomy of Educational Objectives.* New York: Longmans, Green, 1956.

Borg, Walter R., Marjorie L. Kelley and Philip Langer. *Effective Questioning, Teachers Handbook.* Beverly Hills, Calif.: Macmillan Educational Services, Inc., for Far West Regional Laboratory, 1971.

Cook, Ann, and Herb Mack. *Informal Schools in Britain Today: The Headteacher's Role.* New York: Citation Press, 1971.

Eisner, Elliot W. "Instructional and Expressive Educational Objectives: Their Formulation and Use in Curriculum," in *Instructional Objectives.* American Educational Research Association Monograph Series on Curriculum Evaluation, No. 3. Chicago: Rand McNally, 1969.

Gall, Meredith D., Barbara Dunning and Rita Weathersby. *Higher Cognitive Questioning, Teachers Handbook.* Beverly Hills, Calif.: Macmillan Educational Services, Inc., for Far West Regional Laboratory, 1971.

Groisser, P. *How to Use the Fine Art of Questioning.* New York: Teachers Practical Press, 1964.

Koch, Kenneth. *Wishes, Lies, and Dreams: Teaching Children to Write Poetry.* New York: Chelsea House Publishers, 1970.

Kohl, Herbert R. *The Open Classroom.* New York: Vintage Books, 1969.

Morris, Van Cleve. *Existentialism in Education.* New York: Harper & Row, 1966.

Sanders, Norris M. *Classroom Questions: What Kinds?* New York: Harper & Row, 1966.

Siegel, Ernest. *Teaching One Child—A Strategy for Developing Teaching Excellence.* Freeport, N.Y.: Educational Activities, Inc., 1972.

Chapter **8**

Making Learning Relevant

The curriculum is relevant to the child when it deals with his real concerns, enveloping feeling states along with thinking and doing. School experience then becomes a natural part of the child's existence. Relevant learning humanizes the curriculum. As a mediator, the teacher achieves relevance through using methods or technologies that are intrinsically motivating. The child's curiosity is stimulated, he is excited by his explorations and he is exhilarated by personal challenge. Although the range of useful activities is broad, three promising types are illustrated in this chapter: (1) using the real world; (2) simulating the real world; and (3) learning through affective experiences. Brown (1972) has called the last type "confluent" learning, because in it the feeling (affective) and thinking (cognitive) elements flow together. Two types of confluent learning experiences are noted in the literature: synectics (a type of creative endeavor making use of analogies to arrive at creative solutions) and gestalt awareness approaches. However, "real world" experiences and simulated experiences are also valuable in eliciting confluent learning, as are experiences in the arts.

USING THE REAL WORLD

Children learn best from their own participatory experiences, from the opportunity to do and see things firsthand. In the humanistic classroom the four walls will often be pushed out into the out-of-doors and into the community. Children can observe and sometimes participate in basic human activities through on-site visits to businesses and agencies. Parents, senior citizens and artisans may also come into the classroom to share their knowledge and interests.

Wernick, director of the ABLE Program at Northern Illinois University, has developed a model using the "World of Work" as an organizing center for the curriculum of the elementary school. Children gather much of their data directly through field trips. A teacher who used the greenhouse as an organizing center recounted the following experience, which opened many avenues for learning simply through following the lead of one idea:

The whole idea came about when the class was studying living things. The children thought it would be a good idea to plant seeds and watch them grow. So June Hart, my colleague across the hall, and I decided to go along with it. They wanted to learn how to care for the plants so we decided to visit the grower at a greenhouse. The grower was most helpful and the children learned that much goes into producing the flowers sold at the floral shop. . . .

In the discussion that followed the visit to the greenhouse, the children decided to have a greenhouse sale. They made things to sell and brought additional materials from home. In the process of setting up the greenhouse the children learned many things needed to finance new enterprise. They had to have a source of money so a discussion of the need for an initial investment led to the children's each contributing a nickel. This, in turn, brought on a discussion of taking out loans. They had to negotiate with the secretary to get change for the sale. Another decision that required planning was the number of hours they would be open on the day of the sale. When the day came they sold out in one half-hour, so we held a discussion concerning the need for the buyer to predict how much to buy and when to buy for resale.

They made a total of $30. Naturally, there was much talk about how to spend it. Finally, they decided to use it to help stop pollution. An outdoor education teacher who taught in the school was invited to talk with us. The money was used to buy books and filmstrips for the school library.

The children felt so good about the outcome of the sale they wanted to have another sale in the spring. They had learned much from their previous experience so the second endeavor came off more smoothly. This time they made $40 and decided to buy trees for the school yard. A resource person was invited in to advise them on how to buy trees and how to care for them. Since I have a multi-age group, some of the children who were involved last year have already asked to plant seeds this year.

I really think the approach that the ABLE Model Program is advocating is a good one. A teacher can take as little time or as much time as she wishes on the organizing center and the children are so enthusiastic! They learn to make decisions, to plan together, to begin to see the relationship between what they are learning and real life. They are so pleased when a person comes to the class and speaks with them. One of the most rewarding things I learned was that the chil-

dren thought of the good ideas and made them succeed.[1]

In the "World of Work" program, interviews are at the heart of the field site experiences. Children have learned to ask such questions as:

1. What do you do on the job? (Children are interested in how school-taught skills fit in with real work.)

2. Why did you take this job? Did others agree with your thinking?

3. What tools do you use? Is there a special way of talking about your work?

4. What part of your job do you like best? Why? What part of it do you wish you didn't have to do? Why?

5. Who depends upon your work? Upon whom do you depend for your work?

6. What experiences and training on this job might prepare you for some other kinds of jobs should you ever want to change?

7. How does your job affect your personal life? Do you have to work nights? Are you tired when you get home? Do you have noise during the day so that you need quiet at home at night? Do you have a job where you have to be nice to people all day—even people who are crabby and ill-mannered?

8. What inventions could put you out of work?

9. Are people with your kinds of skills usually needed—even when business may be bad? Is your work at all seasonal? Where could you work in this occupation? Is your kind of work limited to geographical areas?

10. What kind of education is necessary for this kind of work? Apprenticeship? Trade school? College? Advanced degrees? Is there any personal quality for this job that is really more important than diplomas?[2]

The ABLE program is built around the concepts of "accessibility" (Where, how and with what can the child learn?); "mobility" (What are the learning possibilities of a given line of work? What interests and ideas might flow together and how can they build on each other?); and "accomplishment" (What can the child do? What can he achieve?).

The following outline shows inherent possibility for content and class activities derived from studying the work of the greenhouse grower:

Accessibility
  Grower
  Greenhouse
  Library Materials
  Posters
  Catalogues of supply houses

Mobility
  Botany
  Chemistry (soil analysis and temperature control)
  Vocabulary development
  Agriculture
  Ecology

Accomplishment
  Report on work hours and duties required of a grower
  Plant seeds and bulbs
  Make a bulletin board showing kinds of soil
  Report on importance of temperature control
  Make a chart showing parts of a flower
  Report on the care of a plant from seed to full bloom
  Describe methods of killing bugs
  Describe methods of fertilization
  Make a picture file showing conditions necessary for growth of plants
  Make a map to show where the most common flowers grow
  Interview parents re: Why aren't there many commercials on flowers?
  Describe how plant leaf looks under microscope[3]

SIMULATING THE REAL WORLD

Many times it is not possible to use the real world, but "real" experience may be simulated through the use of role play, sociodrama, and simulation games. Through role play children may crawl, as it were, into another person's skin and enact his role, entering momentarily into the other's world of feelings. Children may take each other's roles when conflicts occur in school; they may enact an historical event, such as the signing of the Declaration of Independence; they may play out hypothetical problem situations; or they may take other roles in society, such as reversing Black-White roles. For example, the class may be directed to discriminate against all blue-eyed children for a day, denying them the "natural" privileges enjoyed by the rest of the class. The profound impact created by second-class citizenship has been felt by all children who have undertaken this activity (Weinstein and Fantini, 1970).

Role Play Lesson

The following lesson, excerpted from the chapter "Identity Education" in the book *Toward Humanistic Education,* shows the use of role play in getting at the perceptions of people.

The lesson has two purposes: (1) to show that there are different ways of seeing the same situation; and (2) to show that one's state of mind or feeling influences one's perceptions—that, in effect, each person creates his own world out of his own perceptions.

TEACHER	(drawing two vertical lines of different length on the blackboard): What do you see?
STUDENT:	Two lines. One's longer than the other.
TEACHER:	Now think of these lines as two telephone poles. What do you see?
STUDENT:	One's farther away than the other.
TEACHER:	Now try to think again of the lines as two different lengths. How many find this difficult? (Many students indicated that they found it difficult.)
TEACHER:	Now you can see that often when you have a certain idea or feeling it's difficult to see things the way you might if you did not have that idea or feeling.

The teacher now held up two pairs of sunglasses, each with a different color lens. He explained that these were very special glasses, that each pair colored the wearer's view of the world with a particular feeling.

TEACHER:	The first pair of glasses are "suspicious" glasses. When a person wears them, he regards whatever he sees or hears with suspicion. (The teacher asked for a volunteer to put on the suspicious glasses and tell the class what he saw.)

VOLUNTEER:	(looking at two children who were talking and laughing, as he put on the glasses): I wonder if they're talking about me. Are they laughing at me? (The teacher asked that questions be addressed to the volunteer.)
STUDENT:	Who's your best friend?
VOLUNTEER:	Why does he want to know that? Are they going to try to take my friends away?
TEACHER	(holding up a second pair of glasses): I have a second pair of glasses, which are rose-colored. They make whoever wears them see and hear with this feeling: "No matter what anyone says to me, I know they really care for me."

(Teacher asked for and secured the cooperation of another volunteer. Throughout the dialogue that followed the teacher sought to clarify the volunteer's responses by asking: "Are you acting suspicious or just curious?" "Do you really feel that way, or are you exaggerating your reactions?" "Do you really think they might be trying to do that to you?")

In another segment, three students playing the parts of mother, father and child sat around a "breakfast table," directed by the teacher, and were joined by another student, role-playing the second child in the family, who was wearing the "suspicious" glasses. Without really involving the second child in their own conversation, various members of the family directed remarks to him. (The second child was instructed to call out "freeze" whenever he wanted to say what he was thinking.)

SECOND CHILD:	Why don't they say hello? Are they mad at me?
FATHER:	Pass the butter, please.
SECOND CHILD:	He's gonna take all the butter, I bet.
MOTHER:	How do you want your eggs?
SECOND CHILD:	Scrambled, but I bet she won't give them to me. Everyone else has fried eggs.
FIRST CHILD:	What are you going to do this weekend?
SECOND CHILD:	Why does she want to know where I'm going this weekend? They want to follow me around. Or do they just want to get me out of the house? Or are they going to tell me I have to stay home and work?

After a few children had tried this role play wearing "suspicious" glasses, the same situation was repeated with the second child wearing the rose-colored glasses.

To sum up the lesson, the teacher asked the children to make lists of the different kinds of glasses people might wear. They proposed:

show-off	*boasting*	*sissyish*	*nobody-loves-me*
gloomy	*probing*	*yes-y*	*stubborn*
helpful	*boyish*	*flirtatious*	*contented*
scared	*girlish*	*hateful*	*proud*

The children were then asked to produce a list of glasses that would have the opposite effects of the ones named above.[4]

Simulation Games

The simulation game is a technique where elements from real-life experience are simulated into a game with built-in guidelines for the enactment of roles in real-life experience. It is a potentially fruitful source for developing meanings and feelings. The following description of a "Poverty Game" illustrates the principles of simulation.

In this game, people play societal roles of the college educated, high school educated, and school dropouts—each trying to "make it" in society. They are given envelopes with pennies and are instructed to purchase materials in the town's stores in order to make a collage. (Each envelope also contains a Band-Aid, with one type for college educated, one type for high school educated, and still another type for the school dropouts. The players are instructed to place the Band-Aids on their foreheads. The purpose of the Band-Aid is to identify each person's role.) Policemen, officials in employment agencies, storekeepers, and bankers situate themselves in the "town" on one side of the room. The teacher serves as "direction giver" and then as "evaluator," after he calls time.

Equipment Needed:
9 x 12 or larger manila paper (for collages)
Glue
Miscellaneous materials for collage
(string, paper scraps, felt, burlap, feathers, pictures, ribbon, material, yarn)
Envelopes
Pennies
Band-Aids—three different sizes or shapes

Staff Needed:

1. Policemen (At least two, depending on number of players)
2. Employment agencies—two
   Agency "A" (upper class)
   Cater to college or high school graduates; people who have never been in jail; people who do not owe any money. Give only one job per player.
   Agency "B" (lower class)
   Cater to anyone who has not been in jail. Give only one job per player.
3. Storekeepers—two
   (Each has an assortment of collage materials on sale, nothing priced less than 2 cents.)
4. One banker
   (Loan an amount equal to amount of money each person has, or 3 cents.) Grant loans to people who have never been in jail and have some security. Make no loan for more than 3 cents. (Part of loan should be paid back before game is over.)

Prepared Envelopes Needed:

An envelope with pennies is required for each player, set up in approximately the following ratio for 20 players:

3 dropouts with 0 cents
5 dropouts with 1 cent
3 dropouts with 2 cents
3 high school graduates with 3 cents
3 high school graduates with 5 cents
1 college graduate with 10 cents
1 college graduate with 15 cents
1 college graduate with 20 cents

Mark each envelope with the words:
DROPOUT
HIGH SCHOOL GRADUATE
COLLEGE GRADUATE
and indicate the amount of money each has.

Directions for the Players:

Pass out envelopes containing the pennies and Band-Aids to players. Then say: This is the "Poverty Game"—You have been given a sheet of manila paper and an envelope. The envelope is to be carried at all times and displayed on request—consider it your draft card. The people you see on the other side of the room represent a town, including a bank, stores, employment agencies and a police force. The stores will open immediately and the bank and employment agencies when announced.

The object of the game is to make a *Collage*—YOU MUST HAVE A COLLAGE AT THE END OF THE GAME. The money you have been given is to be used to buy materials from the stores for the collage. Some have much money and some have no money. *YOU MUST HAVE A COLLAGE WHEN THE GAME ENDS.*

Directions for Townspeople: (Townspeople should be briefed in advance.)

POLICE

(1) Make sure each person has his envelope.
(2) Record each arrest on the envelope.
(3) Give dropouts and people with no money an extra hard time.
(4) Get people in 3 above as fast as possible—if they are arrested, they can't get a job or a loan and will really feel the pressure of being poor with no hope.

BANKERS

(1) Grant loans only to people who:
   (a) have never been in jail.
   (b) have some security (money or job).
(2) Look at person's envelope:
   (a) Grant loan if person meets requirements.
   (b) Mark amount of loan on person's envelope.
       (Only one loan per person per bank is allowed.)
(3) Loan no more than 3 cents, or an amount equal to the amount of money the person has, whichever is less.

STOREKEEPERS

(1) Keep an eye on your merchandise.
(2) Watch for shoplifters.
(3) Call police if needed.
(4) PRICE NOTHING LESS THAN 2 CENTS.

EMPLOYMENT AGENCIES

(A) Upper-class agency (2-cent jobs)
   Give jobs to:
   (1) college or high school graduates.
   (2) those who have never been in jail.
   (3) those who do not owe any money.
(B) Lower-class agency (1-cent jobs)
   Give jobs to:
   (1) people who have never been in jail.
   (2) people who have never had a job before.
(C) General directions
   (1) Give job if qualified (see above).
   (2) Give money right away.

(3)   Mark envelope (Agency A, 2-cent job, or Agency B, 1-cent job).

(4)   Give only one job per applicant per agency.

(5)   Give a hard time to those who don't qualify; make them feel the pressure.

After the game has proceeded for about 20 minutes, call time. The teacher has the class sit in a circle and each participant holds up his collage for inspection. Regardless of quality or creativity, the teacher downgrades the collages of the dropouts and praises the collages of the college graduates. When the game is ended, the class discusses their feelings.[5]

CONFLUENT LEARNING EXPERIENCES

Gordon (1971)[6] pioneered in the synectics approach to sensitivity and learning, and Brown (1972)[7] and associates used synectics and gestalt awareness approaches in classroom situations during a Ford Foundation Project. Examples from these projects are included in this section to illustrate the principles of confluent education.

The Metaphorical Way of Learning and Knowing

Gordon's approach, developed during 20 years of research in the area of creative process, has been referred to by him as a "metaphorical way" of learning. He claims that "the most important element in learning and understanding is making the strange familiar, because understanding requires bringing a strange or new concept into a familiar context." He also maintains that creative process or innovation results in "making the familiar strange." The use of the metaphor helps in this process.

Two sample lessons follow. In the first, a lesson in mathematics, the teacher helps the students to identify with the concept of "zero" by relating it to something familiar to them. In the second, a writing lesson, children are instructed to search for analogies in order to develop descriptive writing.

Mathematics lesson based on analogies

The teacher explained to the class that she wanted written descriptions of zero in terms of things that were like zero. She got these kinds of responses:

"Zero is a place number . . . in multiplying it holds a place . . . in 5 times 2 we need zero to hold the place in the answer." "It means nothing and something at the same time. . . " "[If you were zero] you could take places like a person who waits in line for a friend holding a place."

"Air is nothing, but we breathe it, so it is something. Zero is like that, too."

"Zero is like a musical note."

The children were able to produce metaphors of the simple comparative form, but they didn't show the analogical connection between the subject (zero) and their analogue. Therefore, the teacher began to draw them out according to the Synectics techniques she had recently learned:

TEACHER: Janet, I asked you what zero was like, and you told me that zero was like a musical note. Do you remember what you meant by that? Can you think of some way that zero is like a musical note?

STUDENT: It gives a tone and a whole note doesn't have a middle to it. There's nothing inside.

TEACHER: Is there any other way that a whole note is like zero?

STUDENT: It's a place holder . . . you have to sing that note. If you skipped the note it wouldn't sound right. If you skip zero when you say a number, say in the thousands or millions, the number wouldn't be right.

TEACHER: Do you think it is exactly the same? What happens if you change the whole note? Say you make a half note out of it.

STUDENT: You would get a different beat . . . if you were singing along you would have to hold that note for a shorter length of time.

TEACHER: Suppose we had a zero. How could we change that zero to change the place it was holding?

STUDENT: To make it increase its value you could put a 1 in front of it and that increases its value by ten.

TEACHER: Do you think there is any similarity between making a half note and making a 10 out of 0?

STUDENT: When you make a 10 from 0, you add to it, and when you make a half note you are really subtracting from it because you are making it lesser.

TEACHER: Is there any way we can make zero lesser?

STUDENT: In subtraction. You could have nothing and owe something. You could owe $3 and have no money, so you would have minus 3—negative 3.

TEACHER: If we go back to our original zero, can we change it in some way that would make it similar to the way we changed the whole note?

STUDENT: Add another 1 to it.

STUDENT: It's really not the same because you just added to the zero where you took away from the whole note.

STUDENT: You could make it a decimal . . . that would make it less. If it was in front of the 1, that would make it less; but not less than zero.

TEACHER: And here we have less than a whole. We started out with a whole note. Do you think that the whole note has given us a new way to look at zero? Do you see it differently?

* * *

(Now the teacher leads the children through a Personal Analogy phase. Without pushing, she draws them into "being" zero:)

TEACHER: Let's try something else. One of you said that zero has no personality, that it would be blank.

* * *

TEACHER: Judy, how would you feel if you got up in the morning and you were zero?

STUDENT: While I am asleep I don't feel anything. I should feel like zero, but I just can't imagine waking up and feeling like zero.

TEACHER: Do you think zero changes when you get up?

STUDENT: While I'm sleeping, I have nothing on my mind at all. When I wake up, there is something that always comes into my mind. I could say my mind's like zero and then when I wake up, something is there.

* * *

TEACHER: Would you say that you felt like zero when you were sleeping?

STUDENT: Maybe sometimes, but not all the time.

TEACHER: Well, let's go back. Sometimes you feel like zero and then when you wake up something happens. What happens?

STUDENT: If I wake up and I was zero I would feel like a nobody. You really wouldn't feel like anybody, because one person really isn't anything like another. Even if you are a nobody you would have to have a different personality than another nobody.

STUDENT: Two people could be very quiet and zero could be a quiet person . . . I think it would be sort of reserved. . . . Zero could be a bookworm, always reading books . . . quiet.

STUDENT: If you feel like a nobody and you go someplace you are hardly noticeable, and if you don't say anything and you're quiet.

TEACHER: Is zero ever not noticeable?

STUDENT: If you are a zero type of person, very few people realize that you're around.

TEACHER: How do you feel when people don't realize that you are around?

STUDENT: You feel like you're not wanted.

STUDENT: I think zero as a person and zero as a number are two different things.

TEACHER: Is there any way we can see zero as a number by looking at zero as a person?

STUDENT: A person could sort of be like a zero. A zero has to take a place in a number. Say this person was very quiet but you couldn't do without this person. Zero is very quiet. You see it a lot, and it is not a very popular number, but you need it.

TEACHER: That does give us a new way of looking at zero. It is something we couldn't do without even though it is quiet. You sometimes don't know it's there, but without it, there are some things we couldn't do.

The class continues with this type of discussion. Some of the children's responses satisfy the mathematical use of metaphor, and others are essentially poetic. In any case, the class as a whole jumps into the metaphorical spirit (and their understanding is increased through the personal identification with zero).

Writing lesson based on analogies

"Noodles, Grass and Shoelaces for Dinner"

TEACHER: Write a paragraph connecting noodles, grass and shoelaces. The following is an example of the kind of connection for which you should be looking: white shoelaces in cheese sauce look like noodles—green noodles on a plate look like grass. *Noodles and grass look like shoelaces. Grass looks like green noodles.*

In the following exercise you will be asked to make unusual comparisons. Look at each common object and then see how strange you can make it. After you have made the comparison, show why there is a connection between the two words. For example: A giraffe is like a rubber band *because* both things can stretch when they want to.

Children's Exercises:

A typewriter acts like Jello *because* when you push down the keys bounce back like Jello.

A fence is like a road *because* they are always going someplace but never moving.

A clock acts like a bicycle *because* you pedal slow and the wheels go fast.

A shoelace is like a snake *because* they look like some snakes crawling all over your feet.

A blade of grass is like a proud soldier *because* they both try to stand up straight.

A telephone number is like your name *because* it helps identify you.

Noodles look like sea weed because they both wiggle.

Ice cream is like a penguin *because* penguins live in a cold climate and ice cream lives in the cold part of the ice box.

TEACHER: Write a paragraph connecting the same three objects (noodles, grass and shoelaces) you wrote about at the beginning of this lesson. Use comparisons to make your connections. *A shoelace that is left on the floor looks like a tired snake. A noodle left in a pot of boiling water looks like a piece of seaweed floating on the sea. Grass looks like a bunch of old retired soldiers.*[8]

Affective Exercises Toward Self-discovery

The two lessons that follow are taken from *Human Teaching for Human Learning.* The concern is with developing awareness. Techniques are used to put the child in touch with himself and his environment.

The Wardrobe of Your Mind

Introduction. *(Seat students in a circle.) Close your eyes a moment. I'm going to close mine too, so no one will be looking at you. You will probably be seeing some yellow or white dots on the inside of your eyelids. Concentrate on those dots for just a moment. Now concentrate on yourself as you really are. Let your mind give to your consciousness some words that describe you. Get in touch with those words and see if they really do describe your true character. When you are satisfied that the words you are thinking of describe you, open your eyes, but remain quiet and don't look around at each other.*

Exercise. *(Pass out scratch paper.) Tear these pieces of paper into eight parts. They don't have to be even parts, because you're going to throw them away in a while. Now, on each of those scraps of paper, write one of the words that came into your consciousness a few moments ago—words that describe your character. If I were doing this I might say I'm pretty honest, that I tend to use people to get what I want, that I'm pushy, that I'm (etc., whatever the teacher feels at that time. GET INVOLVED YOURSELF!) Remember, one word or short phrase on each slip of paper. You are the only one who is going to see these words, so you don't have to be afraid to be honest with yourself. Now read what you have written. Arrange them in order, placing the one you are happiest about or like the most on top, and the one you like least or are least happy about on the bottom. Make a stack of them and place the stack right in front of you. Now for a while confine your eyes to the surface of your desk. Don't look at anyone or anything except the top of your desk and the pieces of paper. Take each piece of paper in order and really spend some time with that word. Stay with it for a few minutes and try on the word just as you try on clothes hanging in your closet. Our characters are like a wardrobe. We are sometimes one way, sometimes another. Today we are going through the wardrobe and examining our clothes and trying them on. Really see how they feel. Become the words you see. Accept them as you at one time or another, then do with the word and the piece of paper what you want to do. Put it back in your wardrobe, tear it up and throw it away, or whatever you wish. All right, you may begin. Take plenty of time with each word.*

Evaluation. *May be done by the students' relat-*

ing their feelings to the group or by writing answers to questions dictated by the teacher.

Trip to Tuckers Grove

We took a field trip to Tuckers Grove to begin our unit on plants. For me this is backwards. I would have done it at the end, but since reading Toward a Contact Curriculum *(Fantini and Weinstein), I'm trying some things—backwards if necessary.*

We didn't say much about why we were going. When asked what we were going to do, we answered that we were going to have a fun day together. We left early, about 15 minutes after school had started. We walked up. Once there we let them run for about 20 minutes. Then we called them into two groups. We went on a nature walk to look at living things. After a while they were really looking. "Look at this, this moss is living." "Look, here's a spider web." "Is it alive?" "No, but the spider who made it was." We began to collect things to look at closely with the magnifying glass. We had magnifying glasses with us, but who wanted to wait his turn out here? They did pass their finds around, though.

After the walk we put our collected items on a table for all to see. They named it the "treasure table." They enjoyed being in groups of six, using the magnifying glasses to see the things they had brought back.

After letting them have free play again, this time on the playground equipment, I announced that I had the blindfolds if they wanted to wear them on the merry-go-round or the swings. They came running! They squealed with delight at the new feeling of motion blindfolded. I was pleased to see how many wore the blindfolds on their own.

After lunch we went on a blind walk. They enjoyed this, too. I noticed many pulling grass and handing it to their blind partner. They touched trees, grass, bushes. I was very happy to get a chance to be led by a child. I laughed at how fast, surely and confidently she walked as she led me. It was Carlene. She seemed to enjoy sharing things with me. I was reminded of the pleasure she got when I first took her on a blind walk a few weeks ago. Now she wanted to take me. She kept me busy with things to feel and smell. As we were

coming down a hill, I slipped and fell. We both laughed at me!

Again I feel an urge to get the mothers in on this. Carlene and I lay there laughing and enjoying each other as mother and daughter, as teacher and student, as two friends. Her mother might also like to experience that feeling. I would like to do this with my own girls.

Unfortunately, the bus came half an hour before I thought it would, and we were not able to continue this activity.[9]

SUMMARY

Sample lessons and activities were presented in this chapter to illustrate personal involvement in learning. The teacher makes learning relevant to the child by putting him in touch with himself and his environment while he learns. The child is active in the process and constantly draws upon his imagination.

Admittedly, the examples provided are limited in scope; for it was not possible to include illustrations covering the wide array of methods known to be useful in humanizing education. Many experiences in the arts—movement, visual arts, music, creative writing, creative drama, for example—contribute to confluent learning. They should be woven into many areas of study as well as treated as separate activities within the curriculum that children may enjoy for their own sake. Experiences in clarifying one's own values are also important in humanistic education. (See the works of Raths, Simon, et al., 1966 and 1972.) The teacher is referred to these and other works annotated in the bibliography at the end of this section to help him locate a wide range of fruitful methods and ideas for teaching.

Notes

[1] Reprinted by permission of ABLE Model Program, Northern Illinois University, DeKalb, from *Career Education Activities through World of Work Resources*, Copyright 1972. Dr. Walter Wernick, Project Director.

[2] Ibid., p. 21.

[3] Ibid., p. 131.

[4] Reprinted by permission of Praeger Publishers from *Toward Humanistic Education: A Curriculum of Affect* edited by Gerald Weinstein and Mario D. Fantini, Copyright 1970 by Ford Foundation.

[5] Contributed by Lynn L. Glaser, Des Plaines, Illinois, "Real School Outside the School" Workshop, Northern Illinois University, Summer 1971. Used by permission.

[6] "The word Synectics, from the Greek, means the joining together of different and apparently irrelevant elements. Synectics theory applies to the integration of diverse individuals into a problem-stating, problem-solving group. It is an operational theory for the conscious use of the preconscious psychological mechanisms present in man's creative activity. The purpose of developing such a theory is to increase the probability of success in problem-stating, problem-solving situations." William J. J. Gordon, Synectics. (London: Collier-Macmillan, Ltd., 1961.)

[7] George Isaac Brown, *Human Teaching for Human Learning: An Introduction to Confluent Education* (New York: The Viking Press, 1972).

[8] Reprinted by permission of Synectics Education Systems from *The Metaphorical Way of Learning and Knowing.* Copyright 1966 by W. J. J. Gordon.

[9] From *Human Teaching for Human Learning* by George Isaac Brown. Copyright © 1971 by George Isaac Brown. Reprinted by permission of The Viking Press, Inc.

STUDY HELPS AND CLASS ACTIVITIES

Annotated Bibliography

In addition to the chapter references, the following are recommended for reading or for use as source books:

Ashton-Warner, Sylvia. *Spearpoint: Teachers in America.* New York: Alfred A. Knopf, 1972.

The author shows a healthy balance between the affective and cognitive in education. Warmth and openness come through in her conversations with children.

————. *Teacher.* New York: Bantam Books, 1963.

A stimulating book explaining the author's organic approach to teaching, based on joy and love and dealing with real life as she works with Maori children in New Zealand.

Baumback, Jonathan (ed.). *Writers As Teachers/ Teachers As Writers.* New York: Holt, Rinehart and Winston, 1970.

The creative aspect of teaching and writing is dealt with in this book, with the idea that teachers "create an occasion where students can come to discovery."

Bluming, Mildred, and Myron Dembo. *Solving Teaching Problems.* Pacific Palisades, Calif.: Goodyear Publishing Company, Inc., 1973.

The authors provide a problem-solving model and emphasize diagnoses and development of plans.

Borton, Terry. *Reach, Touch, and Teach: Student Concerns and Process Education.* New York: McGraw-Hill Book Company, 1970.

Shows how schools can be important to students' personal growth. The philosophy is to "reach students at basic personality levels, touch them as individual human beings, and yet teach them in an organized fashion."

Bruner, Jerome S. *The Process of Education.* New York: Vintage Books, a Division of Random House, 1960.

In this book, the author charted new directions in curriculum reform in the 1960s, renewing emphasis on the structure of the disciplines and the process involved in the discovery of knowledge.

Dunn, Rita, and Kenneth Dunn. *Practical Approaches to Individualizing Instruction: Contracts and Other Effective Teaching Strategies.* West Nyack, New York: Parker Publishing Company, Inc., 1972.

The authors give a step-by-step development of the contract method and detail many other techniques helpful in individualizing instruction.

Hagen, Owen A. *Changing World/Changing Teachers.* Pacific Palisades, Calif.: Goodyear Publishing Company, Inc., 1973.

The major focus in this book is on "question-raising" vs. "answer providing." Many teaching examples offered to illustrate the role of the teacher.

Hertzberg, Alvin, and Edward F. Stone. *Schools Are for Children.* New York: Schocken Books, 1971.

A superb rendition of the British Infant School philosophy related to American education. Practical ways for opening up the various areas of the school curriculum are included.

Holt, John. *How Children Learn.* New York: Dell Publishing Co., 1967.

Holt describes in vivid detail the fascinating and surprising ways in which children learn to talk, read, write, draw, play and acquire other important skills. He shows the decisive difference that flexible and informal teaching can make, and calls for radical change in prevailing attitudes.

Horton, Lowell and Phyllis Horton. *The Learning Center: Heart of the School.* Minneapolis: T. S. Denison & Co., Inc., 1973.

A complete book about the organization of the

learning center and the roles of directors, teachers and pupils in its use.

Hough, John B. and James K. Duncan. *Teaching: Description and Analysis.* Reading, Massachusetts: Addison-Wesley Publishing Company, 1970.

A descriptive and analytic discussion of teaching with emphasis on improvement of teaching through self-evaluation.

Hunkins, Francis P. *Questioning: Strategies and Techniques.* Rockleigh, N.J.: Allyn and Bacon, Inc., Longwood Division, 1973.

The use of the question in the educational environment is discussed in full.

Hyman, Ronald T. *Ways of Teaching.* Philadelphia: J. B. Lippincott Company, 1970.

This author develops the discussion method, the lecture, role-playing, questioning, observing, and evaluating as ways of teaching.

Jones, Richard M. *Fantasy and Feeling in Education.* New York: Harper Colophon Books, Harper & Row, Publishers, Inc., 1970.

A book about the challenge of the "New Social Studies."

Kaplan, Sandra N., Jo Ann B. Kaplan, Sheila K. Madsen and Bette K. Taylor. *Change for Children.* Pacific Palisades, Calif.: Goodyear Publishing Company, Inc., 1973.

A guide and model for the teacher, in which practical ideas are given for individualizing learning, developing and using learning centers, providing for student directed activities, record keeping, and evaluating. Many diagrams and drawings are used.

Lacey, Richard A. *Seeing with Feeling: Film in the Classroom.* Toronto: W. B. Saunders Company, 1972.

Using films as creative vehicles is the approach presented in this book.

Logan, Virgil, Lillian Logan and Lorena Paterson. *Creative Communication: Teaching the Language Arts.* New York: McGraw-Hill Book Company, 1973.

Focus is on creativity in each of the language arts and the right of the child to creative communication.

Mager, Robert F. *Preparing Instructional Objectives.* Palo Alto, California: Fearon, 1962.

A programed book on how to prepare behavioral objectives.

Manning, Duane. *Toward A Humanistic Curriculum.* New York: Harper & Row, Publishers, 1971.

The author of this book deals with person-oriented design of schools, flexible organization, multidimensional grouping and approaches to the various academic disciplines.

McAshan, H. H. *Writing Behavioral Objectives.* New York: Harper & Row, Publishers, 1970.

A small paperback book, which clarifies the meaning and use of performance objectives.

McDonald, Blanche, and Leslie W. Nelson. *Methods that Teach.* Dubuque, Iowa: Wm. C. Brown Company, Publishers, 1972.

A comprehensive compilation of methods and techniques. Uses a prose-outline format. All curriculum areas included.

Moffett, James. *A Student-Centered Language Arts Curriculum, Grades K–6: A Handbook for Teachers.* Boston: Houghton Mifflin Company, 1968.

The author believes in a child-language-centered reading and writing approach. Ideas are given for much discourse and interaction in small-group situations so that the child may expand his own language.

Moustakas, Clark E., and Cereta Perry. *Learning to Be Free.* Englewood Cliffs, N. J.: Prentice-Hall, Inc., 1973.

The authors stress the use of the arts in the classroom for making children more aware of themselves and thus more free. The philosophy fits with the idea of confluent education.

Petty, Walter T. and Mary E. Bowen. *Slithery Snakes and Other Aids to Children's Writing.* New York: Appleton-Century-Crofts, 1967.

The authors develop a philosophy for helping children with creative writing and include practical tips.

Postman, Neil & Charles Weingartner. *Teaching as a Subversive Activity.* New York: Delta Book, Dell Publishing Co., Inc., 1969.

An assault on outdated teaching methods, with proposals on how education can be made relevant to today's world.

Pratt, Caroline. *I Learn From Children.* New York: Cornerstone Library Publications distributed by Simon & Schuster, Inc., 1970.

An old book, republished in paperback because its theory and practice is befitting the new emphasis on the child-centered curriculum.

Raths, Louis E., Merrill Harmin and Sidney B.

Simon. *Values and Teaching: Working with Values in the Classroom.* Columbus, Ohio: Charles E. Merrill, Publishing Co., 1966.

The authors of this book deal with the valuing process and present numerous classroom activities for clarifying values.

Renner, John W., Gene D. Shepherd and Robert F. Bibens. *Guiding Learning in the Elementary School.* New York: Harper & Row, Publishers, 1973.

A common instructional strategy is developed for the various content areas. Inquiry is established as the method to accomplish individualization in the learning process.

Richardson, Elwyn S. *In the Early World.* New York: Pantheon Books, a Division of Random House, 1964.

A beautiful book, showing how a teacher helped young children discover the pleasures of learning by focusing their curiosity freely on the world around them.

Shaftel, Fannie, and George Shaftel. *Role-Playing for Social Values.* Englewood Cliffs, N.J.: Prentice-Hall, Inc., 1967.

A thorough presentation of the values and processes of role playing as a means of helping people get inside the feeling of others and make decisions on the basis of their new insights.

Shumsky, Abraham. *In Search of Teaching Style.* New York: Meredith Publishing Company, 1965.

The author proposes a teaching style that leads learners to divergent thinking.

Silberman, Charles E. (ed.). *The Open Classroom Reader.* New York: Vintage Books, 1973.

A book of readings exploring facets of open education. Contains chapters dealing with the role of the teacher and the various subject areas in the curriculum.

Silberman, Melvin L., Jerome S. Allender and Jay M. Yanoff. *The Psychology of Open Teaching and Learning: An Inquiry Approach.* Boston: Little, Brown and Company, 1972.

A book of readings and classroom activities dealing with the psychology of open learning.

Simon, Sidney B., Leland W. Howe and Howard Kirschenbaum. *Values Clarification: A Handbook of Practical Strategies for Teachers and Students.* New York: Hart Publishing Company, Inc., 1972.

Builds on the values-clarification approach intro-

duced in Values and Teaching *and develops additional techniques.*

Smith, James A. *Creative Teaching of the Language Arts in the Elementary School.* Boston: Allyn and Bacon, 1967.

One of a series of books on creative teaching. Many practical helps for the classroom teacher are given.

Tanner, Daniel. *Using Behavioral Objectives in the Classroom.* New York: The Macmillan Company, 1972.

A small paperback, in which Tanner deals with objectives for both cognitive and affective learning and makes use of Bloom's Taxonomy of Educational Objectives.

Taylor, John L. and Rex Walford. *Simulation in the Classroom.* Baltimore, Md.: Penguin Books, Inc., 1973.

Although it is geared toward secondary education, this book provides an introduction to role play, games, and simulation as learning strategies in education.

Thatcher, David. *Teaching, Loving, and Self-Directed Learning.* Pacific Palisades, Calif.: Goodyear Publishing Company, Inc., 1973.

Drawing on Transactional Analysis, Thatcher looks at the modes of teaching that will enhance the learner's self-esteem and help him become independent and self-directed.

Waskin, Yvonne, and Louise Parrish. *Teacher-Pupil Planning for Better Classroom Learning.* New York: Pitman Publishing Corporation, 1967.

A slim paperback in which the authors present the rationale and techniques of pupil-teacher planning that lead to meaningful classroom experience.

Zahorik, John A., and Dale L. Brubaker. *Toward More Humanistic Instruction.* Dubuque, Ia.: Wm. C. Brown Company Publishers, 1972.

These authors emphasize humanistic behavior in the classroom and include gestalt game approaches, among other methods.

Titles from selected series

Association for Childhood Education International, 3615 Wisconsin Ave. N.W., Washington, D.C.:
New Views of School and Community (1973)
Creating with Materials for Work and Play (1969)
Involvement Bulletin Boards (1970)

Children Are Centers for Understanding Media (1973)
Creative Dramatics (1973)
Games Enjoyed by Children Around the World (1970)
Bibliography of Books for Children (1971)
Guide to Children's Magazines, Newspapers, Reference Books (1972)
Literature, Creativity and Imagination (1973)
Literature with Children (1972)
Some Approaches to Reading (1969)
Feelings and Learning (1965)
Play Is Valid (1968)

Wm. C. Brown Company, Publishers, Dubuque, Iowa. *Literature for Children Series;* Pose Lamb, Consulting Editor:
Carlson, *Enrichment Ideas* (1970)
Chambers, *Storytelling and Creative Drama* (1970)
Montebello, *Children's Literature in the Curriculum* (1972)
Witucke, *Poetry in the Elementary School* (1970)

Citation Press, New York. *Informal Schools in Britain Today.*
The following books in this paperback series give helpful suggestions for open-structured programs:
Biggs, Edith. *Mathematics for Younger Children* (1971)
_____ . *Mathematics for Older Children* (1972)
Harris, Melville. *Environmental Studies* (1971)
Horton, John. *Music* (1972)
Shaw, Peter. *Science* (1972)

Educational Service, Inc., Stevensville, Michigan publish the following Handbooks of Classroom Ideas:
ANCHOR: *Intermediate Language Arts,* Mary E. Platts (1970)
FLAIR: *Elementary Creative Writing,* Zane A. Spencer (1972)
PLUS: *Elementary Mathematics,* Mary E. Platts (1964)
PROBE: *Elementary Science,* Mary Massey Roy (1962)
SPARK: *Social Studies,* Mary M. Roy (1965)
SPICE: *Primary Language Arts,* Mary E. Platts (1973)
STAGE: *Creative Dramatics,* Natalie Bovee Hutson (1968).

Things to Do

1. Divide your class into groups to do research on the following teaching-learning methods:
   Teacher-pupil planning
   Discussion
   Library research
   Group work and pupil reporting
   Synectics and gestalt awareness techniques
   Programed learning
   Use of audio-visual media
   Field trips and resource people
   Inquiry/discovery/problem solving
   Experimentation
   Demonstration
   "Sensory" learning
   Interviewing
   Simulation/role play
   Values clarification
   Expressive activities: Creative dramatics, construction or processing activities (for example, churning butter), art, music, film production, creative writing and others.

   a. Report your findings to the class, *demonstrating* the method you have investigated. Discuss the advantages and limitations of each method.

   b. Develop a filmstrip with overhead transparencies, 2 x 2 slides, or material that can be used in the opaque projector to explain your topic. Design your filmstrip so that individuals or the class can learn from it without a lot of additional explanation.

2. Develop lessons or activities for children, using several of the techniques in 1 above. Tape-record or describe from memory the lesson you have taught. Analyze the lessons in the following ways:

   a. What were the *actual* outcomes? How did these compare with your teaching intents?

   b. What roles did the pupils play? ("listeners," "discoverers," "bait takers"?)
   What roles did you play? ("challenger," "teller," "catalyst," "guide"?)

   c. Analyze the involvement of the children. Did they enjoy the activity as well as learn from it? Why or why not?

3. Design and teach a lesson from a behavioral point of view; that is, organize a lesson around a behavioral objective, such as, "The pupils will successfully perform 10 algorisms involving two-place divisors with 0 in the quotient." Also design a lesson from an expressive objective; for example, "Provide an experience in which children may express themselves in creative dramatics." (See Chapter 7.) Compare and con-

trast the two lessons from the following points of view:

   a. Teacher and pupil roles

   b. Level of pupil involvement

   c. Learning outcomes

4. Begin collecting a file of materials and ideas you can use in your teaching. File pictures in large manila envelopes by categories (children, families, foods, seasons, etc.). (For the sake of flexibility, do not mount!) You may wish to start an "idea box" using 5 x 8 cards. Collect ideas from your reading and from classrooms you visit.

5. Read the *How To Do It* bulletins on *How To Utilize Community Resources* and *How To Conduct a Field Trip* published by The National Council for the Social Studies, 1201 16th St., N.W., Washington, D.C. (25 cents per copy)

   a. Divide your class into small groups to investigate the learning resources of your school community. Construct a 5 x 8 card file listing the businesses, industries, etc.; the locations; telephone numbers; contact persons; things that can be learned from the visit. The groups should make site visits in preparing the cards.

   b. Organize a field trip for children, after doing research on how to conduct a field trip. Follow through from pre-planning to follow-up stages.

6. Tape-record a discussion you conduct with a group of children. Analyze the kinds of questions you have asked. (See Chapter 7.) With what frequency did you use each kind of question? Analyze the involvement of the children in the discussion.

7. Select a segment or chapter from an elementary-school social studies book or a story from a reader. Write a series of questions you would use in discussing this chapter or story with children. See if you can include all the types of questions discussed in Chapter 7. Exchange your set of questions with a small group of classmates. Prepare critiques of each other's sets.

8. Set up an "idea fair" in a classroom or hall. Display concrete teaching aids, teacher-prepared self-help materials, and projects for children, science projects, etc. Include ideas for all curriculum areas. Add children's work from public schools to the collection, if possible.

   Display the kinds of things you would use in language arts, math, social studies, science and creative arts centers in a classroom. Invite other education classes to see your display.

PART III

The Face of Diagnosis

A Child

A child
Is a prayer
Breathed
Without words.

A child
Is a vision
Comprehending
Visions.

A child is a cycle
That generates cycles . . .
An aeon
Among aeons.

A child is a miniature duality
Of heaven and hell.
Seek either . . .
Find him.

Marion M. Van Laningham

Chapter 9

The Phenomenological Environment and the Function of Diagnosis

In school, each child has his own world of personal experience. It is composed of his perceptions of self, of others, of objects, of ideas, of experience. The child brings his own self, his past experience, his present feelings, his abilities and his propensities to act into each emerging situation. In a sense, he creates an environment from his own perceptions. Hence, the phenomenological environment is the child's perceived world—the way things seem to him.

The teacher's role is to interpret what is happening in the pupil's phenomenal field in order to make changes in the external environment that will have a positive impact on the child. In doing so, the teacher looks for the pupil's perceptions of self, of others and of situations. He diagnoses factors contributing to the pupil's success (or lack of it) and tries out new teaching strategies or new modes of relating, as a result of his evaluations. He tries to discover the potentialities of pupils and to uncover blocks impeding each child's access to

them. In fulfilling evaluative functions, the teacher moves into a third dimension of his role—that of an educational diagnostician.

PARADOXES IN RELATING AND DIAGNOSING

Some humanistic educators have deemed the function of "relating" (as discussed in Part I, "The Face of Relationship") and the function of "diagnosing" (to be developed in Part III) to be strange, if not incompatible, bedfellows. However, the school is a place where children congregate for the organized business of learning, and evaluations of their person and progress are inevitable, though often unwittingly done. But evaluation fails to fulfill the functions of humanistic education when children learn negative feelings about themselves as a result of the process. Many teachers, obsessed with grades as controlling or motivating devices, have confused the role of evaluation with grading. In some cases a child lives up to a stereotyped label of "slow learner," "troublemaker" or "ding-bat" that has been stamped on him very early in his school experience. Teachers who hew to the line of set standards for all children, ignoring individual uniqueness and differences, usually account for the negative feelings that arise out of diagnostic and evaluative practices.

The role of the teacher as relator and the role of the teacher as evaluator, or judge, appear to be contradictory—one defeating the purpose of the other. Children feel valued in the presence of a caring adult, but they do not feel safe in the presence of a judge. They are on guard, they are clever in their search for what the teacher wants, and they tend to conform to what they "psych" out as being important in the teacher's eyes. They are afraid to disclose their weaknesses, because they wish always to impress the judge. On the other hand, if children are to develop as real and creative people, they need to be opened to their experience and to feel safe to express themselves, even admitting their weaknesses or their needs. The teacher creates the psychological climate for openness through his own expression of self as a caring person, as we observed in "The Face of Relationship." The question, then, is: How can teachers fulfill a diagnostic role without arousing guilt or destroying a growth-facilitating relationship?

Part of the problem arises when teachers view themselves too much as evaluators and not enough as diagnosticians. An evaluator attaches a degree of worth to what he sees; a diagnostician simply tries to identify conditions, situations or problems by noting signs and symptoms. The diagnostician maintains a neutrality, or a non-judgmental attitude, viewing symptoms as neither good nor bad but as growth-facilitating or growth-inhibiting. He tries to work with either the internal or external conditions in a way that will clear away obstructions, freeing children to use their potentialities in the pursuit of school activities. Children basically *do* want to learn, they become unhappy if they do not achieve, they want a situation in which they feel they are making progress toward a goal that has meaning to them, and they want to feel valued or appreciated for their efforts. In the humanistic classroom, pupils participate with the teacher in evaluation, but the accent is on learning, self-development and the discovery of hidden potentials, not on judging. The child realizes that the teacher is on his side.

Judgments teachers do make often derive from subliminal drives or attitudes, which get in the way of objectivity. Although intuition is used exten-sively in deciding what may be going wrong in the child's existential experience, uneducated intuition may lead the teacher far afield. The teacher develops objectivity in order to put the pieces of a child's confusing life puzzle together. His method for securing data is based on scientific investigation, or the description of observable phenomena, as he seeks knowledge about children, the important inhabitants of the environment.

The purpose of diagnosis is to assess a child's individual needs, learning styles or problems on a qualitative level. Diagnosis is not an end in itself but only a means to bring about more efficient learning; it is a way of helping the teacher understand the child better, so that he can enter into a plan of constructive action on behalf of the child. The teacher as diagnostician seeks not so much to find out what the child knows as to discover the extent of modifiability that resides within him. The teacher is no longer a mere judge, but an interpreter of potential—one who seeks ways to uncover the talents with which each child is imbued.

In the development of their potentials, all children need individual structures and approaches to learning, not just the opportunity to progress at their own rates. Many qualitative factors are involved. If a classroom is to be humanistic or existential, it must appeal to the individuality of each child—through opening many pathways to learning, through providing a variety of interesting things to do, through individually oriented instruction and experiences. Although the task is infinitely complex, the teacher discovers how to work within the classroom environment through exercising his abilities as a diagnostician. Contrary to the belief that diagnostic functions destroy relationships, then, educational diagnosis is the key to creating a more humane environment. The really skilled educational diagnostician is the one who tunes in to each child, and who then uses his knowledge in such a way that he tailors relationships, instructional procedures, and educational experience to the needs of each child.

DIAGNOSTIC INFORMATION SOUGHT BY THE TEACHER

The humanistic teacher takes a holistic approach

as he looks at each child. He sees the child as a unitary being and the child's behavior as subject to the law of multiple causation: The child's social, emotional, physical, mental, perceptual and attitudinal states are viewed within the context in which a child is growing and learning. Factors of both home and school need to be considered.

The teacher holds in mind at least five major rubrics when he fulfills his diagnostic role. First, he looks at the child's person—his life style, his self-concept, his unmet needs and the obstacles to his growth. Second, he looks at the child's potentials—both the apparent and hidden ones, as well as the handicaps and factors that may lead to dysfunction. Third, he looks at the child's learning styles—his modalities, dispositions or "sets" toward learning. Fourth, he sees the child's abilities and achievements within a developmental and experiential framework that helps him to determine whether or not the child is ready to succeed with any new experience. Lastly, he looks at the environment itself and determines whether it is calling forth responses from children that are facilitating growth.

The Teacher Looks at the Child's Person

The child brings a unique biological structure with him into the world, and he develops his "self" in interaction with people who are important to him. The most significant relationships are found in the family setting, and the child's feelings about himself are reflections of the feelings that he perceives his parents have toward him. Later on, siblings, the peer group, teachers and other important adults influence the development of the child's self. Concept of self results, then, from the child's perceptions of the evaluation of others. He sees himself as he believes others see him. Cooley (1902) referred to this phenomenon as the "looking-glass" self. The child imagines the appearance he makes to others, he imagines the other person's judgment of that appearance, and he comes away with a self-feeling that may be associated with either pride or mortification. The amalgamation of these perceptions that is gradually built into the child's self system determines whether or not the child will view himself with esteem. This self-evaluation tends to become uni-

fied into a concept of self that becomes self-maintaining. The child takes on a generalized attitude of approval or disapproval, which defines the extent to which he is able to see himself as capable, significant, successful and worthy.

Most humanistic psychologists accept some theory of self or of self-concept as the key to understanding human behavior. In the literature, references to self-concept, self-perception, self-image and self-esteem are used almost interchangeably. La Benne has summarized these ideas very well. "Self concept," he says, "is the person's total appraisal of his appearance, background and origins, abilities and resources, attitudes and feelings which culminate as a directing force in behavior."[1] It is the person's conscious awareness of what he thinks and feels that determines his performance and action. If children are to behave differently, they need to see themselves differently. High self-regard is the cornerstone to becoming what a person innately can become.

Self-Concept and Achievement

Psychologists believe that man uses only a fraction of the potential that is available to him. Research evidence shows this to be especially true of individuals who see themselves as unable—the "I-can't-ers" of society. For example, a study undertaken at Vanderbilt University showed a differentiation on the basis of self-concept between patients and non-patients; failures in troop training from those who passed; alcoholics from non-alcoholics; delinquents from non-delinquents; and dropouts from those who stay in school (Combs and Snygg, 1959).

Walsh (1956) investigated the difference between high-ability/low-achieving and high-ability/high-achieving boys in handling Driscoll Playkit materials. She inferred self-concept from behavior and reported that low achievers saw themselves as hemmed in, not free, inadequate, rejected and unable to express emotion.

Moustakas (1956), in an action-research program and seminar with teachers, secured data that showed how change in teachers' behavior led to changes in students' perception of self—which in turn altered their behavior.

Davidson and Lang showed that "the more

positive the children's perception of their teacher's feelings toward them, the better was their achievement and the more desirable was their classroom behavior."[2]

Coopersmith (1967) found that individuals high in self-esteem were success-oriented, independent, creative, confident, socially independent, stable, free from anxiety and able to cope with events. Conversely, he found that low-esteem individuals did not trust themselves, were reluctant to express themselves in a group, were listeners rather than participants and tended to be self-conscious and self-preoccupied. Low-esteem individuals suffer from feelings of inadequacy and unworthiness; because they *feel* inadequate, they *become* inadequate. Fearing to reveal their inadequacies, they avoid closeness in their relationships and feel isolated or alienated.

These studies show the tremendous importance of self-concept in the personality growth and educational development of the child. The self of the child is his most precious possession. He brings it with him to school; he cannot park it at the door, contrary to the wishes of many teachers. The child's behavior, aspirations and goals are related to his need gratifications, and the perceptive teacher can tell a great deal about how the child feels about himself by observing him carefully in many situations. His general orientations usually come out in characteristic ways, which show up as constructive, defensive, aggressive or withdrawn behavior, or in other negative or positive manifestations. An increasing amount of evidence indicates that teachers need to become astute diagnosticians of the child's self-image. They should use their findings to alter the school environment, so that children will receive positive feedback, reinforcing a positive rather than a negative self-concept. This is the most important thing a teacher can do to increase the child's achievement or involvement in school activities.

The Teacher Looks at the Child's Potentials and the Factors Leading to Dysfunction

Schools have tended to look at potentials of pupils in very limited academic terms: The giftedness of a child hangs on his verbal abilities. Most intelligence tests focus on the child's ability to use language as a way of processing his world, but many times the test does not square with the child's actual experience and is not a valid indicator of his thinking abilities. Intelligence is much broader than "languaging"; human potential is multifaceted, being made up of a host of gifts that may take many different combinations. Like the infinite variety of snowflakes that fall from the winter sky, no two individuals are identical. However, generalized types of people may be observed. Some tend to be oriented toward people and may be thought of as "people-minded"; some like to work with their hands, to use tools and to construct things—they may be considered "thing-minded"; some like to work in the realm of ideas and may be called "idea-minded"; some people are combinations of these three basic types, but all can make important contributions. The world would not go 'round if everyone were alike.

A friend who is an English teacher told me that recently she met a young man, a former student, in an electrical repair shop. He approached her and said, "You don't remember me, but you flunked me in English. Not only that, I flunked English in junior college, too. But I'm teaching now, I'm teaching people to repair small appliances over at the trade school. I'm not no good at English, but man, I really dig this!" This young man was apparently both thing-minded and people-minded. He has a high I.Q. for doing his own thing with people—and how much society needs good electrical repair men!

Many different kinds of qualities can be assets both to the individual and to society, but people tend to lead from their strengths and cover up their deficiencies. Some people have talents they don't even know about, and they may never encounter situations to bring these talents out. Yet abilities can be strengthened, if the person is encouraged to use them or is convinced of their importance. Schools should be places that help children make use of their assets to the best advantage—but they should also be places that encourage children to bring out reluctant or latent abilities.

Many potentials are readily apparent to the teacher. The children with strong intellectual capacities stand out, because they take the leadership in discussions, read widely or investigate many topics that interest them. Some children are highly inventive or creative; they excel in thinking up things to do—or they get lost in writing poetry and stories, or in doing art work. Some children have outstanding social skills—social stars of the classroom are apparent. Other children are quiet but have great capacity to empathize. Some have exceptionally good physiques or are well coordinated and dexterous, shining in sports activities; others have special talents such as musical ability or organizational skills. Some children sparkle with humor. The child's interests also serve as clues to special abilities. For example, one elementary-school child's interest in maps, which the teacher was wise enough to encourage, led him to become a professional cartographer when he was grown.

Hidden Potentials

The teacher does not have to search for the obvious abilities of children, but he does need to look for the hidden potentials. The fact that a child excels in math, although he cannot read, is a clue to good reasoning ability. The child who can plan and put together a 3-D diorama shows that he has organizational ability, even though he develops a poorly organized report. The child who quickly figures out puzzles or sees the point of a joke shows that he is sharp-witted. The teacher can discover qualitative aspects of thinking, by observing the way a child handles a question or a problem. He should notice when children see relationships, when they are able to synthesize, analyze and remember; he should also observe when they fail to do these things. He should notice whether a child is more fluent in oral or written expression, in reading or in listening. Teachers may be deceived into thinking that certain children are stupid or dull-witted, when perhaps these children have come from backgrounds where there is little intellectual or verbal stimulation. In working with disadvantaged children, Feuerstein (1967) discovered that, when he gave hints to children while they were solving problems or performing tasks, he was able to tap intellectual abilities that would otherwise have gone unnoticed. The child who can make use of a hint has more intellectual capacity than the child who cannot, even though both

might have failed in the task without the intervention of the teacher.

Handicaps and Dysfunctions

The teacher should also be on the alert for major or minor handicaps or dysfunctions that children may have. Physical or motor handicaps, speech impediments, marked visual or hearing loss—like giftedness—may be very apparent. Other problems, such as borderline mental retardation, emotional disturbance or environmental disadvantage, may be more difficult to identify. For example, neurological damage may cause hyperactivity that is unknowingly attributed to emotional disturbance. There is a large classification of learning disabilities or dysfunctions that may be the most difficult of all to diagnose. It includes disorders that result in dysfunction of basic psychological processes involved in understanding or using spoken or written language. Some authorities estimate that as many as 15 to 20 percent of all children in elementary classrooms may have learning disabilities of some sort.

The Association for Learning Disabilities has offered the following definition of the disabled learner: "He is a child with normal intelligence who has learning disabilities of a perceptual, conceptual, or coordinative nature. . ."[3] Listening, thinking, talking, reading, writing, spelling or arithmetic disorders may be involved (Kirk and Kirk, 1971). Defective auditory memory, auditory association, space orientation or the like may be responsible for arithmetic disabilities. Writing disabilities may be related to a deficit in motor encoding or other psychological functions. Reading disabilities may result from deficits in psychological development. Children may be dyslexic (i.e., have reading problems due to psycho-linguistic or perceptual disorders) even though they have normal intelligence, and this can be very deceiving.

The following signs or symptoms, especially if they occur in combinations, should make the teacher suspect a learning disability: hyperactivity; faulty perception (beyond age 8), such as confusing *d* with *b* or *p* with *q*, or saying *52* for *25;* clumsy and uncoordinated motor activity; emotional instability—unpredictable emotional reactions, or impulsive and erratic behavior; distractibility and short attention span; poor memory and inability to make appropriate associations; unorganized thinking and slowness in concept formation.

The Teacher Discovers the Child's Learning Style

Classroom teachers are often frustrated by the fact that they must approach children in many different ways in order to provide successful experiences for all. Many times teachers approach a child's learning problem through trial and error in order to find something that will work. Although educators give much credence to the notion of working with the child's learning style as a basis for individualizing instruction, a great deal of investigation remains to be done to make this concept operational for teachers.

In the literature, some writers look at learning style to denote differences in the ways children perceive and discriminate phenomena. There are auditorial and visual differences in perception and also differences in perceiving ideas depending upon the child's past experience, prior knowledge, or mental outlook. Other writers associate learning style with the way in which the child classifies and orders his environment in the process of integrating sensory inputs and new ideas into his thinking. Others equate learning style with personality orientations and mental sets or outlooks. Rosenberg (1968), for example, described learning styles using the categories of "rigid-inhibited" (the child who has a strong need for structure); "undisciplined" (the child who seeks immediate gratification of needs); "acceptance anxious" (the child who is over-anxious in pleasing others, especially authority figures); and "creative" (the child who is open to his experiences and his feelings and hence is able to approach his learning freely).

Some clinicians have found the concept of "learning modality" to be a useful guide in determining methods for teaching children with special problems—and, although much remains to be discovered about the learning modalities of children, there is evidence to indicate that some children do tend to process information visually, while others predominantly use their auditory sense. Still other children make use of their kinesthetic sensitivities and learn best through a tactile approach. Teachers must remember, however, that all people use all these modalities. The concept is useful in looking for children who may have a definite preference in one direction that the teacher may understand and take into account in providing for the learning needs of the child.

Gould[4] reported major differentiations between "seeing" learners and "hearing" learners, which teachers can observe in the classroom. The seeing learner acquires knowledge through visual channels; he understands and processes his world by visualizing it. The hearing learner relies predominantly on auditory channels; he understands his world by verbalizing about it. Usually, he translates visual stimuli into words before he can deal with them. Fernald (1943) demonstrated a third modality, that of kinesthetic learning, through a tactile approach in remedial reading that was based upon tracing letters with the finger. This method proved to be effective with some children who could succeed through no other medium.

Intelligence comes in many assortments, and it is misleading to calculate a child's intellectual capacities merely on the basis of I.Q. scores. Teachers who pay attention to differing learning modalities and who use multi-sensory approaches will tap and develop more intellectual and creative capacities than will those who stick with one approach, especially if this approach is predominately verbal.

Recognizing Visual Modality

Gould[5] reported that, although the seeing learner may be a bright child, he is often clumsy in his verbalizations, so that he does not appear to be as intelligent as he really is. On the Wechsler Intelligence Test he tends to score relatively high on performance compared with his score on the verbal scale. In a testing situation, the seeing learner will pause after a question has been asked and will consider his answer carefully. He is easily distressed by time pressures, and results on timed tests may therefore be inaccurate.

The seeing learner does not feel a need to talk and he sees a problem through before he wants to talk about it, so he tends to be a quiet child. When he does speak, he speaks deliberately. If the seeing learner has average intelligence or better, he will enjoy reading and will advance well with it. especially if the "look-say" method is used. He tends to visualize the whole word and store it in his memory.

The seeing learner is frequently overlooked in school, because he does not present his intelligence in a verbal manner. Numbered among the late bloomers, many seeing learners have talents in art, mathematics, science and descriptive writing that really do not begin to show up until junior-high or high-school levels.

The visualizer readily orients himself to new situations. Being adaptive in social skills, he generally keeps out of trouble. He is not likely to be overstimulated by free play on the playground, but when he does get upset, he needs support through physical contact.

Recognizing Auditory Modality

The hearing learner scores relatively high on the verbal scale of the Wechsler Intelligence Test, according to Gould[6]. He responds to time pressures favorably and is not upset by a testing situation. The hearing learner has an adequate vocabulary and enjoys reading. Reading, in fact, is his best subject—but he finds writing and arithmetic more difficult because of his inability to visualize. The hearing learner, therefore, makes better progress in math if he can do his learning on a verbal level.

Hearing learners have been known to say that they don't know what they think about things until they hear themselves say it. Therefore, all of their verbalized working through of problems and explorations in the realm of ideas give the impression of being foolish and disorganized, simply because the teacher hears the child in the process of problem solving. But if the teacher listens long enough, he finds that the child reaches the correct solution eventually; then the teacher realizes that the child is not as foolish as he originally appeared to be. "Both in writing and in arithmetic, the hearing learner will want to talk, breathe, or at least move his lips." When the hearing learner has a problem, the teacher must talk to him about it. The hearing learner needs to have new situations explained to him. The teacher should therefore never show the hearing learner anything without at the same time talking.[7]

The major differences between the seeing learner and the hearing learner are summarized in Table 3, under four categories.

TABLE 3. DIFFERENCES IN SEEING LEARNERS AND HEARING LEARNERS

	Seeing Learner	Hearing Learner
1. Impulsivity	Little difficulty, for he visualizes the consequences of behavior. He can empathize deeply with others.	Can't look before he leaps. Tends to move too fast, both physically and verbally.
2. Excitability	Has difficulty expressing feelings to others. Tends to burst into tears in reaction to strong feelings. Tends to internalize his feelings and act them out in a generalized kind of behavior.	Overreacts to stimulation, change or any type of disorganization. Does silly, impulsive things; often can't explain his behavior.
3. Distractibility	Seldom is distracted if he has a book or pencil and paper before him, but may be distracted by things he sees. Finds it difficult to shift from one stimulus to another.	Is more easily distracted by sounds than by sights. More easily distracted if not permitted to verbalize things to himself.
4. Organization	Very well organized and well oriented in time. Finds it easy to plan his day. Is neat and notices how people and things look.	May be disorganized. Organization is difficult. Finds it difficult to organize on paper and to organize his time.

The Teacher Assesses the Child's Readiness

Factors such as the child's past experience and achievements, his interests, attitudes, special aptitudes and developmental growth—including intellectual capacity, auditory and visual perception, emotional stability, social status and peer relationships, energy levels, physical dexterity, motor coordination and health—need to be considered in determining a child's readiness to learn new concepts and skills or to undertake new activities. Readiness implies that a child may enter into a new experience equipped with all the requisites necessary to cope successfully. It is an important factor in building a success identity. Teachers, therefore, need to be well aware of the child's state of readiness, so that they may expose him to new experience in the depth and quality that are appropriate to him. The field of child growth and development is too vast to review here, but familiarity with theories and research evidence concerning this field is an essential backdrop against which the teacher designs school experience for each child.

The Teacher Looks at the Educational Environment

An important function of diagnosis is to determine the effects of school experience on the child. The teacher needs to decide what the actual learning outcomes are and then determine whether they are in harmony with the overall goals of self-development of the child. Teaching methods and social relationships need to be examined and related to both academic achievement and personal growth. The child needs to learn, but he also needs to feel good about what he learns and about himself as a learner during the educational process.

If a child is not functioning well, his dynamic syndrome of self-perceptions, personality and learning sets—which is brought to or evoked by the environment—needs reassessment. The diagnostic process is not complete until the total constellation of factors operating within the child's life space are looked at. Hypotheses about what is cause and what is effect should not be made without identifying all possible interrelating factors. Only then can intelligent changes be made in the child's environment, offering him new options to function in growth-facilitating ways.

In Chapter 10, "The Teacher and the Tools of Diagnosis," we will examine the diagnostic process in more detail, describe the diagnostic tools available to the teacher, and inventory the behaviors that carry out the teacher's function in diagnosis.

Notes

[1] Wallace D. La Benne and Bert I. Greene, *Educational Implications of Self-Concept Theory* (Pacific Palisades, Calif.: Goodyear Publishing Co., Inc., 1969), p. 10.

[2] Ibid., p. 25.

[3] See Jeanne McRae McCarthy, "How to Teach the Hard to Reach," *Grade Teacher*, Vol. 84, No. 9 (May/June, 1967), p. 98, for an expansion of this definition and down-to-earth descriptions of characteristics of children with learning disabilities. Available in reprint form from *Teacher*, 22 W. Putnam Ave., Greenwich, Conn. 06830.

[4] P. Gould, "The Seeing Learner and the Hearing Learner," mimeographed speech, 1964.

[5] Ibid.

[6] Ibid.

[7] Ibid.

References

Blitz, Barbara. Chapter 6, "Learning Styles," *The Open Classroom: Making It Work*. Boston: Allyn and Bacon, Inc., 1973, pp. 184-213.

Combs, Arthur W., and Donald Snygg. *Individual Behavior: A Perceptual Approach to Behavior*. Rev. ed. New York: Harper & Brothers, 1959.

Cooley, C. H. *Human Nature and the Social Order*. New York: Scribner, 1902.

Coopersmith, Stanley, *The Antecedents of Self-Esteem*. San Francisco: W. H. Freeman, 1967.

Fernald, Grace M. *Remedial Techniques in Basic School Subjects*. New York: McGraw-Hill Book Company, Inc., 1943.

Feruestein, Reven, and H. Shalom. "Problems of Assessment and Evaluation of the Mentally Retarded and Culturally Deprived Child and Adolescent. The Learning Potential Assessment Device." Paper presented at the First Congress of the International Association for Scientific Study of Mental Deficiency, Montepellier, September 10-12, 1967. Symposium No. 8.

Gould, P. "The Seeing Learner and the Hearing Learner." Mimeographed speech, 1964.

Kirk, Samuel A., and Winifred D. Kirk. *Psycholinguistic Learning Disabilities: Diagnosis and Remediation.* Urbana: University of Illinois Press, 1971.

La Benne, Wallace D. and Bert I. Greene. *Educational Implications of Self-Concept Theory.* Pacific Palisades, Calif.: Goodyear Publishing Co., Inc., 1969.

McCarthy, Jeanne McRae. "How to Teach the Hard-to-Reach," in *Grade Teacher,* May/June, 1967.

Moustakas, Clark E. *The Teacher and the Child.* New York: McGraw-Hill Book Co., 1956.

Rosenberg, Marshall B. *Diagnostic Teaching.* Seattle: Special Child Publications, 1968, pp. 38-63.

Walsh, Ann M. *Self Concepts of Bright Boys with Learning Difficulties.* New York: Teachers College, Columbia University, 1956.

Chapter 10

The Teacher and the Tools of Diagnosis

There are many occasions for informal diagnosis in the classroom. The teacher diagnoses continuously as he helps the child with his thinking, guides him in pursuing an interest, unsnarls a learning task, or relates to the child in a special way when the child has an apparent need.

Sometimes the teacher looks more deeply into areas of personal or educational concern and follows the scientific process of problem solving in order to make a formal diagnosis. He senses a problem through observing the child in various circumstances over a span of time. Seeing something amiss in the child's academic, social or personal life, he begins to observe more closely, making notes that he carries around in his head.

In puzzling situations, the teacher may decide to write anecdotal accounts of the child's behavior or to use various forms of self-report, sociometric devices and tests. After a period of time, the teacher begins to see relationships and makes hypotheses (at least tentative ones) concerning the child's potentials, his needs, his learning styles and his problems. In other words, the teacher begins to

interpret data by seeing the relationships that exist. Out of his diagnostic assessments, the teacher formulates a plan to help the child individually. Sometimes the teacher realizes that the problem is beyond his area of expertise, and he will then refer the child to the school social worker, learning disability teacher, speech correctionist, the family physician or other professional.

The teacher also sees the ongoing evaluation of the child's educational experience as part of his diagnostic role. Diagnosis is a matter of looking for the elements of the child's experience that are not fitting him, or of determining where the child's educational experience is leading him. The teacher does not wait to make a formalized compilation of his findings; he begins to follow his hunches in daily activities and gets additional feedback. Formal diagnosis, then, entails the whole process of (1) gathering data about the individual and his learning; (2) synthesizing and interpreting all the available facts and making hypotheses or educated guesses about the individual's potentials, achievements or problems; (3) developing a plan to meet the child's needs; (4) making referrals to other professionals when necessary; and (5) continuously evaluating the educational process, in order to guide the child or change his environment to increasingly fulfill his needs. As in any problem-solving activity, these steps are not necessarily followed sequentially—there is working back and forth—but in general, these are the steps a teacher takes in formalized diagnosis. The diagnostic tools the teacher employs and the processes he pursues are the subject of this chapter.

WAYS OF GATHERING DATA

As an educational diagnostician, the teacher gathers data about the child to determine his developmental growth patterns, his self-concept and the use he is making of his potentials. To make his knowledge as accurate as possible, the teacher will employ several methods for gaining insight into the child's behavior—but probably the most important thing he will do is to observe the child in day-to-day activities.

Informal Observation

Informal observations are focused primarily on the child's personal adjustment to himself and others; on his goals, aspirations and need-fulfilling behaviors; on his life style and coping mechanisms; and on his learning patterns and his hidden potentials. Research indicates that observations of experienced teachers are as accurate in determining a child's readiness for an activity, such as learning to read, as are formal methods (including testing). Observation may well be the most helpful technique in diagnosis, because the teacher sees the child as a person, not as a statistic.

In observation, the teacher becomes aware of the child's interests, his potentials and his physical and mental sets; these are taken into account in guiding the child's learning. The teacher continuously looks for answers to questions: What are the interests of individual children? When the child has a choice, what kinds of activities does he seek out on his own? What kinds of books does he choose? What things does he bring with him from home? What does he talk about when he is engaged in conversation? What subjects does he bring up in discussions?

How does the child express himself in creative work? What is his most fluent mode of expression: Talking? Writing? Painting and drawing? Working with his hands? What do his creative works say about his interests or his conception of himself?

Is his creative writing autobiographical? What does it say, directly or indirectly, about the child? What moods are expressed in the child's art? Which children are spontaneous and creative and under what conditions?

How does each child tackle problems? Which children are impulsive, confident, fearless? Which ones need coaxing and a great deal of support? Which are self-starters? Which enjoy working independently? Which need a great deal of guidance? Who are the good problem solvers? Who does not know where to begin?

What kinds of questions do different children ask and what depth of thought do these questions reflect? What ideas do individuals bring out in group discussions? Which children are the "idea" people? Which are the most fluent in generating ideas? Who contributes and who hangs back?

What are the levels of thought processes in which different children engage? Who can deal with abstract ideas? How well do specific individuals comprehend? What are their language patterns and levels of vocabulary in oral and written communication? What kinds of help do individuals seek? Which children need only hints and suggestions? Which ones are working with concepts, skills and materials at a frustration level?

Which children have poor memories? Which ones have difficulty in making associations, in assimilating their learning? In integrating knowledge?

When a child is being helped, how does he respond? Is he quick or slow to get the point? In group teaching, which children catch on quickly? Who are the mental dropouts? Which children are always "with it"? Which children have great staying power? Which children have very short attention spans or low frustration tolerance levels and under what conditions?

Which children show difficulty with visual-perceptual work, such as reversing letters in writing? Who has difficulty copying? Who doesn't hear phonetic combinations? Which children lose interest when they are required to listen?

Which children have high energy levels? Which ones are lethargic, pale or physically run-down? Which children have poor motor coordination? Which ones are dexterous? Who has poor posture?

In his observations, the teacher also looks for

the child's attitudes toward himself, his life style, his personal integration or adjustment, and his social relationships. The teacher is on the lookout for answers to the following questions:

Does the child like his own appearance? Does he have confidence in his abilities? If not, in what areas of living does he lack confidence? Is the child outgoing, reserved or withdrawn? How does he respond to authority—is he hostile, compliant or accepting? Does he constantly seek teacher approval? Does the child behave differently in one set of circumstances than in another? Is what he says about himself congruent with the way he behaves—does he make remarks about being dumb when in fact he is bright? About being a failure when he is usually successful?

Are there children who appear tense? Bite their nails? Have facial tics? Do certain children cry easily? Retaliate? Become angered upon slight provocation? Are there children whom you seldom notice, who fade into the woodwork?

Which children are the leaders? Do they lead in most cases, or does the activity make a difference? Which children are the social "stars?" Which ones are usually left out or have no friends? What seem to be the dominant values of the group: Social acceptance? Solving problems through fighting? Being clean or sloppily dressed? Being successful in school? Being good in sports? Are there children who are not swayed by the values of the group? Are any becoming independent thinkers?

How do children perceive their peers? Are some children perceived as being "better" than others? Do some children assume social roles as bully or scapegoat? Do some children take pride in being trouble-makers or in deviating from the group?

When individual children or the group become upset, what are the precipitating circumstances? What were the antecedents of the event? What does this say? Are there patterns of circumstances that bring on emotional upset?

Are there similarities or differences in personal behaviors of given children in academic, social, creative or physical activities? What are these differences saying?

Do the children with academic or self-concept problems have special problems at home? How can I find out? How is the community environment affecting the child?

Anecdotal Records

In puzzling situations, teachers need to go beyond their informal observations and record descriptions of children's behavior in varying situations over a period of several months. Later, as the teacher goes over his notes, he sometimes sees connecting links in the child's behavior that he has heretofore missed. These links may yield important clues to the child's self concept, goals and interests, or they may reveal information about his social, personal or intellectual needs.

A good anecdotal record gives a true vignette of a child's behavior. The following information should be noted:

1. The setting, including the date, the place and the situation in which the action occurred.

2. The actions of the child, the reactions of other people involved and the response of the child to these reactions.

3. Accurate quotation of what is said to the child and by the child.

4. "Mood cues"—posture, gestures, voice qualities and facial expressions that give cues to how the child felt. (Interpretations of feelings are not given, but only the cues by which a reader may judge what they say.)

5. Enough description to cover the episode. The action or conversation is followed through to the point where a little vignette of a behavioral moment in the life of the child is presented.[1]

Note how these characteristics are exemplified in the following anecdote:

Setting	December 5, 1972, 10:30 A.M. Chris came up to me in the first-grade area after recess and handed me a slip of paper on which she had written her reading words.
Direct conversation	"Very good Chris," I said. "When did you write these?" "At recess," she answered promptly.

Teacher reaction	"Don't you play with the other kids at recess?" I asked.
Mood cue and reaction	Chris *glanced at me furtively* and replied, "They won't play with me. I always stay by myself and play by myself."
Teacher reaction	"But maybe you could take the first step and join in with the other kids, instead of waiting for someone to take the first step," I said, encouragingly.
Mood cue	Chris *shook her head vehemently* and said in no uncertain terms, "I don't want to play with them, because they don't want to play
Descriptive action	with me." Then she scampered away.

The teacher does not confuse description with interpretation or evaluation, nor does he characterize the child's personality by one particular trait. The following types of anecdotal entries preclude objective data and should be avoided:

1. Evaluative statement--anecdotes that judge a behavior good or bad. Sample: Gary was always at my desk during mathematics. When I asked him to go to his seat, he showed a bad attitude.
2. Interpretive statement—anecdotes that explain the child's behavior on the basis of a single fact. Sample: We are making our Christmas presents, and Carl is most uncooperative. This is because his parents are divorced.
3. Generalized descriptive statements—anecdotes that characterize behavior in general terms. Sample: Larry is always annoying the boys in the milk line.
4. Anecdotes that omit a description of the setting; behavior that is acceptable in one setting may be most inappropriate in another. Sample: Marvin defended his point of view vigorously for five minutes.[2]

The teacher does not attempt to make an evaluation until behavioral patterns are evident. After keeping anecdotes for several months, the teacher may attempt to answer the following kinds of questions: How does the child really view himself? What feelings does he have toward his peers, family, and other significant adults? What are the goals of the child's actions? What are the child's assets and liabilities? What does he have going for him, and what is working against him? What are the child's values, and how do they color his behavior? How does the child usually cope with frustrating situations? Under what faulty assumptions is the child operating?

Time Sampling

Busy teachers may not have time to keep extensive anecdotal records. As a short cut, some teachers have used time samples in which they jot down entries on a card every few minutes during a segment of the day when they are free to observe. Entries such as these yield fruitful information, if they are made intermittently over a period of weeks or months. Behavior samplings may be made of the group or of individuals. In the following account written by a student teacher, notice that the focus is on one child:

Time study: November 17, 1972

9:30   *Anne is bent over her desk, concentrating on working math problems.*

9:35   *Judy, sitting next to Anne, asks Anne a question about the math assignment. Anne raises her head, gives Judy what appears to be a curt answer, and curls even closer around her paper.*

9:42   *Anne finishes notebook, smiles as she puts it in her desk.*

9:44   *Begins to twist in her chair and tap feet against chair, while looking around the room.*

9:45   *Teacher calls Anne to ask if she has finished her math. Anne says, "Yes."*

9:48   *Anne leaves her chair and slowly walks over to her teacher. She asks if she may go to the Learning Center early, since she is finished with her work.*

9:50   *Anne comes up behind me in the Learning Center, grabs my hand, and explains proudly that she finished her work early so she came for cooking class early.*

9:53   *Washes hands and rushes around putting utensils out, happy and smiling.*

9:57   *Volunteers to go and bring another second grader to the group.*

10:01   Anne brings Vicki into the kitchen and they both get ready to begin class.

The Springfield Interest Finder

This inventory, which is used to obtain an index of children's interests, yields a surprising amount of information. The child responds easily, and he usually will not regard the questionnaire as "nosey." Some teachers have adapted the original "Springfield Interest Finder," making inventories more directly related to the exact information they are seeking.

Name:_____ Age:_____ Sex:____
Date:_____Teacher:_____ School:____
My three wishes:

What I'd like to learn more about at school:
What I don't care to study about:
What I like best in school:
What I like or dislike most at school:
What I like best outside school:
What I like least or dislike most about home:
What I want to be or do when I grow up:
The most interesting thing I have done at our school during the past week or so:
One of the places I especially like to go is _____.
                                                   (name of city)
One of the happiest days in my life:
My three best friends in my room (boys or girls):[3]

Studying Children Doing Creative Work

It is important for teachers to observe children under varying conditions while they are involved in different kinds of tasks. A child may behave quite differently on the playground than he does in the classroom. His approach to academic work may show marked difference from the way he approaches expressive, creative undertakings. One of the best opportunities for finding clues to the child's self-concept or his creative and mental "sets" is through observing him work with creative media and examining his creative products. Some teachers purposely structure situations in creative dramatics, role playing, art, movement and dance in order to observe reactions of specific children.

A sixth-grade teacher, for example, made a resumé of clues from observing children in an art class:

1.   What a child draws may show his interests.

2.   The skill with which a child uses his tools may indicate his special abilities.

3.   Some children finish work neatly; some are easily satisfied with any kind of product.

4.   Some children voluntarily do work over when the result is not good; others refuse to try again.

5.   Some children say, "I can't draw," or "I can't paint," and refuse to try.

6.   Some children destroy what they have done, or do not want anyone to see their work.

7.   Most of the children like to use color rather than black and white.

8.   Some of the children who are painfully careful and neat use colors sparingly and show little spontaneous originality. Some of the most creative children are untidy in their work.

9.   Children like to consult one another when drawing, painting, working with clay, etc.

10.   A child's work may, but does not need to, have meaning for someone else. If a child tells the teacher or the class about his picture, the teacher may get an insight into how the child thinks or feels about a particular situation, or she may get an insight into the home or other out-of-school situations.[4]

Carlton and Moore designed a study in which they used self-directive dramatization with groups of children as a way to gain information regarding self-concept. They formulated questions that would direct a teacher to look for behavior without being too judgmental and that would minimize the danger of misinterpretation. Teachers made observations in reference to the following questions, as children informally dramatized the stories they were reading:

A. Associating with Others

  1. Does he withdraw from the teacher?

  2. Does he withdraw from the other children?

  3. Does he withdraw from the teacher and the other children?

  4. Does he want to be with the teacher all the time instead of with the other children?

5. Does he try to gain favor by agreeing, by giving gifts or through flattery?

6. Does he give one the feeling that he is shy—talks almost in a whisper, tiptoes about the room?

B. Attitude Toward Himself

1. Does he need praise in order to complete his work?

2. Does he brag about what he can do?

3. Does he express opinions about himself?

4. Does he refuse to do things because he thinks he does not do them well?

C. Attitude Toward Others

1. Does he refuse to give help if a child asks for it?

2. Is he unkind to a new child, or to any child?

3. Does he show signs of being jealous—of a child's new clothes, or praise given another child?

4. Does he want to do all the talking?

5. Does he refuse to listen when others talk?

D. When Things Do Not Go Right

1. Is he eager to "tell on" another child?

2. Does he refuse to apologize if he hurts a child's feelings?

3. Does he blame someone because he does something wrong?

4. When his feelings are hurt, does he hold a grudge?

5. Does he pout a long time when something displeases him?

6. Does he act impulsively—hit someone, cry?

7. Does he argue with other children?

8. Does he demand that other children give him what he wants?

9. Does he get angry when his suggestions are not accepted?

E. In Daily Routine

1. Does he want to be first in everything—getting a drink, giving an answer?

2. Is he unwilling to take turns?

3. Does he do things to attract attention—make faces, talk loudly, "steal the show"?

4. Does he refuse to make contributions to classroom activities?

5. Does he often fail to finish what he starts?

6. Does he refuse to share things with the other children?

7. Does he try to boss the other children?[5]

Teachers not only gained insight into behavior by using this technique but were also surprised to find that informal dramatizations actually had a positive effect in changing self-concepts. They saw significant change in the five questions checked most often: (1) Does he give one the feeling that he is shy? (2) Does he need praise in order to complete his work? (3) Does he try to gain favor by agreeing, by giving gifts or by flattery? (4) Does he express opinions about himself? (5) Does he withdraw from the other children?[6]

Teachers sometimes structure creative writing projects around topics such as "My Favorite Pastime," "If I Had Three Wishes," "If I Could Change Myself," "If I Were a Teacher," "What I Am Afraid Of" or "The Story of My Life," to obtain insights into the child's self. Children also project their feelings and values when they talk or write about pictures. Pictures of situations that might arise at home, on the playground or in the classroom are good subjects and may include children of different racial or ethnic origin. When reading the child's stories for diagnostic purposes, the most important thing to look for is what the child chooses to tell. Does the child feel good about his life? Does he mention his family and, if so, which members are referred to most frequently? What are the child's fears? What are his utopias?

Sociometric Studies

Sociometry is a method of studying interpersonal relationships in group settings. The teacher asks questions requiring children to select certain of their peers with whom they would like to work or play. Children might be asked to respond to any of the following: List in order of preference three classmates you would like to have seated near you. Name three people with whom you would like to work on our social studies project. Whom would you like for a buddy on our field trip to the printing plant? Sometimes hypothetical questions are asked: What three people would you like most of all to have at your birthday party?

The teacher uses the information to plot a sociogram, which depicts graphically the social structure of the class. Friendship choices plotted among a group of girls might appear as in Figure 2.

If the teacher wishes to improve social relationships, he will try to structure situations in which isolates are placed with social stars or people of high acceptance, and he will integrate cliques into other groups. Children will realize that there are others they could enjoy if they took the time to develop new friendships. It is important that the isolate be cast in a favorable position and that he not be placed with people who totally reject him.

Different kinds of sociometric questions will elicit different kinds of responses. Note what may be inferred by the following questions:

Whom would you like to have for chairman of the game committee? (Leadership qualities)

Whom would you like to have in your research group? (Academic qualities)

Three choices:

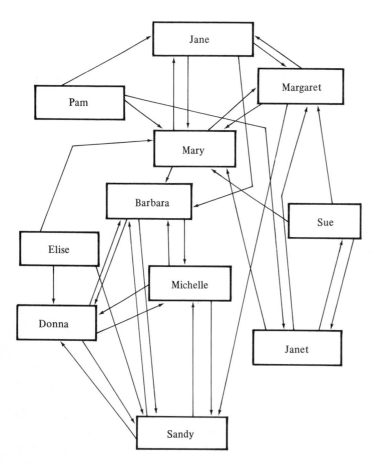

Interpretation:

1. Mary is the social star. Several children would like to be associated with her. Barbara is the second most frequently chosen girl.

2. Barbara, Michelle, Donna and Sandy constitute a clique of mutually chosen friends who are not striving to enter any other social group.

3. Pam and Elise are isolates who are trying to enter other groups but are chosen by no one else.

Figure 2. Sociogram of Friendship Choices

Who are your three best friends? (Social qualities)

Who would be the three best representatives to the Student Council? (Leadership qualities and trustworthiness)

Teachers should be careful not to invade the privacy of children or make them feel that they are expected to reject some of their peers. Unless the teacher puts his findings to some practical use, children may perceive sociometric questions as phony or nosey. To avoid this, the teacher may say, "Name three people in order of preference with whom you would like to work in our next social studies project. I do not promise to give you all of your choices, but I do promise to give you at least *one* of your choices." Then the teacher must stand behind his word.

Answers to sociometric questions often verify what the teacher already knows. Occasionally, however, he discovers a neglected child or sees something in the social fabric that has gone unnoticed. Some teachers make sociograms to confirm their observations and find the technique reassuring, especially when they are troubled about the social dynamics of the class.

Parent Conferences

The parent conference can be used to obtain further information about the child, including parental expectations and the quality of family relationships. Good conferences are two-way affairs. Parents have as much or more to contribute than do teachers. The teacher makes parents comfortable with this knowledge and helps them feel that they are a part of the educational team. Humanistic teachers are friendly and open. They establish a basis for trust by relating authentically to parents. The Dale Carnegie how-to-win-friends-and-influence-people "sandwich technique" may be a helpful pattern, provided it rings true: The teacher leads off with a positive statement about the child, then discusses areas of concern, soliciting the parents' insight and help. He seals the conference on another positive or hopeful note.

Some teachers like to include the pupil in the conference. A teacher I know seats the parents and then asks the child to draw up a chair, paying special attention to where he places it. The secure child generally deposits the chair an equal distance from parents and teacher, and appears unencumbered during the conference. A child feeling the need for parental protection places the chair near one of his parents. (The teacher notices which one.) If the child wants the teacher to defend him, he places his chair near the teacher. These are significant attitudes to detect, and they give the teacher clues for approaching the parents as well as providing insight into the child.

Files of Representative Work

Many teachers keep files in which they periodically place samples of the child's work. These concrete examples help to communicate the child's progress to parents. Even more instructive may be the feedback to the child and teacher of the progress (or lack of it) the child is making as he compares his work from September to midyear or to end-of-the-year samples.

Teacher-prepared Diagnostic Materials

Perhaps the best diagnostic materials are the ones the teacher prepares himself. If the teacher wishes to know whether the child has mastered a specific skill, such as placing the zero in a quotient correctly, he may set up a sequence of algorisms leading step-by-step from simple to complex operations. By checking the child's work, he can tell exactly where the breakdowns occur.

A simple method in discovering a child's reading level is to have him read selected pages from books that gradually move from easy to more difficult material. When the child begins to miss as many as three words on a page, he has reached his reading instructional level. Further observation of the child in the act of reading will give clues to self-confidence, word attack skills, eye movement, speed and ease of reading, and other areas of performance. Questions geared to differing levels of thought, ranging from simple recall to interpretation, evaluation or creative solutions can indicate the quality of a child's thinking.

Standardized Tests

Teachers need to be aware of the limitations of tests as well as of their potential usefulness in revealing factors that are necessary for accurate diagnosis of the child's academic or personal experience. Most schools periodically administer batteries of achievement and psychological tests or reading inventories to get information about academic progress or I.Q. potential. Group tests are usually not as accurate nor as definitive as tests administered individually by the psychometrist or school psychologist. Children with special problems, therefore, often need to be referred for individual testing.

The teacher does not use test results as the sole criterion for assessing the child's abilities, but always looks at tests in relationship to his own observations. Sometimes teachers stereotype a child in terms of his test scores, which may not be true indicators of the child's potentials although the teacher relates to him as if they were. Test data are passed from teacher to teacher, sometimes prejudicing a teacher even before he works with the child. The teacher communicates his low estimate to the child in subtle ways, and the child lives up to the teacher's expectations. Rosenthal and Jacobson (1968) showed the dramatic effects of "self-fulfilling" prophecy in *Pygmalion in the Classroom.* Children tabbed as "bloomers" improved markedly as compared with those whom teachers believed were mediocre or low in I.Q. potential. The actual test data indicated the children were about equal in intellectual capacity.

The value of standardized tests lies in the analysis and use made of the results. Neighborhood cultural patterns are important to consider. Children from environments where little intellectual stimulation is available should not be underrated, even though their scores do not compare favorably with those of children who live in a community where educational advantages abound. How the child feels on the day the test is given can change his score drastically. I.Q. results may fluctuate within a range of 20 points for any one child, depending on the circumstances under which the test was taken. Insecure children and those who panic under time pressures are usually known to the teacher who considers the child's personality and mental or emotional set in relationship to test results.

In any classroom, patterns of errors made by individuals or groups are more significant than actual scores. The teacher can often discover deficiencies in teaching or learning by noting the areas where individual children or the class are weak. It is important that the teacher spot weak points revealed in subtest items and analyze them carefully, to determine what needs to be taught or retaught.

Most test booklets provide a page where a profile or graph may be drawn, showing pictorially how a child has responded in relationship to each category of items tested. This is a useful tool to the teacher in interpreting test results, for he can tell at a glance the general trend of the child's performance. Percentile and achievement scores turned up in testing should always be looked at in relationship to the child's total person. The teacher needs to ask the question: What does this score mean for this individual or this group? He refrains from labeling the child or the group and views all data as tentative. He looks for new evidence in his informal observations that will help him interpret test data more accurately in terms of what the data mean in relationship to a given child. The humanistic teacher views all data uncovered by a test as tentative; he does not permit the data to stereotype his perception of any child.

Cumulative Records

Many humanistic teachers view cumulative records disparagingly, feeling that past records lock the child into unfortunate growth patterns that brand him permanently. Perhaps this attitude says more about the growth of the teaching profession than it does about the purpose of cumulative records.

Teachers who are professionally educated and who have freed themselves from psychological hangups should be able to handle information professionally without prejudging a child. Medical information and knowledge of the school communities in which the child has lived, for example, can be very enlightening. When studying a child's record, the teacher needs to consider the limitations of past test scores and to notice comments about the child that are *judgmental* vs. those that are *descriptive*. In writing comments for folders, the teacher observes the same principles that guide him in writing anecdotal records—the child's personal style and developmental characteristics are always recorded in descriptive rather than interpretive terms. Information should include the total development of the child: social, emotional, physical and attitudinal, as well as academic.

It may be better for the teacher to gain his own first impressions of each child before consulting the folders, but after the first month of school, the cumulative record may be consulted and information compared with any other data the teacher has observed.

DIAGNOSTIC ASSESSMENT

Accumulated data lead the teacher to hypothesize about each child's work and person. However, the teacher should avoid making hasty judgments or judging on the basis of limited data. Valid interpretations result from looking at the growth of the total child and noticing factors that are interrelated. Some children, though progressing satisfactorily or even doing very well, may actually be underachievers.

The teacher must, therefore, look at the child's developmental growth patterns and notice the interrelationship of physical, social, emotional and intellectual factors. If the child is having academic problems, is it due to poor self-concept? Is he a slow learner, or does he actually have a learning disability? Are the materials the child is using too difficult, so that he is working at a frustration level? Is a physical or health problem involved? Is the hyperactive child emotionally disturbed, or is there neurological damage? Do informal observations of the child's thinking abilities correlate with test data on his learning potential? Is a particular learning style or modality indicated—visual, auditory, kinesthetic? What kinds of materials has the child been working with, and how are they related to his best mode of learning? What *specific* learning problems does the child have?

Kirk and Kirk (1971) emphasize that in making a diagnostic analysis it is important to notice the intra-individual differences involving learning problems that reside within each child. For example, it would be important to notice behaviors of the child that indicate impairment of receptive processes (attaching meaning to what is seen and heard), expressive processes (expressing ideas verbally or in written form) or organizing processes (integrating ideas into one's thinking). Children with learning problems usually have a deficit in one of these areas. If a child has good abilities in one area while experiencing difficulties in another, an unevenness may show up in his ability to cope with academic tasks. In diagnosing, the teacher must decide what impairments are related to other impairments. It may be discovered, for example, that a child is having difficulty in reading because of inadequate oral language experience. On the other hand, his inadequacy may be related to visual-perceptual problems.

The teacher looks at all his data and makes a summary of the symptoms and factors that have inhibited the child's learning and personality development. He pinpoints any interrelated factors he sees and notices how they are related to specific problems or disabilities a given child may have. At this point, the teacher is ready to determine whether the child is gaining access to his potentialities. He must decide where the child is functioning and design corrective procedures from this baseline. Even though the teacher has made his best judgment, he keeps an open mind and may change his hypotheses after he has begun a corrective plan. The teacher must base his teaching plans on the right premises. This is the reason the diagnostic assessment is so important.

DESIGNING CORRECTIVE PLANS

Several principles inhere in translating diagnostic assessments into educational plans that will help the child.

Involvement

First of all, the child must be involved. Children are aware of their problems, and their unhappiness usually shows up in some sort of emotional or social manifestation. The teacher who tries to gloss over the problem and pretend it does not exist is only kidding himself and the child. Ego-building tactics usually fail, if the basic problem is not dealt with. Therefore, the teacher discusses the problem with the child openly. The teacher communicates his understanding and his concern, but he also communicates his belief in the child and his faith in the child's potentials. He refrains from telling the child to try harder, but suggests instead that there is something in the environment, in the books and materials, or in the teaching approach that is not suited to the child and is not helping him.

Cooperative Development of a Plan

On the basis of their talk, the teacher and the child agree to try a new plan. This plan is aimed at helping the child with his special problem (for example, word recognition), and it begins at the level where he functions adequately. It also provides a wholesome involvement with life-related activities that are a part of the ongoing classroom experience. It is important to make short-term plans with concrete goals, so that the child is able to see his own progress; this approach allows the teacher and child to restructure the learning situation frequently. If the middle-grade child is working on sight vocabulary from the Dolch list, for example, three new words per day for one week might be a realistic goal. If the child manages this goal, he may choose to master five new words per day the following week. The goal can be specified and there is evidence, that the child can see, confirming the fact that he is making progress. Seeing one's progress toward a goal is in itself a powerful motivator. The child begins to experience success, and he wants more of it. The teacher carefully watches factors such as attention span and the complexity of the learning situation, but he also allows the child to do some self-pacing, to find his own best level of involvement.

Programed materials are often helpful, for they break concepts or tasks down into sequential units, so the child does not miss essential aspects in learning a concept or a skill. The program also serves as a monitoring device to the child, giving feedback on his responses that he, himself, can recognize. Sometimes these convergent materials can be obtained commercially; in other cases the teacher constructs his own, to insure that they are tailored to the child and that they adequately develop the concepts or skills the child is learning. When purchased materials are used, the teacher investigates them carefully, making sure they are teaching what they are purported to teach. The many enjoyable reading and math games available on the market serve well as self-motivating practice

tools. However, the teacher looks carefully at the psychology behind the games, to make sure they are doing the job intended.

Task Analysis

Sometimes it is necessary for the teacher to analyze minutely the task with which the child is coping. If the child is having problems with spelling, it may be that he actually is not hearing the sounds or that he is not relating the sounds to specific consonants, vowels or digraphs. The child may need extra phonetic practice to succeed with both word recognition and spelling, and special practice may need to be given in these aspects every time a new word is introduced. The sample math lesson in Chapter 7, "The Teacher as Mediator," is another example of task analysis, for each element of the task is broken down in sequence.

Use of Feedback

Feedback is important in the learning process, especially for the child who finds learning difficult. When the teacher is giving a child feedback, it is important to concentrate on his successes and progress. In going over a work page, for example, the teacher may say, "You got seven of the examples correct!" rather than, "You missed 13 examples today." It is better to say, "Good, you topped your score this week—you learned three more addition facts than you did last week," than to say, "You missed 12 out of the 20 facts on this sheet." The teacher analyzes the nature of the errors with the child, and reteaches concepts and skills that have not been mastered. Then new practice activities are assigned to detect deficiencies that may remain. New tasks are made either more simple or more complex, depending on the feedback obtained from the child's prior work. In a one-to-one tutoring situation, there is continual feedback between the child and the teacher in order to correct the child's inadequate responses before he undertakes new steps.

Teaching to Modalities

We noted in Chapter 9 that some children learn best through a visual modality, some through an auditory modality and still others through a tactile or kinesthetic modality. If, for example, the teacher finds that a child is an auditory learner rather than a visual or tactile learner, he will give the child guided practice in visual intake to strengthen this modality. However, he will not ignore the auditory approach. If the child is a poor reader, he will be encouraged to use his auditory facility to obtain information in science and social studies through listening and telling about what he knows, rather than through reading and writing about it. The child needs to have weak learning modalities strengthened, but he also needs to feel success through using his best available powers.

Children Learn Through Being Tutors

Experienced teachers have found that children with learning problems often benefit from teaching a skill they have mastered to someone who is less far along. Experiments have been conducted in some low economic neighborhoods, for example, where upper-grade underachievers have been sent into primary grades as reading tutors, with astounding results for both the "teachers" and the "taught." In other cases, reluctant middle-grade readers have advanced proudly when they are sent to the kindergarten to read stories. When a child becomes a successful tutor, at least three things happen: (1) he rethinks the processes of the skill and then communicates these processes to another; (2) he experiences the exhilaration of involvement and the command that he has over his skill; and (3) he realizes that other children have problems and are in need of help, and that he is not alone in the learning world.

MAKING REFERRALS

Sometimes classroom teachers do not have the expertise necessary for diagnosing or coping with behavioral problems that are caused by neurological dysfunctions, learning disabilities, emotional disturbance or other severe deficits. The educational background and experience of the teacher cannot possibly enable him to be knowledgeable in all problem areas, nor does his training necessarily give him the specialized skills he needs as a therapist or remedial teacher. The teacher does, however, need to recognize when he is able to help and when he is not. He also should be aware of all the available ancillary professionals in the district

where he teaches, and he should use the official referral procedures of his school (for ethical as well as legal reasons). When making referrals, the teacher functions in four important ways:

1. He shares all the information he has accumulated concerning the child. Every shred of information available about the child should be given to the professional, to help speed up the diagnosis or to make it more accurate and complete. (The professional will then not waste time uncovering information that has already been compiled.)

2. He clarifies the reason for the referral. If it is a problem of disruptive behavior the teacher cannot tolerate, he makes this known. If the child has a puzzling learning problem that the teacher cannot solve, he makes this known; if he suspects neurological damage, he makes this known. The ancillary professional can proceed more effectively when he knows why the teacher feels the need of specialized help.

3. The teacher explains the procedures he has used in working with the child before referral. This is important information to the specialist, for it may show what is left to be done, what needs to be undone or what new alternatives need to be sought.

4. He uses feedback from the helping professional in altering his relationship with the child or in adjusting his teaching procedures. If the child remains in the classroom, periodically visiting the helping professional, the teacher should find out how he should deal with the child, and how he and the specialist may best function as a team working in behalf of the child. Sometimes children are referred to more than one specialist, and the teacher may be asked to participate in a "staffing," in which information is shared in a group meeting involving all the helping professionals. If new procedures are agreed on, the teacher then has the responsibility for carefully noting and reporting the child's behavior and his reactions to these new solutions.

Inexperienced teachers sometimes refuse to seek help from a specialist because they feel that their inability to cope is a stigma, but the enlightened teacher will realize that there are times when he cannot cope and that he is acting sensibly and humanely when he puts the child in touch with a specialist. The mature teacher can make referrals without feeling that his status is threatened.

CONTINUOUS ASSESSMENT OF THE CHILD'S EXPERIENCE

Although many children have been harmed by evaluation, the educational process would be incomplete without it. There is a human tendency to value, and each person wants to know where he stands. People need standards in order to function, but academic standards should be unique to the individual. Damage results when children are evaluated against set norms and are made to feel inferior because their performance is not up to some adult's expectation. It must be conceded, also, that children have their own levels of aspiration and can feel defeated when they do not attain a standard they have set for themselves. However, unrealistic levels of aspiration indicate poor adjustment to the realities of life; they usually result when parents hold unrealistic expectations for their children or when they withhold praise and approval. The behavior of teachers may also contribute to the child's skewed aspiration for himself: The child may undershoot or overshoot, depending on the feedback he has received from his phenomenal environment and the level of self-assurance he has attained.

It may sound paradoxical to say that teachers should attempt to use evaluation to correct these flaws. Instead of experiencing failure, children will feel intrinsically rewarded and fulfilled, if evaluation is used constructively to help each child recognize his own strengths and weaknesses and accept them for what they are. This recognition leads the child to appreciate his true attainments. As was pointed out in Chapter 9, the teacher does not judge the child but helps him identify standards, goals and expectations that are suitable to him. School should not be a race in which each child tries to keep up to or ahead of the next fellow; rather, it should be an excursion in which each child savors his school world while looking through realistic glasses. The child enjoys what he sees, because it is qualitatively suited to him. The teacher helps the child decide whether he is, *for*

him, doing good work. Gradually, the child begins to form his own independent judgments.

The teacher can have the child compare his work to other work he has done, especially earlier work he has attempted. The teacher might tape the child's reading at an early period and share it with him later in the school year. The child's written expressions and art products are easier to retrieve. Some of the more mature children may seek the teacher's critical analysis of their work in relationship to specific models in art, music, or literature. But in this case the child is ready for criticism, because he has asked for it; he has the confidence and courage to place his creations alongside those of the experts to see what he can learn from them.

The teacher looks at the total environment and notices its effects on each child. He can discern some of the changes that have taken place in children's attitudes, their thinking and their growth in achieving skills, but he cannot discern the whole picture—some changes are never visible. He looks at his own methods, actions and interpersonal relationships to determine the effects his behaviors are having on individual children, and he decides whether the visible evidence is in harmony with his philosophy of education. However, if the teacher views his role as a creator of environment, his major concern is that children are interacting dynamically, and he knows that the subjective experience of each child will be different. Only a part of educational experience can be evaluated objectively. Therefore, judging educational outcomes must necessarily be a subjective process; it is like looking at one's creation to see whether it is good or unsatisfactory.

Perceptions of Learners as Feedback to Teachers

The perceptions of learners are probably the most accurate guides to the teacher in ascertaining the quality of educational experience. The teacher may wish to have children respond to the following *Pupil Perception Inventory* (if they are fourth grade or higher), noting whether the feedback he receives is what he hopes for.[7] The teacher makes his own key; he decides which responses fulfill his aims.

PUPIL PERCEPTION INVENTORY OF CLASSROOM ENVIRONMENT

Directions: Here are some statements about how you may feel about school or the teacher. There are no right or wrong answers. Notice there are two statements for each number, one marked "a" and one marked "b." Pick out the statement, "a" or "b," in each pair that is most like what you think or feel is true and put a check on the answer sheet beside the right letter. For example, if you think your teacher lets you do things in your own way, place a check beside 1.a. on your answer sheet. NEVER mark both "a" and "b."

Example:

Statements   Answer Sheet

1. ____ a. My teacher lets me do things in my own way.   1. _X_ a.
   ____ b. My teacher makes me do things his way.   ____ b.
2. ____ a. Each day seems to pass quickly.   2. ____ a.
   ____ b. Time always seems to drag.   _X_ b.

1. ____ a. My teacher lets me do things in my own way.
   ____ b. My teacher makes me do things his way.
2. ____ a. Each day seems to pass quickly.
   ____ b. Time always seems to drag.
3. ____ a. My teacher gives me the help I need to keep going.
   ____ b. My teacher expects me to keep going on my own.
4. ____ a. We often do new and exciting things in school.
   ____ b. Each day is usually like the one before.
5. ____ a. Most of the time, I look forward to going to school.
   ____ b. Most of the time I wish I could stay home from school.
6. ____ a. Things usually run smoothly in our classroom.
   ____ b. There is usually much confusion in our classroom.
7. ____ a. My teacher always makes us finish an activity even when we are not getting anything out of it.
   ____ b. My teacher lets us quit an activity if we are not getting anything out of it.
8. ____ a. Our teacher shows us how to do the things we need to know in a new activity.
   ____ b. Our teacher doesn't show us how to do the things we need to know in a new activity.
9. ____ a. The things we need for an activity are usually around.
   ____ b. We often can't finish an activity because we don't have the things we need.
10. ____ a. Our teacher lets us quit an activity or discussion if something interesting comes up.
    ____ b. Our teacher makes us stick to a discussion or activity until it is finished.
11. ____ a. We know what our teacher expects when we begin an activity.
    ____ b. We don't know what our teacher expects when we begin an activity.
12. ____ a. We always follow a set plan when carrying out an activity.
    ____ b. We make plans for an activity but sometimes change them as we go along.

13. ____ a. Our teacher usually solves our problems for us.
    ____ b. Our teacher helps us solve our problems together.
14. ____ a. I am usually excited about an activity when it is over.
    ____ b. I am usually not very interested by the time we finish an activity.
15. ____ a. Practice activities are usually fun to do.
    ____ b. Practice activities are usually boring.
16. ____ a. There are always interesting things to do in the classroom when I have finished by work.
    ____ b. Usually there is nothing interesting to do when I have finished my work.
17. ____ a. I always have some time during the day when I can choose an activity I like to do.
    ____ b. I never have free time to choose things I like to do.
18. ____ a. We are free to move around in our classroom.
    ____ b. Our teacher stops us if we move around a lot.
19. ____ a. We are free to talk to other children so long as we are not disturbing others.
    ____ b. We are not allowed to talk to others while we are doing our work.
20. ____ a. Our teacher changes the lesson or activity when we are getting bored.
    ____ b. Our teacher makes us keep on doing the same thing in a lesson or activity even if we are bored.
21. ____ a. Our teacher is excited about the things we do in school.
    ____ b. Our teacher is bored with the things we do in school.
22. ____ a. Our teacher has lots of good ideas.
    ____ b. Our teacher doesn't have very many new ideas.
23. ____ a. We have both quiet times and active times in our classroom.
    ____ b. Our classroom is always quiet or always noisy.
24. ____ a. The class has lots of ideas that we use in our activities.
    ____ b. Our teacher thinks up all the ideas for activities.
25. ____ a. The children in our class get along well together.
    ____ b. The children in our class don't get along very well together.
26. ____ a. I have plenty of time to do my work in school.
    ____ b. I feel rushed and nervous at school.
27. ____ a. Our class usually feels nervous and tense.
    ____ b. Our class is usually relaxed and happy.

SUMMARY

The teacher may use the following inventory to analyze his own behavior as an educational diagnostician.

THE TEACHER AS "EDUCATIONAL DIAGNOSTICIAN" IN THE PHENOMENOLOGICAL ENVIRONMENT OF THE CLASSROOM

I. As an educational diagnostician, the teacher gathers data about the child, to determine his developmental patterns, his potentialities, and his growth toward fulfilling his potentialities.

   A. The teacher observes children informally to get clues about each child.

      1. The teacher becomes aware of the child's interests, potentialities and his physical and mental "sets"; therefore, he:

    a. notices interests of individual children and the kinds of activities each child seeks out on his own.

    b. notices how the child expresses himself in creative work and other activities; looks for the mode of expression in which the child is most fluent.

    c. notices which situations call forth spontaneous expressions in the child and which situations inhibit him.

    d. notices the way a child approaches or tackles problems.

    e. notices the kind and quality of questions the child asks, the kind and quality of his ideas, and the contributions he makes in the group.

    f. looks for the level of a child's thought processes in his oral and written responses and communications.

    g. notices the kinds of help the child seeks and the responses he gives when he is being helped.

    h. notices which children are catching on, which are dropping out, which children are attending.

    i. notices the child's visual-perceptual, auditory and motor reactions, and recognizes unusual responses.

    j. notices the child's physical energy, motor coordination and posture.

2. The teacher becomes aware of the child's attitudes toward himself, his life style, his personal adjustment (or integration) and his relationship to the group; therefore, he:

    a. notices the child's attitudes toward his own body, his abilities, his "self," other people and authority; notices stereotypes and incongruent behavior.

    b. recognizes tensional outlets in children as well as withdrawing, aggressive or defensive behavior.

    c. notices the child's tendency to lead or to follow.

    d. notices the dominant values of the group and the children who are independent from the dominant values.

    e. notices how individuals are perceived by the group.

    f. notices the role(s) each individual tends to play in the group.

    g. notices the antecedents and precipitating factors of an episode of behavior that is upsetting to the child or the group.

    h. looks for similarities or differences in the child's characteristic behavior in different settings— academic, social, creative, physical.

    i. becomes aware of home and community social factors that affect the child.

B. *The teacher uses tests to expand his knowledge of the child's potentialities and to pinpoint under-developed areas of growth, if the need is indicated.*

1. The teacher chooses tests appropriate for a given need and administers them with care; therefore, he:

    a. helps the child understand the purpose and expectations of testing and makes the child feel comfortable with the testing process.

    b. follows directions exactly as given in the test manual.

    c. has all the necessary tools and materials on hand.

    d. gives full attention to pupils being tested and does not allow himself to be interrupted when administering a standardized test.

    e. encourages the efforts of the child during testing without revealing the exact response.

    f. scores standardized tests carefully and accurately, and if possible has them checked by someone else.

2. The teacher gets below the surface when analyzing data from standardized test results; therefore, he:

    a. looks at the cultural patterns of the neighborhood in relationship to any standardized test.

    b. considers the physical and emotional health of the child in relationship to the child's performance.

    c. looks for patterns of errors made by individuals and groups.

    d. analyzes test items in relationship to each child and analyzes test results of the group as a whole.

    e. analyzes test results in relationship to his teaching; determines what he has failed to teach or in what way he has failed to reach the child.

    f. makes individual profiles of test results; notices atypical scores on subtests.

    g. interprets percentile and achievement scores in terms of what the scores mean to that particular individual or group, and views these data as tentative.

C. *The teacher uses other formal methods of collecting data when the need is indicated and checks these data against his informal observations and test results; therefore, he:*

    1. keeps anecdotal records that *describe* (rather than judge) behavior.

    2. uses sociometric devices with discretion; gives the child a real purpose for doing a sociometric activity and protects his privacy.

    3. prepares his own diagnostic materials, which get at specific factors in the child's perceptual, cognitive and/or skill development.

    4. devises specific tasks in which the child demonstrates his understanding of a problem or concept; his powers in absorbing information, in expressing himself, and in integrating ideas and information; and/or his ability to perform specific skills.

    5. notices *how* the child approaches a specified task and raises questions with the child about the task to get at his level of thinking.

D. *The teacher studies data from cumulative records with reservations and considers this material only in relationship to other observed factors; therefore, he:*

    1. consults records after he has time to gain his own impressions of each child.

    2. refrains from labeling or judging a child on the basis of information contained in records.

    3. looks for patterns in the child's academic and personal growth (behavior) that have shown up over a period of time.

    4. notices factors in the child's background which may contribute to his present academic and personal adjustment.

II. **As an educational diagnostician, the teacher interprets personal and academic growth of the child within a constellation of related factors and makes a diagnostic assessment; therefore, he:**

1. assesses the child's developmental growth patterns—physical, social, emotional, mental—and looks for all the factors that contribute to a child's behavior.

2. looks for relationships in data; discovers patterns in the child's behavior and areas of blocked or unused potential; notes "typical" behavior of the child.

3. sizes up basic personality orientations of each child.

4. analyzes the child's behavior in terms of his self-perceptions, personality orientations and the needs he is trying to satisfy.

5. tries to discover the basic learning style of the child; looks for learning modalities—visual, auditory, kinesthetic—and determines whether these are integrated within the child.

6. looks at the results of tests in relationship to other observed factors about the child, such as chronological age, general school performance, emotional growth.

7. identifies specific learning problems and sees relationships between these and the child's learning style.

8. analyzes the learning processes of the child having difficulties and decides whether the child's problem is in attaching meaning to what he sees and hears, in expressing himself, in organizing and integrating ideas into his thinking, or some other factor.

9. makes a summary of the symptoms and contributing factors that have inhibited the child's growth and learning.

10. pinpoints the relevant factors related to specific problems/disabilities a given child may have and sees how these are interrelated.

11. makes hypotheses regarding where the child is in his personal and academic development, what his needs are and what he is ready for; determines whether a child's problems are due to physical, environmental, or psychological and aptitudinal factors.

12. decides whether a child is gaining access to his potentialities.

13. keeps an open mind about the child and views his hypotheses as tentative.

III. **For children with special needs, the teacher as educational diagnostician organizes individual programs based on diagnostic assessments; therefore, he:**

1. helps the child understand his problems, hangups, and stages of progress in the learning process, and uses data obtained from tests, daily work or other sources when doing so.

2. lets the child know that failure does not lie in the child but in failure to provide for his needs.

3. involves the child in a plan to overcome his problems; helps the child see where he is and cooperatively plans a balanced, life-related program that gives special attention to skills or abilities that are underdeveloped.

4. helps the child make short-term plans and concrete goals, individualized to his own needs.

5. structures the learning situation according to the child's attention span, rate of learning and other variables that are affecting the child's ability to cope; keeps the learning situation simple enough for the child to cope successfully.

6. tailors a program to capitalize on the child's abilities, while at the same time giving the child special work in the areas of his needs.

7. analyzes tasks to see what abilities are required; provides for instruction and practice in each ability in which the child is deficient and then helps the child integrate the ability into tasks that are more complex.

8. develops and/or uses self-monitoring instructional materials and helps the child develop a system to check on the correctness of his own responses.

9. elicits feedback from the child as the plan progresses—gives feedback to the child to help him assess his own progress.

10. helps the child see his strengths when giving feedback.

11. helps the child use feedback from his performance to determine what his next steps should be.

12. sets up situations where the child who is being helped may teach another who is less advanced in a particular skill.

IV. **When the teacher, as educational diagnostician, has exhausted his own resources, or when he needs data he cannot obtain by himself, he makes appropriate referrals of the child to other "helping" professionals, such as special teachers, school psychologist, remedial teacher, social worker, nurse, physician, or counselor. When making referrals, the teacher:**

1. shares information he has accumulated concerning the child.

2. clarifies the reason for the referral.

3. explains the procedures used before referral.

4. uses feedback from the helping professional in altering his relationship with the child or in making adjustments in his teaching.

V. **As an educational diagnostician, the teacher evaluates the educational experience of the child; therefore, he:**

1. decides what the actual learning outcomes are and determines whether these outcomes are in harmony with overall goals of self-development of the child.

2. decides whether given methods or planned experiences have been effective in reaching educational outcomes.

3. analyzes the social-emotional climate of the classroom group and its effect on each child.

4. looks at his own language and behavior to determine whether he is fulfilling the role of one who helps and guides rather than being simply a judge.

5. becomes aware of his own feelings and behavior in his interactions with a child or group, and evaluates how this is affecting the educational process.

6. refrains from judging or stereotyping the child on the basis of his past record or other prejudicial factors, such as family background.

Notes

[1] Daniel A. Prescott, *The Child in the Educative Process* (New York: McGraw-Hill Book Co., 1957), pp. 153-154.

[2] Don C. Dinkmeyer, *Child Development: The Emerging Self* (Englewood Cliffs, N.J.: Prentice-Hall, Inc., 1965), p. 59.

[3] Reprinted by permission of the publisher from Arthur T. Jersild and Ruth J. Tasch, *Children's Interests and What They Suggest for Education* (New York: Teachers College Press, copyright 1949 by Teachers College, Columbia University), p. 2.

[4] Reprinted by permission of the publisher from Millie Almy, *Ways of Studying Children* (New York: Teachers College Press, copyright 1959 by Teachers College, Columbia University), pp. 31-32.

[5] Lessie Carlton and Robert H. Moore, *Reading, Self-Directive Dramatization and Self Concept* (Columbus, Ohio: Charles E. Merrill Publishing Co., 1968), pp. 25-27.

[6] Ibid., p. 47.

[7] Dorothy I. Seaberg, *Pupil Perception Inventory of Classroom Environment: Choreography, Form A* (Unpublished, 1972).

References

Almy, Millie. *Ways of Studying Children.* New York: Teachers College Press, Teachers College, Columbia University, 1959.

Carlton, Lessie, and Robert H. Moore. *Reading, Self-Directive Dramatization and Self Concept.* Columbus, Ohio: Charles E. Merrill Publishing Co., 1968.

Dinkmeyer, Don C. *Child Development: The Emerging Self.* Englewood Cliffs, New Jersey: Prentice-Hall, Inc., 1965.

Jersild, Arthur T., and Ruth Tasch. *Children's Interests and what they Suggest for Education.* New York: Bureau of Publications, Teachers College, Columbia University, 1949.

Kirk, Samuel A., and Winifred D. Kirk. *Psycholinguistic Learning Disabilities: Diagnosis and Remediation.* Urbana: University of Illinois Press, 1971.

Prescott, Daniel A. *The Child in the Educative Process.* New York: McGraw-Hill Book Co., 1957.

Rosenthal, Robert, and Lenore Jacobson. *Pygmalion in the Classroom.* New York: Holt, Rinehart and Winston, Inc., 1968.

Seaberg, Dorothy I. "Pupil Perception Inventory: Choreography, Form A." Unpublished, 1972.

Chapter 11

Diagnostic Study of Jeffrey Clark[1]

Jeff is a very immature little boy. He is small for his size, and he also has a short attention span. He would rather play with toys when his work is done than read or do special interest activities. When playing with other children at recess, he is quite "physical." He likes to run, play tag, or swing on a swing when he is outside. He loves to make noises and repeat them over and over. At recess he may even act out the noises he is making.

In the classroom, Jeff takes his work seriously and really tries. He is not a discipline problem. He is discouraged easily and will often sit staring at his work, hoping I will notice he needs help. If I don't, he will start conversations with those around him or begin to make funny noises. At this point, he will mark anything and turn it in. Jeff usually confuses the directions.

In reading, Jeff responds well in one-to-one teaching. He enjoys working for rewards such as stars, smiling faces drawn on his paper, and candy. Jeff likes working with me. Even the simplest tasks are frustrating, but when we work together like

this the interest level is longer because he doesn't have to wait for help.

Both the reading teacher and I have tried many approaches. He can do simple discrimination tasks where he must mark like and non-like items. He has begun (slightly) to learn through associating pictures and letters when reading. He has great difficulty drawing from his own knowledge and applying what he knows. He cannot recognize letters and sounds from groups of letters. He does not seem to have much memory. He is very "hot" and "cold" in his learning. One day he knows what is going on and the next day he is lost. Copying anything down on his own or from the board is also a big problem.

When Jeff tackles a task, he seems to be really concentrating on what he is doing. At times he appears to be dazed, lost in thought. There is usually no expression on his face at all. He will sit this way when he is not sure of the answer. Often it continues until I ask him if he is stuck. Then I get a vertical shake of the head.

In reading, Jeff has learned a few sight vocabulary words through the method of constant repetition. He likes and can read simple, first preprimer stories. Sometimes he reads them over and over. But again, he is very hot and cold on what he remembers and forgets. For some reason, if I say,

"Find 'look,' Jeff," he can find it. In contrast, if there is a "look" flash card, he may pick it up and have no idea of what it says. He seems to have no independent "association" techniques for figuring out words on his own.

In math, Jeff can do simple addition and subtraction problems. He does this out of routine, not because he really understands the processes. This shows when I take him out of his math book and give him the same types of problems—he can't seem to do them. However, I do take it slow in math. It is individualized and he does find success.

Phonics is Jeff's biggest problem area. Both the reading teacher and I worked until Christmas trying to teach him his vowel sounds. He can do long sounds alone, short sounds sometimes, but neither when combined. We are now trying to teach him the alphabet so we can begin consonant work. He can say most of the alphabet but writes only a few letters correctly. He can write a few letters at random but usually cannot name the sounds.

There is no one approach that works best with Jeff. He does best with visual discrimination tasks and auditory repetition activities. Anything involving memory is very difficult. Sometimes learning through games works and sometimes it doesn't. Jeff cannot work independently.

This year we discovered Jeff needed glasses. This did cut down on the wiggling, but I still feel he does not see things as we do. He has so much trouble copying anything.

PINPOINTING THE PROBLEM

1. *Is the problem related to Jeff's interests?*
   I do not feel the problem is related to Jeff's interests. He does not seem to get bored—just frustrated. Jeff likes:
   a. animals
   b. motorcycles and bicycles
   c. playing guns
   d. riding on his family's boat
   e. math
   f. swinging
   g. his family

2. *Is the problem related to Jeff's personal adjustments or integration?*
   Jeff is always very cooperative and eager. He has little trouble moving from one activity to the next. The only trouble is when we do "active things." Jeff gets a little too active—sometimes very silly.

3. *Is the problem related to Jeff's social relationships?*
   No. Jeff gets along and is liked by the other children. When playing group games, he is usually picked. (He is *seldom* picked for academic activities.)

4. *Is the problem related to Jeff's unmet emotional needs?*
   Jeff gets frustrated and tense at times. This usually happens when he has been scolded. He may even get a little mad and push or hit another child. He does not take criticism well and he does not like to be pushed around. In groups, if I take it nice and slow, play games and make small challenges, Jeff usually does not get frustrated. When on his own again, he gets discouraged easily.

5. *Is the problem related to Jeff's perception?*
   Yes! Jeff often reverses letters. He does not always perceive things the way others do.

6. *Is the problem related to physical health or disability?*
   It might be—his glasses don't seem to correct his perceptual problems. His general physical health is good, however.

7. *Is the problem related to intellectual capacity?*
   Jeff has a very short attention span. I am very concerned about his memory ability. He forgets so easily from one day to the next. However, when given the *Primary Mental Abilities* test for grades K-1, Jeff scored:
   Verbal meaning – 6 years, 4 months
   Perceptual speech – 6 years, 2 months
   Number facility – 6 years, 10 months
   Spatial relationships – 7 years, 8 months
   Total: 6 years, 8 months.
   His chronological age at test time was 6 years, 4 months.
   On the *Basic Reading Test* from Scott Foresman's *Before We Read,* Jeff scored in the 20–25 percentile range.

   These data show an average intellectual capacity and indicate that Jeff's reading and memory problems arise from a different cause.

OBSERVATIONS CONCERNING JEFF'S PERSONAL AND ACADEMIC DEVELOPMENT

Informal Observations of Interests and Potentials

1. *What types of activities does Jeff seek out on his own?*

   Jeff usually chooses manipulative games and items. It varies from day to day, but he usually chooses blocks, Tinker Toys, puzzles or Lincoln Logs. He usually builds cars, trucks or motorcycles of some kind; he enjoys vocalizing sounds to accompany the objects he makes. When he uses Lincoln Logs, he usually makes houses.

   Jeff also enjoys art projects that involve paper, scissors and glue. His ideas do not usually come from the other children. He likes art because this is probably his most successful subject. The other children also think Jeff is good in art.

2. *What mode does Jeff use to be expressive? What situations inhibit his spontaneous expression?*

   a. Expressive means
      (1) Art.
      (2) Manipulative items. } These are things where there are no right or wrong answers.
      (3) Active games and gym.
      (4) Making noises—it relieves him.
      (5) We talk every morning before we settle down. Jeff loves to talk about what happened last night or over the weekend.

   b. Situations inhibiting expression
      (1) Anything that requires him to write.
      (2) Even when someone else does the writing, Jeff finds it difficult to make up a story. He does not always speak in complete sentences. He seems to be at a loss for words. (except when he talks about his family).
      (3) He has difficulty seeing stories and inferences in pictures.

3. *What are the different ways Jeff tackles a problem?*

   Jeff usually doesn't tackle a problem on his own. He usually waits for step-by-step questions. If Jeff does not know the answer he puts his head down and sits quietly. Then I ask, "Don't you know, Jeff?" or "Don't you understand?" Then he shakes his head and we try a new approach.

   When working at his seat, Jeff starts in very quickly and works very deliberately for a few minutes. Then when he gets to a part he doesn't understand, he just quits. He seldom asks for help. He turns his work in and goes and plays.

4. *What are the kinds and quality of questions Jeff asks?*

   This is a problem area. Jeff does not ask questions. Usually one of the children or I spot Jeff having problems, and we go and help him. I'm not sure Jeff knows what to ask. He does ask for help with knots in his shoe or for help with a stuck zipper.

5. *What kind of help does Jeff seek? For what reasons? What are his responses to help?*

   Jeff seeks help from most of the children around him when it comes to problems with words or puzzles. He seldom seeks help on his seat assignments or boardwork activities. He seldom copies anyone else's work just to get it right.

   The children are good to Jeff and often help him. Sometimes they help a little too much and do his asking and thinking for him.

   Jeff responds well to most help. He likes being and talking with people rather than working alone. He reacts with a smile to praise, but he never gets really excited. I can tell he is proud of some of the things he has done, but he seldom shares anything academic with anyone else.

6. *What are Jeff's visual-perceptual responses?*

   a. Jeff reverses many letters; for example, *b* for *d, ƨ* for *z.*
   b. He usually confuses *m* and *n.*
   c. He always mixes up capitals and small letters when he writes, and cannot write a complete alphabet of either capitals or small letters.
   d. The other day he copied my name, Pyfer, off the board as "Rute."
   e. He has great difficulty copying sentences off the board, reversing words as well as letters.
   f. I feel he cannot "zero-in" on what he sees. He seems to be easily distracted by everything around him.

The reading teacher and I have been trying to teach Jeff the alphabet, but there seems to be a real block. We have great difficulty getting him to read, write or say his alphabet. Jeff can sing the "alphabet song," however. This helps him in writing it down, but he has to start the song at the beginning. He cannot continue correctly, starting from a random letter. There are certain letters that always cause him trouble (*h,* and the tail end of the alphabet). His memory is good one day but not the next. I feel we are progressing, but *ever so slowly.*

7. *What are Jeff's auditory responses?*
Auditory responses are probably Jeff's best responses. There are not so many things that distract him. He can repeat sounds (except *th*). He can say most vowel sounds when told, for example, that the *i* is short or the *e* is long.

Jeff has progressed in hearing short or long sounds. He can sound out simple words if I use short-sound words. In long-sound words he forgets to count the vowels.

8. *What is the nature of Jeff's physical energy, coordination and posture?*
Jeff is very wiggly. He can't sit still or stand in a line very long without making noise or touching others. He usually plays active games rather than sitting quietly and reading. He does, on occasion, like to look at pictures or color. On the playground, if he is not running, he is swinging. These are his two favorite activities when he is outside. Jeff's posture, walk, run and general coordination are good.

Jeff is very social on most occasions. He loves to talk to anyone who will listen. He loves to scrub the top of his desk. Sometimes I think he gets crayon on it so he can get out the soap and scrub.

Weather affects Jeff. He is usually quite wiggly on stormy and snowy days.

INFORMAL OBSERVATION CONCERNING SELF, OTHERS, THE TEACHER

1. *How does Jeff respond to others?*
Fine, so long as the children do not "put down" what he is doing academically. On the playground, things are great (unless he is angry). He has shown progress in controlling his roughness since Christmas.

2. *How does Jeff feel about his own body? His abilities? His self?*
Jeff will not admit he is having troubles, but it shows on his face and his body. Jeff is unhappy about himself academically. He once told me he wished he were a smart little girl in the next room.

Jeff had trouble writing his own name—especially his last name—at the beginning of school. He still forgets his last name from time to time, and he does not know his birthday.

3. *What are Jeff's tensional outlets?*
   a. Noises! He makes things (mostly vehicles) out of Tinker Toys and then sounds appropriate noises.
   b. On the playground he runs.
   c. When he is mad he pushes.

4. *When does Jeff lead? When does he follow?*
Jeff leads as a "room captain" once every two weeks. He is the helper for the day. Sometimes he leads in gym. (He is a good runner.) Sometimes he leads in art.

In any other group activity, Jeff is always a follower.

5. *What is Jeff's home background?*
Jeff lives with his mother and father. His mother is a housewife and his father is a welder. They live only a few blocks from school, so the children walk to school. Jeff has two brothers and two sisters, all older than he. The eldest boy is in a special classroom for children with learning disabilities.

Jeff is usually very clean and so are his clothes, although many of them seem too small for him. He has good bathroom habits. He also takes pride in keeping his desk clean inside. On top it is another story! He makes messes but he does enjoy cleaning them up. He seems to enjoy the physical activity.

Jeff likes his family. He talks a lot about his father and his cat. Once in awhile he talks about his sister Cathy; otherwise, he does not talk about his brothers and sisters. The family seems to do things together. Jeff frequently talks about going out in their new boat together.

GATHERING DATA THROUGH TESTING
The Primary Mental Abilities Test

1. *What patterns in the neighborhood do not coincide with the standardized test?*
   Jeff has trouble with these words:
   spear   brave
   dome   taxi ⎫ We are a farm community.
   beast

2. *What are Jeff's problems?*
   Jeff does not always listen to the whole sentence.
   Examples:
   a. In response to "What keeps a house dry?" he marked a raincoat.
   b. In response to "Sally tried on a new dress she wanted to wear to a party," he marked a girl holding a dress.
   Jeff had difficulty in the perceptual speed test. When only 1-1/2 minutes were allowed, he got nervous.

3. *What was the condition of Jeff's health at the time of the test?*
   Jeff's health at this time was good. The only factor that might have influenced the test is that he took a long time to complete it, and he was limited just to the time he normally has for his remedial reading class.

4. *What were his strong areas?*
   a. Spatial relationships. For example, he correctly marked the triangle as the element necessary to complete the square.

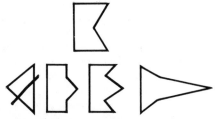

   b. Number facility

5. *What were his weak areas?*
   Timed activities and verbal meaning.

The Check Test of Long Sounds
In October, Jeff had trouble marking all the vowels. He was not sure of his sounds at all. (He does know long $\bar{o}$.)
   In January, Jeff was improving. He knew long $\bar{a}$, $\bar{o}$, and $\bar{u}$ most of the time.

Results of the Basic Reading Test to Accompany *Before We Read*, Scott Foresman

1. *What cultural patterns of the neighborhood do not coincide with the standardized test?*
   There were no obvious patterns that would cause trouble.

2. *What conditions might have influenced the test?*
   The whole class took the test at this time. Jeff might have felt rushed. His health was good.

3. *What were the strong and weak areas?*
   The strong areas were sentence meaning and sensory images. The weak areas were visual perception. (But he has really improved in this area.)

Other Methods of Data Collection

1. I used the board a lot when working with Jeff to see how he was doing in various areas. I also used many games and worksheets geared to his needs.

2. I used two interest inventories.
   a. From the "Pupil Report of Interests and Activities" taken from the reading book, *Peppermint Fence,* I found that Jeff's interests were very "young."
      (1) He likes to play with toys.
      (2) In free time, he rides bikes, but is not interested in anything academic.
      (3) His interests were active—building, playing, riding. (He said he had no books of his own.)
      (4) His free time at home was spent watching television, especially cartoons.
      (5) His choices in rank order were interesting:
         (a) play outside
         (b) go to the movies
         (c) watch television
         (d) listen to the radio
         (e) read books.
   b. Results of the "Springfield Interest Finder."
      (1) *My three wishes:*
         (a) real motorcycle ⎫ Hard to do.
         (b) jeep

(c)   Santa Claus suit (Didn't know why.)

(2)   *What I'd like to learn more about in school:*
"Learn more math." (Math is his favorite subject.)

(3)   *What I don't like to learn about:*
Spelling (It's hard to do.)

(4)   *What I like best in school:*
Reading

(5)   *What I like least or dislike most at school:*
Lunch (Because you get hungry.)

(6)   *What I like best outside school:*
Swing

(7)   *What I like least about home:*
He likes everything.

(8)   *What I want to be when I grow up:*
A policeman (They get to ride on a motorcycle and go through red lights.)

(9)   *What did I enjoy doing the most last week?*
Playing with my cat.

(10)   *One place I really like to go is* "to my cousins."

(11)   *One of the happiest days in my life:*
Go on our new boat.

(12)   *My three best friends in my room (boys or girls)·*

Tim	(Yet these children do not
Dan	play with Jeff. These are
Troy	the popular boys. He plays with Scott.)

Results of sociometric questions:

(1)   *What two people would you like to play with?*
(a)   Jeff chose Mike B.
(b)   No one chose Jeffrey Clark.

(2)   *What two people would you like to sit next to you?*
(a)   Jeff chose Troy and Mike B.
(b)   No one chose Jeffrey Clark.

(3)   *What two people would you like to work with on a science project?*
(a)   Jeff chose Renée and Penny.
(b)   No one chose Jeffrey Clark.

(4)   *What two people would you like to work with on an art project?*
(a)   Jeff chose Renée.
(b)   Scott chose Jeffrey Clark.

(5)   *What two people in our room are your best friends?*
(a)   Jeff chose Troy and Tim (the two most popular boys).
(b)   No one chose Jeffrey Clark.

(6)   *What two people would you like on your team in gym?*
(a)   Jeff chose Dan and Tim.
(b)   No one chose Jeffrey Clark.

(7)   *What two people do you think are responsible enough to take care of the room?*
(a)   Jeff chose Troy.
(b)   Brenda chose Jeffrey Clark.

The Alphabet
Upon request, Jeff will write the alphabet in order. Yesterday he wrote: A,B,C,D,E, F _, _, i, _ K,L,M,N,O,P _, r,s, _ u _ w _, _ ꙅ.
Jeff mixed capitals and smalls.
He called "m" n.
He reversed z.
He knew "k" after I pointed out he had the letter in his name.
Jeff missed g, h, j, q, t, v, x, y, z.
Upon repeated trials, Jeff will write the alphabet in order getting more right than he did the time before. Today he wrote: A,B,C,D,E,F,G,H,i _, K,L,M,N,O,P, _, R S, V, u, W, T, X, _ ꙅ.

As you can see, we did not reach our objective. This time he missed different things. Jeff thought "v" was "t"; "w" was "v"; "T" was "w". He left out "J", "Q" and "Y" altogether.

Jeff commented, "Maybe next time I will get them all," so he tried again. This time he wrote the alphabet as follows: A,B,C,D,E,F,G,H,i _, K,L, M,N,O,P, _, R,S,T,U,V, _, _, _, ꙅ.
He had trouble with j, q, w, x, y, z.

REFERRAL FOR SPECIAL EDUCATION SERVICES

Statement of problem as seen by the school
(1) Jeff has great difficulty copying sentences from the board. (2) Jeff still has many letter reversals after constant practice. (3) Jeff has memory trouble—one day he remembers, the next he doesn't. He has trouble recalling sounds, the alphabet, the spelling of his own last name. He

looked at my name on the blackboard and copied it as "Rute." My name is Pyfer.

Additional comments

Jeff will be retained. I would really like him tested so we can help him get off to a good start next year. Both the reading teacher and I have made such slow progress. Jeff has great trouble learning. We have tried many approaches. There is no one best approach; different things work at different times. Jeff is easily distracted. He has trouble keeping his eyes on what he is doing. He will be working along and then all of a sudden make funny noises. He cannot sit still for very long.

WHAT GROWTH HAS JEFF MADE?

Jeff continues to find success, but at a very slow pace. He has learned that some things we do in school are fun. He enjoys reading and especially doing math.

In reading, Jeff has begun to build a small sight vocabulary that he seldom confuses. He can read chart stories that go along with our series with few mistakes. He is beginning to see details in pictures and has even begun to make inferences about what is happening in the story. His oral reading is still pretty much "word calling."

In math Jeff can recognize dimes, nickels, pennies. He knows their worth and can make simple change. He can count by tens and do simple 10's addition problems.

In phonics Jeff knows his short and long sounds most of the time. He is beginning to spell simple, short-sound words by phonics. He is beginning to understand rhyming words.

Comments:

Jeff still cannot work independently.

He still continues to make noises.

He still cannot seem to learn the alphabet. Because of this, Jeff finds consonants, sound association, blends and writing very difficult. The reading teacher and I feel we need more help.

Although I have filled out a form for "special services," I feel I waited too long to get outside help. The reading teacher and I wanted to try

everything we could before we sought other help. I am still very concerned about Jeff's perception and his memory. Jeff will be retained and will go to the other first-grade class. I hope that next year special services will help Jeff's teacher with his learning disabilities.

SPECIAL PROGRAMS TO MEET JEFF'S NEEDS

NOTE: Help the child find success.

Have him help in plans.

Set short-term goals together.

Ask him what he thinks he needs help with.

Jeff has received much special help. I have individualized his math and his reading. He is coming along in math but both reading and phonics are a real struggle.

Boardwork activities and papers are special for him. His activities are also shorter and so are his group sessions.

For a while Jeff was playing with another little boy named Scott, who also has trouble in some areas. During the period when the friendship was strong, I put Jeff and Scott in a special group together to play educational games.

The reading teacher and I have worked together throughout the year. Her comments follow:

Report on Jeffrey Clark from the Remedial Reading Room

Jeffrey is and has been attending remedial reading class for 20-minute periods each day since the beginning of the school year. He was referred to me by his teacher when it became apparent that he had difficulties in mastering the appropriate materials for his grade level.

Assuming that Jeffrey's problem stemmed from input disorder, I began with a multi-sensory approach, using three-dimensional letters, motor-associated learning, and audio-visual aids. Although some progress was noted after using these methods, I began to feel that perhaps part of Jeffrey's problem had to do with his inability to reproduce previously learned material. Because the communication process was involved, efforts were made to elicit the proper responses through oral repetition and exercises that use the process of elimination.

Among the areas emphasized were vowel letter recognition, vowel sounds, consonant letter recognition and consonant sounds. Through slow and painful steps requiring two months of intensive concentration, Jeffrey eventually mastered the names of the vowels. His short-term recall ability varied greatly. A back-tracking procedure seemed to dominate his learning, thus hindering his progress in new areas.

In retrospect, Jeffrey's response time has improved and, to a lesser degree, so has his attention span. Although some progress has been achieved, Jeffrey will continue to need remedial help, because his learning problems interfere with his academic gains.

Sally Hedrick
Remedial Reading Teacher

SUMMARY

The case study presented in this chapter illustrates the baffling problems presented by a child with a learning disability. Although Jeffrey Clark has normal intelligence, a number of symptoms indicate he has a learning problem connected with an input disorder. His dysfunctions may be summarized as (1) visual-perceptual (which showed up when he copied from the board, when he reversed letters, especially the letter *z*, and when he failed to distinguish between capital and small letters) and (2) memory dysfunction as indicated by the repetitive practice needed to fix letters of the alphabet in Jeff's mind. (He easily forgot and could not retain learnings from day to day for lack of associative powers.) Jeff's learning problems probably caused him to be easily distracted, to attend sporadically, to be very wiggly, and to be erratic in his learning.

In the realm of personal aptitude, Jeff might be classified as "thing" minded. The account showed he enjoyed manipulative physical activity. Constructing things with his hands and doing art work were the activities he liked to do best. Having difficulty with the verbal mode, Jeff probably needed to express his ideas through making things and by drawing rather than by talking. Jeff's physical orientation may indicate that more kin-esthetic methods needed to be used in teaching him, as mental processing may work best for Jeff through this mode. Jeff also seemed to be "people" minded. He enjoyed people and liked to talk about things he did' at home. In these instances he proved to be quite verbal. Basically, Jeff had good social relationships both at home and at school.

Clearly, this was a case that needed to be referred to a learning disabilities specialist. Mrs. Pyfer and the remedial reading teacher have garnered a great deal of information about the child which will be useful when shared with the learning disabilities specialist and should give a head start in planning for Jeff's needs the following year.

Without referral to a specialist equipped to do individual testing, it is impossible to make an accurate hypothesis that can be used to formulate a program to meet Jeff's learning needs. The study shows that the teacher provided the supportive relationship Jeff needed and that she was doing commendable work with him given the limitations of her own knowledge and training in working with children having special handicaps. The example provides a point of reference for inexperienced teachers who are trying to work through a learning problem with a child in the regular classroom.

Notes

[1] Paper contributed by Donna Pyfer in the author's course, "The Teacher in the Elementary School," Northern Illinois University. Used by permission.

STUDY HELPS AND CLASS ACTIVITIES

Annotated Bibliography

In addition to the books listed in chapter references, the following are recommended:

Adler, Alfred. *The Problem Child.* New York: G. P. Putnam's Sons, 1963.

The life styles of difficult children are analyzed in specific cases in this book.

Almy, Millie, et al. *Young Children's Thinking.* New York: Teacher's College Press, Columbia University, 1961.

Report of studies of some aspects of Piaget's theory of intellectual development, especially the idea of "conservation."

Chesler, Mark, and Robert Fox. *Role-Playing Methods in the Classroom.* Chicago: Science Research Associates, 1966.

A how-to-do-it book on the techniques of role playing. The thrust of the book is to show how role playing can be used as a technique in improving the learning atmosphere in the classroom.

Cunningham, Ruth, and associates. *Understanding Group Behavior of Boys and Girls.* New York: Bureau of Publications, Teachers College, Columbia University, 1951.

An action research study. The findings have interesting and valuable implications for the grouping of pupils, classroom teaching, group dynamics, and learning. Almy's Ways of Studying Children, mentioned in Part III, "The Face of Diagnosis," is the updated version of this work. Many techniques are included for getting data about children.

Dean, Joan. *Informal Schools in Britain Today: Recording Children's Progress.* New York: Citation Press, 1972.

A very practical and helpful little paperback giving illustrations of ways to keep records of children's progress.

Dunne, Lloyd M., et al. *Peabody Language Development Kits, Levels 1–3.* Circle Pines, Minn.: American Guidance Service, 1967.

Good materials for improving integrative language skills.

Erikson, Erik H. *Childhood and Society.* New York: W. W. Norton and Co., Inc., 1963.

In this classic work, students will find Chapter 7, "Eight Ages of Man," particularly helpful.

Fox, Robert. *Diagnosing Classroom Learning Environment.* Chicago: Science Research Associates, Inc., 1966.

A paperback manual that has many helpful suggestions to the teacher for getting feedback from children on their perceptions.

Frostig, Marianne, and David Horne. *The Frostig Program for the Development of Visual Perception.* Chicago: Follet, 1964.

A teacher's guide to developing visual perception in children.

Frostig, Marianne, and Phyllis Maslow. *Learning Problems in the Classroom.* New York: Grune & Stratton, 1973.

The authors present both theoretical knowledge and practical suggestions for teaching with particular reference to children with learning difficulties.

An invaluable aid to the classroom teacher with limited knowledge in the field.

Gordon, Ira J. *Studying the Child in School.* New York: John Wiley and Sons, Inc., 1966.

A rich source of models for studying children, based on newer concepts of child development. Ranges from rather simple to somewhat sophisticated designs.

Guszak, Frank J. *Diagnostic Reading Instruction in the Elementary School.* New York: Harper & Row, Publishers, 1972.

Addressed primarily to the diagnostic reading teacher or specialist, this book is also helpful to the classroom teacher in dealing with reading problems. Also helps the classroom teacher understand the role of the special reading teacher.

Harris, Albert J. ed. *Casebook on Reading Disability.* New York: David McKay Company, Inc., 1970.

Contains 16 case studies in reading diagnosis. A very complete inventory of standardized tests is given in the appendix.

Havighurst, Robert J. *Developmental Tasks and Education.* New York: David McKay Company, 1952.

The author points out important tasks that the individual faces in his development. A developmental task is midway between an individual need and a societal demand.

Ilg, Frances L., and Louise B. Ames. *Child Behavior.* New York: Harper & Row, Publishers, 1955.

A practical handbook on child behavior during the formative years from birth to ten. "Ages and stages" approach.

Jenkins, Gladys, et al. *These Are Your Children.* Chicago: Scott Foresman and Company, 1966.

This readable book describes and illustrates all four basic aspects of child growth and development—physical, emotional social and mental—throughout the "ages and stages."

Johnson, Doris, and Helmer Myklebust. *Learning Disabilities: Educational Principles and Practices.* New York: Grune and Stratton, 1967.

A basic text in the field of learning disabilities.

Kierschenbaum, Howard, Sidney B. Simon and Rodney W. Napier. *Wad-Ja-Get? The Grading Game in American Education.* New York: Hart Publishing Company, Inc., 1971.

A discussion of grading and its effects upon students. Alternatives to the grading system are examined.

Koch, Charles. *The Tree Test*. Berne, Switzerland: Hans Huber Publishers, 1952.

Draw-a-tree, draw-a-house, draw-a-man technique. The tree test is an aid in psychodiagnosis and should be interpreted by a skilled diagnostician.

Lowenfeld, Viktor, and W. Lambert Brittain. *Creative and Mental Growth*. 5th ed. New York: Macmillan Company, 1970.

A book in art education that has a great deal to say about creative development.

McCarthy, James J., and Joan F. McCarthy. *Learning Disabilities*. Boston: Allyn and Bacon, Inc., 1969.

This overview of the field presents a unified approach to the problem of learning disabilities. Views of 13 leading practitioners are evaluated. Differential diagnosis and educational procedures are among the topics covered.

Missildine, W. Hugh. *Your Inner Child of the Past*. New York: Simon and Schuster, 1963.

The author of this book deals with the idea that the conflicts internalized in the past stay with the individual as he gradually becomes a "parent" to himself. Self-understanding is the key to the avoidance of becoming victimized by the past. Helps the teacher understand the child as well as himself.

Piaget, Jean. *The Child's Conception of the World*. Paterson, N. J.: Littlefield, Adams and Co., 1969.

_____. *Judgment and Reasoning in the Child*. Paterson, N. J.: Littlefield, Adams and Co., 1964.

_____. *The Language and Thought of the Child*. New York: The World Publishing Co., 1969.

_____. *The Origins of Intelligence in Children*. New York: W. W. Norton and Co., Inc., 1952.

A study of Piaget's theories will help the teacher understand intellectual growth as a developmental process and gain insight into how children think.

Raths, Louis E. *Meeting Needs of Children: Creating Trust and Security*. Columbus, Ohio: Charles E. Merrill Publishing Company, 1972.

The author discusses eight fundamental needs of children and how the teacher might deal with them.

Redl, F., and C. Wineman. *Children Who Hate*. Toronto: The Free Press, 1965.

A sensitive analysis of the antisocial behavior of children in their response to the adult world.

_____. *Controls from Within—Techniques for the Treatment of the Aggressive Child*. Toronto: MacMillan Co., 1952.

A sequel to Children Who Hate.

Strang, Ruth. *Diagnostic Teaching of Reading*. New York: McGraw-Hill Book Company, 1964.

Much can be learned about the diagnostic process in general through reading this book. Checklists and reading profiles are provided.

Bibliography of Standardized Tests

California Test of Personality. California Test Bureau, Division of McGraw-Hill Book Co., Del Monte Research Park, Monterey, Calif. 93940

Primary, Elementary, Intermediate, and Secondary. Provides scores on self-adjustment and social adjustment. An analytical group personality questionnaire.

Culture Fair Intelligence Tests. Forms A, B. Institute for Personality and Aptitude Testing. 1602-04 Coronado Drive, Champaign, Ill. 61820

Group test of general intelligence. Does not require reading.

Dolch Basic Sight Word Test. Garrard Publishing Co., Champaign, Ill. 61820

List of 220 basic sight words arranged on one sheet for testing.

Durrell Analysis of Reading Difficulty: New Edition. Harcourt Brace Jovanovich, Inc., 757 Third Ave. New York. 10017

Tests oral and silent reading, listening comprehension, word analysis, phonics, pronunciation, writing and spelling.

Marianne Frostig Developmental Test of Visual Perception. (Ages 4–8) Follett Publishing Co., 1010 Washington Blvd., Chicago 60607

Five subtests: eye-motor coordination, figure-ground, constancy of shape, position in space, spatial relationships. Group test.

Goodenough-Harris Drawing Test. Harcourt, Brace & World, Inc., 757 Third Avenue, New York. 10017.

Provides objective method for scoring children's drawings of the human figure as a measure of non-verbal intelligence.

Illinois Tests of Psycholinguistic Abilities, Revised. Ages 4–9. University of Illinois Press, Urbana, Ill. 61801.

Measures abilities basic to communication. Individually administered by experienced diagnostician.

Inventory of Language Abilities. Educational Performance Associates, Ridgefield, N. J. 07657.

A screening device for use by the classroom teacher in identifying children with possible language learning disabilities.

Iowa Every-Pupil Tests of Basic Skills. Houghton Mifflin Co., 2 Park St., Boston, Mass. 02107

Test A, silent reading, and Test B, work-study skills.

Lorge-Thorndike Intelligence Tests, Multi-Level Edition. Houghton Mifflin.

Grades 3–13. Contains eight levels of difficulty. Provides verbal, non-verbal and total scores.

Metropolitan Achievement Tests, Revised (1958–1962). Harcourt.

Primary I and II Batteries and Elementary, Intermediate and Advanced Reading.

Metropolitan Readiness Tests, 1965 Revision. Harcourt.

Word meaning, listening, matching, alphabet, numbers and copying.

Monroe-Sherman Group Diagnostic Reading Aptitude and Achievement Tests. C. H. Nevins Printing Co., Pittsburgh, Pa. 15219

Grade three and up. Contains both achievement and aptitude tests.

Otis Quick-Scoring Mental Ability Tests. Harcourt.

Alpha Short Form *for grades 1–4,* Beta Test *for grades 4–9.*

Peabody Picture Vocabulary Test. American Guidance Service, Inc., Circle Pines, Minn. 55014

Vocabulary test requiring the choice of one out of four pictures. Ages 2–18.

Picture Story Language Test. (Myklebust, 1965) Grune and Stratton, Inc., 381 Park Ave. S., New York, N.Y. 10016.

A developmental scale for written language development and disorders of written language.

Revised Stanford-Binet Intelligence Scale, Third Edition (1960). Houghton.

Individual test of general intelligence to be used by trained psychologists only.

Slosson Intelligence Test. Slosson Educational Publications, 1961–1963.

Brief individual test of intelligence designed to be used by relatively untrained examiners. Should be used as a preliminary screening procedure only.

Spache Diagnostic Reading Scales. California Test Bureau.

Individually administered. Battery contains word lists, graded reading passages and phonics tests.

Wechsler Intelligence Scale for Children (WISC). The Psychological Corp., 304 E. 45 St., New York, N.Y. 10017

Individual intelligence scale for use by trained psychologists only.

Wepman Auditory Discrimination Test. Language Research Associates, 950 E. 59 St., Chicago. 60637.

Child distinguishes whether or not two spoken words are the same or slightly different. Ages 5–9.

Wide Range Achievement Test, Revised Edition (1965). The Psychological Corp.

Individual test of word recognition, spelling and arithmetic computation. Ages 5 to adult.

Things to Do

1. *Action project:* Study a child and involve him in a plan of action to meet his need.

   a. Select a child you would like to know better and make a diagnostic study of him. Try to uncover his potentialities, his learning style, and his life or personality style, and try to involve him in a plan that will help him meet his needs. While your plan is in operation, try to assess whether it is, indeed, meeting the child's need. Make shifts and changes as you go along.

   b. In studying the child, gain as much information about him as you can through the process of observation. See the section "The Teacher as an Educational Diagnostician," page 130, and follow the steps suggested there. You will want to observe the child in as many kinds of situations as possible and may need to keep some anecdotal records. Try to discover the following things about the child:

   (1) interests

   (2) creative abilities

   (3) intellectual capacities, including problem-solving abilities

   (4) unique potentialities; special talents; personal bent toward "things," "people" or "ideas"

   (5) learning style

   (6) energy level

   (7) physical and perceptual abilities

   (8) self-concept and life style

(9) social relationships; leadership

(10) defense mechanisms

(11) value orientation

c. Make an assessment of the child's self-development as well as his academic progress and achievement in all areas. If you feel that testing is necessary, arrange for this, taking note of the role-function behaviors given in "The Teacher as an Educational Diagnostician." Develop some of your own assessment devices to find out the kind of academic help this child needs. Make use of your findings in developing the plan involving the child. Evaluate the plan at the conclusion of the project.

2. *Action project:* Diagnose a particular problem of a child and set up a corrective plan.

a. Identify a particular problem that a child is having—it may be difficulty with some academic area such as reading, spelling, or math; or it may be a problem in getting along with his friends. Find out all you can about the child's problem and involve him in a plan to overcome it. Consult the role-function behaviors in "The Teacher as an Educational Diagnostician" for suggestions of actions to take. Find the answers to these questions:

(1) Is the problem related to the child's interests?

(2) Is the problem related to the child's personal adjustment or integration? Social relationships? Unmet emotional needs?

(3) Is the problem related to perception?

(4) Is the problem related to attention span?

(5) Is the problem related to physical health or disability?

(6) Is the problem related to intellectual capacity?

b. In addition to observation, make use of appropriate standardized tests; design your own activities in which you can observe the child's behavior more closely. Set up tasks for the child that call for the abilities you are trying to study. Observe the child in the performance of these tasks and analyze areas of difficulty.

c. Make diagnostic hypotheses about the child's personal and academic development. (See "The Teacher as an Educational Diagnostician.")

d. On the basis of your hypotheses, involve the child in a plan of both formal and informal experiences to help him. Set up a way for the child to gain feedback, to set goals and to determine progress toward these goals.

e. Involve other professionals if necessary.

f. Evaluate the educational experience you have developed with the child. What changes do you need to make? What do you *now* need to provide for the child? How do you need to *involve him* now? Have you been playing the role of a "helper" or a "judge"?

3. *Library research:* Make a study of various methods for gaining diagnostic data in order to help children with their problems. Explain in written form what these devices are and how to use them in order to gain the benefits you are looking for. You may want to include all of the following means of diagnosis and others you read about, or you may wish to pick one or two methods you are especially interested in and do a deeper study in these areas:

Children's art

Children's creative writing

Bibliotherapy

Standardized testing

Sociometric and self-reporting devices

Task Analysis

Role play and creative dramatics

PART IV

The Face of Choreography

EPILOGUE

Dear Reader,
I cannot write an epilogue. There is no conclusion
to education, there is only a process, and the
process has no conclusion.

A process of emerging education.
An experimental approach to learning.
The integration of the "I" and the "educator."
The "I" as the creator, I, creating an environment
*   for discovery.*
The when, where, and how of learning.
Cooperative living . . . The child and the adult.
I and thou.
The poetry of self.
My own rhythm.
Resting.
Flowing.
The heat of energy awakening the dormant "I."
I am flowing, I am dancing. I am singing, I am
*   crying.*
Together and apart.
The flow of in and out contracting and expanding.
One generation flowing, into the other.
Getting through the impasse, transcending the
*   status quo.*

The dance is to educational experience as
choreography is to teaching. The following poetic
vignettes suggest why:

. . . [The dance] moves in a self-contained realm of
its own and implies no reason, no tendency toward
completion. A formula for pure dance should
include nothing to suggest that it has an end. It is
terminated by outside events; its limits in time are
not intrinsic to it; the duration of the dance is
limited by the conventional length of the program,
by fatigue or loss of interest. But the dance itself
has nothing to make it end. It ceases as a dream
ceases that might go on indefinitely: it stops, not
because an undertaking has been completed, for
there is no undertaking, but because of something
else, something outside it has been exhausted.

            Paul Valery, Aesthetics*

                    * * *

            Janet Lederman, Anger and the Rocking Chair**

The Collected Works of Paul Valery, edited by Jackson
Mathews, Bollingen Series XLV, Vol. 13, *Aesthetics,*
translated by Ralph Manheim, pp. 206–207. (Copyright
© 1964 by Bollingen Foundation, reprinted by permission
of Princeton University Press.

**From *Anger and the Rocking Chair* by Janet Lederman.
(Copyright 1969. Used by permission of McGraw-Hill
Book Company.)

Chapter 12

The Aesthetic Environment of the Classroom and the Function of Choreography

A discussion of humanistic education would be incomplete without looking at its aesthetic effects in the life of the child. In the "Fourth Face of Teaching," analogy with choreography explains the function of the teacher as a "composer" who facilitates the possibility of aesthetic experience. In dance as well as in teaching, choreography is a flexible, creative art that involves far more than merely assembling movements or manipulating the environment. The dance assumes a form that has unity and gives illusion of "aliveness" (Hawkins, 1964). An educational experience comes to life when the learner taps his creative and rational powers. When the dancer choreographs his own movements, he is a creator as well as an aesthetic object. When the pupil choreographs his own learning, through the facilitating function of the teacher, he too is a creator, and his educational experience evokes beauty and joy both for himself and for his teacher. His experience projects itself into a pleasurable and hence an aesthetic event in the life of the classroom.

SIGNIFICANCE OF CHOICE

In the political environment the teacher's concern is with the child's individuality, his adequacy and his ability to be involved with others. In the technological environment the teacher's concern is with the child's thinking and creative powers. In the phenomenological environment the teacher's concern is with discovering the child's potentials as well as the blocks that may be impeding his growth. As the political, technological, and phenomenological environments blend into the aesthetic, the teacher's overriding concern is that the child begins to make decisions and choices—that he learns to assume responsibility within a context of freedom, circumscribed by interdependent life. The child knows why he is doing an activity—it is primarily for himself, not to please the teacher. As he gains experience, he can decide how to go about doing his tasks and possibly when and where to do them. Because as he is freed to use his potentials and to work according to his own rhythms, the child feels adequate, he senses a connectedness with his peers and he comes to feel that he is an able doer in control of his own school world. The affect of satisfaction preempts his feelings about school. He is aesthetically involved.[1] Relevance, creative expression and freedom, then, circumscribe the aesthetic dimension of classroom life.

AESTHETICS AS A THEORETICAL FRAMEWORK FOR STUDYING TEACHING AS ART

Aesthetics, as a field of study, is involved with the mental and emotional responses to the beauty in art. Valery (1964), a noted authority in aesthetics, says that in its original derivation, *art* means "way of doing," but little by little the word has been limited to mean the "ways of doing that involve voluntary action or action initiated by the will." Art is action that aims to conjure up or arouse perpetual desire. "Here we capture the production of a work of art in its very germ," says Valery. The man who sets out to make a work of art strives to captivate the beholder. He aims to "create a necessity; to promote infinite developments in someone. The true creator is the one who makes others create."[2] Art, then, may be viewed as a formula for action. The teacher-artist devises a plan for stimulating the child, for calling forth an emotional response. His aim is to create a necessity—a thirst for learning, for doing, for creating—so that the pupil is impelled to act and to become his own creator.

According to Valery, three interdependent yet distinct agents must be considered in studying art—the artist, the work of art and the audience. We may reason that the artist is the teacher and the audience is the pupil—but what is the work of art? And what is the nature of the transformation which makes the art felt? The answer to these questions must be found in the environment that the teacher creates. But pupils participate in this creation, too; they feed back their reactions and initiate plans, and the sensitive teacher-artist in turn becomes audience, responding and creating anew. A continual chain of events, steeped in affect, evolves. The feelings of satisfaction, enjoyment, involvement and sensory impressions experienced by pupils and teacher constitute a fourth dimension, a new environment that breaks out of the political, the technological and the phenomenological, which intermingle dynamically and globally, as wheels

within wheels moving toward climax, evoking aesthetic experience for all involved.

Teachers and learners grapple together in their authentic struggles to be, to do, to learn, to create. The teacher choreographs the environment as he weaves his relationships and his mediational and diagnostic acts into an open structure through which he confronts the child. The teacher works with a universe of people, materials, events, feelings, ideas and actions[3]—the raw materials of the environment—blending them into a unity that is felt by both teacher and child. The global environment, like a mosaic, is subtly blended; its "pieces" appear as one overall, harmonious design. Only the impact of the whole is felt.

Relationship of the Technical and the Emotional in the Creation of Art

The arts, as represented by the dance, have both technical and emotional aspects; so does teaching. In choreography of the dance, aesthetic effects grow out of the function of the dance as interpreted by the dancer. The dance becomes an aesthetic object by maintaining the simplicity and form derived from its unity, variety, continuity and climax (Hawkins, 1964). The literature of aesthetics suggests that beauty, harmony, balance, rhythm, tempo, contrast, sequence, transition, repetition and freedom are other intrinsic qualities that serve as the threads of the aesthetic experience (Hyman, 1968).

In designing educational environment, the teacher as choreographer weaves in these qualities, too. Because responses and feeling are private matters, the educational experience is individual and personal to each pupil, whose sensitivity to function (purpose) and to form is determined largely by his own frame of reference—his own internal rhythms and his propensities to act. The teacher serves as catalyst, facilitator and guide. If, as choreographer, the teacher is imaginative, sensitively aware and spontaneous in his approach to pupils and events, he encourages self-initiative; he may also change an activity, alter the pacing of it, or confront the children with new experience when boredom, overstimulation or frustration set in.

Choreographing Teacher Behavior

As composers, teachers create the aesthetic environment through choreographing their own behaviors as relators, diagnosticians and mediators. The teacher aims to move children into the center of action while he takes a peripheral, facilitating role. Children come away from a skillfully choreographed educational experience feeling, "We did this ourselves."

The following analysis may help the reader visualize the major functions of the teacher arising out of his roles as relator, mediator and diagnostician, as these roles are brought to bear on the artistic management of classroom life. The implied pupil roles are set in the right-hand column.

As a Choreographer the Teacher-Artist is . . .	As a Creator the Pupil-Artist is . . .
A *designer of structure*—he structures learning situations according to the individual needs of pupils *and* the type of experience undertaken.	A *hunter* and *explorer*—he seeks to satisfy his needs and is on the lookout for things that interest him.
A *confronter*—he provides dissonant situations and provocative questions to pique the child's interest—to throw him out of equilibrium, temporarily.	A *decision maker* and *chooser*—he makes choices of things to do or ways to do them. He accepts the challenge of dissonance, disequilibrium or ambiguity and finds creative solutions to problems.
A *travel agent*—he is available for consultation. He responds to the vague notions of where the child says he wants to go. He contributes ideas, raises relevant questions, lends his expertise and, like the travel agent, helps the child plan a flexible itinerary with suggestions for getting the most out of the trip.	An *experimenter* and *discoverer*—he experiments with his environment and discovers meaning for himself; discovering concepts is like encountering life.
A *diagnostician*—he zeros in on the specific problems the child is having and helps to unsnarl the difficulties. He gives suggestions for next steps.	An *examiner* and *receptor*—he examines and takes in from his environment, and he works new ideas and impressions into his thought processes.
A *record keeper*—he keeps track of where each child is and uses the record for future planning.	A *questioner* and *actor*—he questions and acts upon the objects, materials, ideas in his environment and forms new gestalts in his thought processes.
A *contriver*—he contrives experience to simulate the real world.	
A *scrounger*—he is on the lookout for materials that have a conceivable use and brings them into the classroom.	An *investigator*—he satisfies his curiosity through investigating questions and topics of interest, the things that grab him.
A *guide*—he has been down the road before and helps the child find his way through uncharted courses, problems, ideas, concepts.	An *expresser*—he gives expression to his creative urges through various art media and communicates his feelings through the expressive arts—movement, music, plastic arts, creative dramatics.
An *encourager*—he is there to lend support when the child hits a snag and is losing faith in himself.	A *communicator*—he learns to communicate his feelings and ideas through language and written media.
An *appreciator*—he shows his enjoyment of the child's learning, his creations, his progress.	A *constructor*—he constructs realia and three-dimensional artifacts to demonstrate his understanding of an idea, or to make things he can use in his learning environment, or simply to express himself.
An *intervener*—he sees when and how he can intervene in the child's experience, to raise the significant question at the right time, to make suggestions of where to go next.	A *responder*—he sees and appreciates the good and beautiful in classroom life.

An *improviser*—he composes on the immediate, the unexpected happening that has relevance for the child right now.

A *model*—he knows that he teaches through example. He is an enthusiastic learner, and a human relator in the classroom.

RECOGNIZING AESTHETIC DIMENSIONS OF CLASSROOM LIFE

The teacher, as choreographer, relies heavily on intuition, and not just on technical know-how, in creating an educational environment. Choreographers and other directors of the performing arts believe their artistic response to problems results from intuition, rather than from technique. However, techniques are totally at the choreographer's command, probably reduced to a subliminal level, so that intuition is free to take over when he is working with the performers (Zinsmaster-Seaberg, 1972). There is reason to believe that teacher-artists rely heavily on intuition, too. Many master teachers say they do what comes to them naturally; they are not able to analyze their teaching acts.

When so much depends on intuition and the "if-ishness" of existing situations, how can the class-room choreographer determine whether his actions have been aesthetically relevant? There is no exact way of knowing, but he can tell to a large degree by the "feel" he gets from the pupils. Reflection on the following questions may help:

Was there a variety of offerings in the day's activities, and did the children have an opportunity to contribute and choose from these offerings? Was the day integrated, and did the children see a purpose for what they were doing? Did they feel a natural transition from activity to activity, or did they feel hemmed in by the clock or a rigid schedule? Did boredom set in because activities were not properly paced, or did children become frustrated because they were not allowed to pace themselves?

Was the day structured openly so that children could follow their own timing? Did the day's experience take on form and shape? Did the children see a link between this day and other days, and did they sense beginnings and temporary endings—knowledge of something attempted, some-

thing done? Did the learning have validity—did the doing make sense? Was it purposeful? Meaningful? Were the materials relevant to the children's concerns? Did the children practice skills as variations on a theme? (That is, was there meaningful repetition of skills and the application of knowledge to new contexts?) Was there a sorting out of the important from the less important or the irrelevant? Was there a readiness for action? Did each child start where he was, without fear of censure?

Was there a balance in activities? Was the school day heightened with contrasts so that the children felt an ebb and flow of quiet and active moments? Did they feel a movement toward climax, falling action, and the denouement of given experiences?

Did the children experience harmony in their interpersonal relationships. Was there a flexible mix of individual, small-group and large-group activities? Were any temporary interest groups started? Were any disbanded because children had completed their plans? Did the class meet at any time as a whole, because of a child's request? Was a wide variety of materials in several media available?

Did I, as a teacher, intervene strategically? Did I know when to stay out as well as when to intervene in a child's learning process or in his personal problem? Did I confer frequently with individuals, and did I get around to all the children who needed me? Did I plan cooperatively with individuals, groups or the whole class, or did I impose my ideas on them?

The teacher, as choreographer, creates an overall classroom tone that is energetic, active, dynamic, enthusiastic, harmonious, and hence aesthetically pleasing. When the atmosphere is sterile, anxious, dull, raucous or placid, children most likely are turned off. The environment that does not give them a stimulating emotional lift is devoid of aesthetic quality.

SUMMARY

In the humanistic classroom, the aesthetic or affective dimension of education emerges as the center and core of the child's existence. The child feels in command. He has a dynamic sense of being in touch with himself and his ongoing contemporary world. He acts upon his own universe of materials, events, feelings, ideas and people. The environment confronts him; it is he who must decide, choose and do. But in the doing, his desire for more is not surfeited, his thirst for knowledge is not quenched, his urge to create or investigate is not sated. Like the dance, his experience is continuous, with no impelling end.

In the chapter that follows, a more detailed analysis will be made of the teacher-artist at work, showing what he does choreographically to call forth aesthetic response in the child.

Notes

[1] The reader may wish to consult the entire issue of *The Humanities Journal,* National Association for Humanities Education, Vol. VI, No. 3 (May 1973) for a discussion of synaesthic education—which would, if more consciously developed, push out the boundaries of the aesthetic environment of the classroom. Synaesthesia is defined as "a process whereby one perceives his environment with all his senses, at times individually but more often simultaneously. What he sees he can also actually hear and feel and unconsciously empathize with on the basis of his past experiences. Sights are often perceived as sounds, feelings and smells; while sounds are perceived as visions, motions and tastes; and smells are perceived as tastes, sounds and viscerally. Synaesthesia is primarily an interaction of conscious and unconscious sensuous experiences resulting in impressions perceived symbiotically."

[2] *The Collected Works of Paul Valery,* edited by Jackson Mathews, Bollingen Series XLV, Vol. 13, *Aesthetics,* translated by Ralph Manheim (Copyright 1964 by Bollingen Foundation, reprinted by permission of Princeton University Press), p. 143.

[3] M. H. Abrams describes the universe of the artist as consisting of "people, ideas, and feelings, material things, and events, and supersensible essences," in *The Mirror and the Lamp: Romantic Theory and the Critical Tradition* (New York: The Norton Library, W. W. Norton & Co., Inc., 1958).

References

Abrams, M. H. *The Mirror and the Lamp: Romantic Theory and the Critical Tradition.* New York: The Norton Library, W. W. Norton & Co., Inc. (Copyright 1953 by Oxford University Press. First published in the Norton Library by arrangement with Oxford University Press, 1958).

Hawkins, Alma M. *Creating Through Dance.* Englewood Cliffs, N. J.: Prentice-Hall, Inc., 1964.

Hyman, Ronald T. (ed.). *Teaching: Vantage Points for Study.* New York: J. B. Lippincott Company, 1968.

Lederman, Janet. *Anger and the Rocking Chair.* New York: McGraw-Hill Book Co., 1969.

Rogers, Carl R. "Toward a Theory of Creativity," in *Creativity and Its Cultivation,* Harold H. Anderson (ed.). New York: Harper & Row, Publishers, 1959.

Seaberg, Dorothy I., and Wanna M. Zinsmaster. "What Can Teachers Learn from Directors in the Performing Arts?" in *The Elementary School Journal,* Vol. 72, 4 (January, 1972), 167–175.

Valery, Paul. *Aesthetics.* Translated by Ralph Manheim. Bollingen Series XLV. New York: Pantheon Books, 1964.

Weinstein, Gerald, and Mario D. Fantini. *Toward Humanistic Education: A Curriculum of Affect.* New York: Praeger Publishers, for the Ford Foundation, 1970.

Wolfson, Bernice J. "Pupil and Teacher Roles in Individualized Instruction," in *The Psychology of Open Teaching and Learning,* Melvin L. Silberman, Jerome S. Allender and Jay M. Yanoff (eds.). Boston: Little, Brown and Co., 1972.

Chapter 13

The Teacher-Artist
at Work

Who is the teacher-artist? As Valery suggests, he is the one who stimulates his audience—the pupils—to create, to be involved, to learn. The teacher-artist has the rare gift of intuiting when and how to plug the child into his own creative circuit, to release him to his own powers. He puts the child in the driver's seat to choreograph his own dance.

Like directors in the performing arts, creative teachers inspire their pupils and develop a personal style from their own unique abilities, traits and intuitive powers (Seaberg-Zinsmaster, 1972). As choreographers, teachers approach their jobs as creative problem-solvers who work from the inside out with the "givens" of any classroom situation.

The teacher-artist knows himself and is aware of his strengths, weaknesses, defenses; thus, he finds his own best ways of working. Being psychologically free, he expresses his originality in the classroom. He creates an open environment through democratic leadership and humanitarian example, inducing harmony into the interpersonal scene. Beyond this, the teacher's enthusiasm, excitement for learning, and humor contribute special qualities

that bring zest into classroom life. Gestures, facial expressions, intonation, manner of speech, and the enthusiasm with which the teacher identifies with subject matter are all felt in the aesthetic environment.

The teacher-artist lives his work, and for him life in the classroom is an adventure. He shares his life experiences vividly, letting his pupils know he is a real person. The child reciprocates by admitting his own experience and his feelings into the environment. The teacher discovers his pupils and encounters interesting facets of the world with them, leaving behind the scope and sequence charts in the wake of creative experiences that require the functional use of skills. He shares his pleasure and excitement over good literature, and children learn to look upon books as friends to know and value. He is interested in current happenings in the community, the nation and the world, and his pupils are stimulated to think critically about these happenings. He enjoys living things and shares in the children's pleasure as they feed the hamsters, water the plants or watch the chicks hatch. As Curran suggests, creative teachers bring a passion to the events in the classroom. "They sense the same tingle at the spine a seaman, hunter, or explorer [feels] as he pushes into the unknown."[1] The teacher-artist believes it is natural for children to be curious, and he takes it for granted that pupils coping with real problems, real interests or real concerns will want to learn, discover and create. In the aesthetic environment, self-discipline based on intrinsic motivation replaces suppressive control. Pupils who feel understood and psychologically safe are free to launch out and express themselves creatively. They find they can take risks within a climate of acceptance and freedom as they test their powers. Little by little, they learn to trust their own judgments and can embark on learning voyages of their own.

CHOREOGRAPHIC FUNCTIONS OF THE TEACHER-ARTIST

The teacher brings about aesthetic effects through managing the environment artistically. He choreographs his interventions and relationships to fit situations in flux. Intuitive insights enable him to blend the elements of a learning situation into a pleasing and unified whole, or to change things that are not working. Classroom choreographic functions are three-fold in nature: As choreographer, the teacher (1) structures the environment to facilitate open-endedness, enabling each child's experience to become personal and individual to him; (2) he facilitates the integration of educational experience, weaving all activities meaningfully into an open evolving environment; and (3) he synchronizes the "here and now" of classroom events to bring about unity, variety, continuity and climax.

CHOREOGRAPHING AN "OPEN-STRUCTURE" LEARNING ENVIRONMENT

If the ultimate function of education is to develop self-actualizing individuals, the environment must provide a divergent framework that enables children to become autonomous. Autonomous living requires both freedom and responsibility, leading to interdependent as well as independent living. Within the social reality of the classroom, children learn that "my freedom ends where your nose begins," or that "my freedom to choose not to work does not give me the right to keep my neighbor from working." In a humanistic classroom, all children need to be guided into increasing degrees of autonomy, but they must move according to their own stages of readiness and internal integration.

Because individuals need freedom of structure in order to grow, there need to be as many structures as there are people in the room. Such structures include provisions for the child's self—his interests, abilities, needs, ideas; for access to supplies and materials; for places to work and people to work with; and for ways of solving problems. The teacher provides for a variety of structures to cohabit the environment simultaneously, so that each child can find his own best level of functioning. Some children need direct intervention and prescribed learning materials; other children are "soloists" and need unhampered autonomy. Some need the support of a group; others may need to work alone. As a choreographer has said, "You see what the people can do. Some people will take direction, and some are better if you don't direct them—if you let them play around. Some actors love to improvise and some don't and so you have to really feel your way."[2] In the classroom, each child has his own dance, but all the children together make the finale.

Ways of Scheduling

In an atmosphere of freedom, the teacher-artist attempts to help the child find the structure with which he is most comfortable. This means giving the child support in finding his own direction. Some humanistic teachers are opening up structures by giving children a hand in planning their schedules, allowing for independent choices in activities or topics of study.

To loosen up structure, the teacher plans a daily schedule with the class, which he posts on the board. The schedule may have both stationary parts and movable parts. It allows for both whole-class and small-group activities, as well as for work done individually and handled through consultation with the teacher.

A schedule may look like this:

9:00 - 9:15   *Class planning time.*
9:15 - 10:15   *Individual reading, spelling, writing or math activities. Conferences.*
10:15 - 10:30   *Recess.*

10:30 - 11:45	*Social studies or science interest groups and/or independent study. (Access to the learning center if there is one.)*
12:45 - 2:00	*Individual reading, writing, spelling or math activities. Conferences.*
2:00 - 2:30	*P.E.*
2:30 - 3:15	*Free choice activities. (Children avail themselves of materials in interest centers in the classroom, read books, go to the learning center or catch up on work they have missed.)*

In schools that follow team- or cooperative-teaching plans, class schedules may appear as blocks of time within which children have options, thus:

9:00 - 9:15	*Class planning time with teacher-adviser.*
9:15 - 10:30	*Language arts block. (Provision for individualized reading and other language activities, work in small groups and pupil-teacher conferences.)*
10:30 - 10:45	*Recess.*
10:45 - 12:00	*Mathematics block. (Provision for individual progression, conferences and work in small groups.)*
1:00 - 2:00	*Fine and applied arts block. (Choices of modules or alternated activities in arts and crafts, industrial arts, creative dramatics, movement education, music, cooking, sewing, etc.)*
2:00 - 2:15	*Recess.*
2:15 - 3:15	*Social studies/science block. (Often done in relationship to a learning center if there is one.)*

In providing for individualized schedules, the teacher has each child plan his day and write his personal schedule in a notebook or on a sheet of paper that is kept in the child's own file. The teacher decides with the class who will have conferences on a given day. The teacher may also designate special-help groups for children with common problems. In other words, the daily schedule includes the ways the teacher intends to use his time, the scheduled class activities and the open times in which children schedule their own work. Within limits, children may choose when they will do their math, reading, spelling and other language activities. The teacher's schedule becomes a framework within which each child works. Therefore, scheduling practices in an open structure usually specify that:

1. Children keep either a notebook or a file folder in which their daily schedules are posted. They also record the work they have completed. This material is used during conference time with the teacher.

2. Children are their own time keepers.

3. Schedule boundaries are flexible—an activity missed because another activity was extended by heightened interest, special problems, or miscalculation in timing can be made up tomorrow.

Ways of Grouping Flexibly

The teacher provides for individual progression in the attainment of skills—reading, spelling, computation—but he also groups and regroups for various purposes. Sometimes the whole class works together, using the unit approach in studying a problem or a theme, and individual side-studies or small interest groups spin off from the organizing center. For example, a sixth-grade glass tackled the problem: "How can I read a newspaper intelligently?" This problem led to whole-class discussions, as well as to the identification of sub-problems that were pursued by the whole class, by small groups and by individuals. The unit culminated in the production of a newspaper, which called for differentiation of tasks; small teams prepared different sections of the paper—news items, sports section, editorials, feature columns, want ads, market reports, cartoons and so on.

Small interest groups or mini-courses are also popular, especially in the science and social studies curricula. In these cases groups are formed on the basis of common interest and may become more numerous as interest spreads. Usually such groups are self-contained, and there is no attempt to share learnings with the class as a whole. Sometimes children think up topics of study, and sometimes the teacher suggests topics and children choose those that interest them most.

In skills areas such as reading and math, the teacher organizes small groups for instruction or for the reinforcing of a skill or concept. These groups, of short duration, are organized by the teacher in terms of common problems the pupils have.

In a learning environment with an open structure, groups are temporary and are constantly changing. Some groups are developed under the teacher's direct supervision, usually because more than one child needs help with the same concept or skill. In other groups, the teacher helps children identify interests; in still others, the teacher suggests interests and the children make choices.

Teacher-Pupil Conferences

In the individual conference the teacher helps the child evaluate his work according to a standard that is realistic for him. Individual goals are set; new plans are made. The teacher uses his time wisely and efficiently by observing the following practices:[3]

1. The teacher uses the sampling method. By looking at representative samples from the child's total work, the teacher sees problem areas and the general quality of work being done. The child chooses what it is he will share. For example, he may present a piece of original writing or a page from a workbook to discuss with the teacher.

2. The teacher may ask the child to demonstrate a skill. The child perhaps reads an exciting paragraph from a story he has enjoyed, or perhaps he works out a problem so the teacher can diagnose his needs. The teacher asks questions to get at comprehension, interpretation and underlying relationships involved.

3. The teacher identifies types of problems the child is encountering. He gives the child individual help and possibly supplies him with extra practice materials. Sarah may have a special spelling or word-recognition problem; Jim may need help with locating words in the dictionary; Barbara is experiencing difficulty in locating information for a report. Lynn has problems organizing her thoughts into a coher-

ent written paragraph; Kevin needs help in interpreting story problems; Jack needs suggestions for an independent project in social studies.

4. The teacher keeps conference time open-ended. Some children need more time than others. Equal opportunity to learn does not mean the teacher will spend equal time with each student. Needs of children are qualitative. Some children merely need to be recognized and challenged; others have instructional needs in the basic skills. In the open-structured environment, children are working with their own needs. The teacher emphasizes quality and creativity in work, not quantity.

6. The teacher shows interest and gives encouragement. All children need recognition and encouragement, but especially the child who finds learning difficult. The teacher recognizes that if a child's performance is not up to his usual form, there are reasons, and if the child is encouraged he will prevail. The teacher's comments are tailor-made to fit each situation.

EXAMPLE OF A WHOLE-CLASS ACTIVITY ENTAILING "OPEN STRUCTURE"

In the following discussion of children's research on ponds, the reader becomes aware of the amount of personalization and individualization that can occur, even in a whole-class activity, when structures for learning are kept open. In this example, the children developed their own ideas for projects and side-studies, which resulted in self-imposed demands.

A Unit on Pond Life — Grade Three

The children's interest level was even higher than I had anticipated. As a result, even children who ordinarily have difficulty reading and comprehending the third grade basal used at "reading time" eagerly delved into reading the supplementary and informational books in the science corner. They were so involved in why they were reading that, without even thinking about it, they naturally employed such techniques as using context clues and the dictionary to understand a new word and comparing different sources to validate their information. They didn't have to be "tested" for a measure of their comprehension; they were so eager to share their discoveries and newly achieved understandings that class discussions were rich with their informal contributions, and their growth was quite apparent.

At the children's request, special time had to be set aside for the sharing of oral and special written reports in small interest groups or with the entire class. The students extended the unit's content as they became more involved. They then located and brought in additional references and resource materials. Not only did the children contribute informational books to the science corner, but also fiction stories and poems they encountered or had at one time heard and enjoyed, and now wanted to share. Individual differences were evidenced in the ways the children chose to record and share their work; some limited themselves to oral contributions or discussions; some made written reports; others displayed their findings pictorially; and still others composed more extensive comparisons of one form of pond life with another.

The children eagerly anticipated and readily participated in activities involving the class as a whole. Much to my surprise, however, with almost no particular prod, suggestion, or stimulation from me to initiate such action, every child in the room found an area which interested him to such a degree that he began investigating it on his own. Either, as was the case for one boy in particular, they were further exploring a related previous interest (he kept snakes and a crayfish as pets at home), or they became aware of a new area which appealed to them and aroused their curiosity.

In a learning atmosphere such as this, the children quickly became aware of the value of their classmates as irreplaceable sources of information, and of the role of sharing of both their materials and themselves. I feel that the nature of this learning atmosphere was one of the strongest features of the unit, for it was almost solely responsible for the growth which resulted in the children's knowledge, skill, and understanding.

As the various areas of independent research were drawn together in class discussion and viewed as a whole, the children were able to understand and see into not only the depth of the individual aspects of pond life, but also the interrelationship of the nature and activities of all life in a pond. Gradually, then, they became aware of broader, more basic understandings of their environment and the ways of nature. They then related this to themselves and asked such questions as, "How does this affect us?" and "What can we do about it?" The children's conversations and the discussion which accompanied the posing of these questions revealed how vital and meaningful the experiences and resulting understandings associated with this unit were to them.

The culminating activities served well in their role to summarize and draw together what the children had done. However, the children were not "saturated" with the subject. Some questions were left unanswered. Some things we did not have time to do. New, more mature levels of curiosity were sparked. These things will provide new inroads to avenues of interest to be travelled and explored at some future time. For some of the children this may be very soon; for others, it may not be until perhaps another teacher someday says, "Tell me, what do you know about ponds?"[4]

INTEGRATING AND SYNCHRONIZING THE SCHOOL DAY

The teacher-artist heightens aesthetic experience through integrating and synchronizing classroom events. He is sensitively involved with children and has an intuitive feel for materials, ideas or activities that fit a given child or group at a given time.

Integration

To provide a unified experience, the teacher-artist develops activities with children that integrate several academic disciplines in a meaningful way, as units, themes or topics unfold. (This principle was illustrated in the unit on pond life.) Although isolated lessons are taught and children work with programed materials or worksheets to master skills, these activities flow naturally into the evolving environment. Through open scheduling, no child is locked into a reading or math group, but each progresses in his own style and at his own rhythm and rate. The child is not forced into the "Dick and Jane" book—reading materials are either selected to fit the child or he selects his own. Some children acquire information about a social studies topic by looking at picture books; others read the encyclopedia.

When children are wrapped up in activities that are meaningful to them, the demands of the activity circumscribe behavior. Pupils adhere to limits that are natural and necessary to accomplish interesting work that fulfills their purposes. Limits are elastic, not rigid; set rules need not govern the order of the day. Different activities make different demands on both pupil and teacher. Some activities, by nature, require movement, talking and other noise. Some activities demand a quiet atmosphere. The demands of the environment are like the built-in controls of a game. Children accept them because they see the necessity—the game would be no fun and would have no challenge without rules. Children become self-disciplined when they have a personal investment in the learning environment and are motivated by self-interest to follow through.

The teacher-artist keeps things moving by anticipating logistical problems. He thinks ahead: What books, materials and equipment are needed? How can the children obtain access to them? How can things be arranged so that pupils don't get in each other's way? What materials can be handled on a self-serve basis? What elements can be reduced to a routine, so that both pupils and teacher can invest their energies in thinking, solving problems and carrying out activities? What materials must the teacher prepare in advance? What problems will the pupils encounter when they undertake an activity? Do they have the skills necessary for success in the activity, or are there skills that must first be taught?

If a new technique is needed, such as handling tools, the teacher gives the child experience that will enable him to use the technique successfully. Sometimes problems need to be resolved before an activity can get underway: Some children really do not know what is expected of them; not everyone feels confident; the class is upset because of an occurrence on the playground; individuals need more experience with a skill. In these instances, the teacher takes care of the immediate problem before he asks the children to move ahead.

Synchronization

Synchronizing the elements in the unfolding classroom environment is an important choreographic function. Unity, harmony, balance, freedom and other aesthetic effects are largely dependent upon the teacher's artistic management. He must be flexible and adapt to events as they occur. The teacher-artist senses when things are not going right, and stops or changes things when necessary. If he sees that an activity is not "coming off," he does not hesitate to scrap plans—even though he may have spent long hours developing them.

The teacher-artist works with the "here and now" of the classroom and moves with the moods and emerging interests of individuals and groups. He adroitly handles distracting situations and turns them into learning experiences. He figuratively goes out the window with the children to see the fire engine whizz by, and he uses the noisy bulldozer scooping out dirt in the vacant lot across the street as a stimulus for learning about the building trades, problems in housing, zoning laws or interior decorating.

The teacher-artist also improvises on the contributions children make and recognizes a good lead when he sees one. The snake or the butterfly that is brought to school, for example, becomes the object of scientific study. If children bring in snapshots, books, stamp or coin collections, or other hobbies, the teacher integrates them into the day's activities. When children offer ideas and suggestions, the teacher builds on these. But the teacher also offers ideas to children, such as titles for stories, suggestions for projects, topics for investigation. Then the children improvise on the teacher's themes.

When the teacher imposes on the children's learning, he does so with an eye to specific situations and individuals. Limits are set to enhance or execute an activity, not for the sake of limits themselves. Sequence comes naturally out of the dictates of activities. Sometimes ideas are followed randomly. Children are not forced into set patterns but find their own rhythms and follow their own sequences in a self-paced environment.

Although the teacher takes a leadership role, he quickly sees when he can move out to the periphery of action while the children choreograph their own show. Furniture is placed in the classroom to permit freedom of movement and interest groupings. The teacher's desk is probably off in a corner and the teacher, though present, may not be readily visible when a visitor enters the room. Interest and work centers, especially if they display children's work artistically, add aesthetic quality and give children the feeling that school belongs to them.

Although children in a humanistic classroom are helped to choreograph their day by planning their own schedules, the teacher enters at strategic points to keep things moving. Perhaps there is need for more variety of offerings, perhaps a greater balance in active and quiet activity must be introduced to bring about unity, harmony or climax. The teacher is sensitive to boredom but is also aware when children are overstimulated; he either provides for more active involvement or tames the situation down through introducing quiet times.

The teacher does not worry unduly when he sees children frittering time away but recognizes that, like the orchestral composition that takes on mood and vitality through sensitive placement of sustained tones or even silence, so humans need time merely "to be." Activity then becomes vital, in contrast. When certain children seem always to be at loose ends, the teacher asks himself "why?" and then may talk with the child and suggest individual plans. As the teacher-artist choreographs, he finds what movements he can make so all the dancers are contributing to the show.

When activities are teacher-directed, the way materials and experiences are put together, timed and paced are crucial in their effects. Interest is often won or lost on the basis of timing and pacing, but the key to artistic pacing is building it into the activity so the participants are not aware of it.

Although the teacher may engage the children in an activity with an overall plan in mind, he finds that he must make changes as the lesson unfolds. He observes the children while they are involved with materials, discussions and activities, and picks up clues for restructuring events as the experience moves along. Sometimes he discovers that the children do not have the skill to handle an activity; he must then intervene with direct

teaching, or provide formats for practice so that the children may consolidate their learning and go on. Teaching involves some imposition by the teacher, but it also allows great latitude for creative response and the manipulation of materials and ideas by the child.

An in-service teacher who studied her own choreography by recording observations has verified many of the above factors. She summarized her findings as follows:

What makes a good day?

1. Flexibility.

2. My good mood.

3. Meeting the children's needs and requests.

4. Exciting activities.

5. Quiet times and loud times.

6. Taking advantage of the weather for projects.

7. Off-the-cuff teaching when the time and the excitement is right.

8. Excitement and interest on my part.

9. My being organized as well as ready for the unexpected.

10. Creative activities.

11. Not too much seat work.

What makes a troublesome day?

1. My being crabby.

2. The program being too rigid.

3. Not stopping when the children were bored.

4. Not stopping but being pushy when the children were tired.

5. Too many noisy activities in a row.

Comments:

I was surprised to find out how much *I* determined what the day would be like. Whether I was crabby, happy, quiet or excited really influenced them. I was glad to see that stopping an activity in the middle had little influence on them. That pleased me.

In order to illustrate the functions involved in

integrating and synchronizing the day, a running commentary detailed by Miss S ___ is offered below. Choreographic actions are dubbed into the right-hand column.

Classroom Commentary (Miss S)	Choreographic Actions
It is amazing how many influences there are on how children react—the weather, too little or too much sleep, fights, atmospheric conditions, parents (illnesses, working or not working, interest or non-interest in their child), new hair cuts, new clothes—just about anything influences a child's behavior.	SYNCHRONIZING: The teacher senses children's reactions to situations and adapts activities to moods, anxieties, fatigue, or other physical or psychical manifestations.
My teaching methods and aids are always handy to be put into action without any hesitation. But if I plan on using one way of teaching and see blank expressions, I think nothing of changing. The same thing can be taught many different ways, and all children don't learn in the same way. Some learn better visually, others perceptually and still others auditorily. So to change ways doesn't hurt anything. Some concepts I teach all three ways, to be sure that everyone learns something at least once, with repetition providing reinforcement for those who already understand.	INTEGRATING: The teacher lets his methods flow naturally out of his knowledge and understanding of the problems and goals he has in mind, the individuals and materials with which he works, and his own personality and talents.
In working with the children from day to day, I encounter varying moods and situations that dictate my approach. The following are typical examples:	SYNCHRONIZING: The teacher trusts his intuition when he senses things are not going right, adapts to events as they occur, makes changes in his plans as the creative response of individuals emerges abandons plans even though their development has consumed time and energy.
I. Snowy day, children unusually excited, physically active.	He senses whether the child is ready for an activity or whether other problems need to be resolved before an activity can get under way.
On days like this they are interested in being out-of-doors and playing. So we began with an active game in our reading group. To try to settle them down would have been futile, so we played our alphabet-twister game. They couldn't goof around with this too much, because that would cause them to lose the game. After a while, though, they started showing loss of interest by being too rowdy. So we changed. We went to our large piece of paper and played our made-up game, "What's My Letter?" I started off with a letter of my choice. A child who could recognize my letter came up, rewrote it, and put his own letter on the paper. Another child guessed it. Hopefully, everyone had a chance to come forward and try to stump the others. They really enjoyed this game! It beat sitting at their desks and practicing to write letters.	INTEGRATING: The teacher lets authority and limits flow from the nature of the activity pursued by the children.

SYNCHRONIZING: The teacher moves smoothly from one activity to another, sensing when children need to change from quiet to active, or from active to quiet.

Manages time flexibly and moves with the mood of individuals or groups; stops work before the saturation point is reached, when interest is high. |

Group activity with the whole class again meant some type of active game. Most of the time it was "Doggy, Doggy, Where's Your Bone?" (When children are allowed to choose the game, then they don't usually complain.) With their milk, we tried to have a movie, which usually makes them content to be sitting for ten to fifteen minutes.

Takes a peripheral role as he moves children into the center of action.

II. *A day when they were very talkative and high strung.*
They just didn't want to stop talking. As soon as I realized this, I brought out the large paper, and we created our own story. Some kids can really get going on this and tend to monopolize the story, so a rule was made that each person had to contribute at least one sentence in each story. Then these stories were typed, duplicated, and passed out for everyone to take home. On these creative days, flexibility is a must. When they want to talk, I don't like to stifle them. During milk we had a social hour—they can really come up with the conversations. On a day like this we might also go on make-believe trips—sometimes lion hunts—which they really enjoyed.

Senses when children need to move from an active to a quiet activity.

SYNCHRONIZING: The teacher adapts to events as they occur, makes changes in his plans as the creative responses of individuals emerge, abandons plans even though their development has consumed time and energy. Improvises as he follows the lead of children, receives ideas from children and improvises on them, gives ideas to children and lets children improvise on them. Manages time flexibly and moves with the mood of individuals or groups.

III. *A day when they seemed very depressed.*
On these days I really racked my brain to think of fun things to do. For reading, we sometimes played a fishing game with a real fishing pole and a magnet. It is supposed to be for learning initial sounds, but they didn't know them well, so we used it for an oral game too. The child would pick up a shape and would have to say, "I picked up an orange fish." (Or a yellow house, or a brown log.) They really went crazy with this game.

SYNCHRONIZING: The teacher senses whether the children are ready for an activity . . . he adapts to moods and other physical manifestations. He improvises as he follows the lead of children; he gives ideas to children and lets children improvise on them.

IV. *Rainy, lousy day. Anxious children.*
They couldn't be out-of-doors at all, so I needed to keep them a little more settled, because they weren't able to run off their steam outside. We worked in our regular ABC workbooks,—just one or two pages, then they got bored. The highlight of this day was when we decided to make our own alphabet books. We thought up our own titles and wrote them on our own books. They couldn't wait to finish these and take them home. We took turns naming different letters and learned how to write them by

SYNCHRONIZING: The teacher senses children's reactions to situations and adapts activities to moods, anxieties, fatigue, or other physical or psychical manifestations.

Capitalizes on teachable moments and improvises as he follows the lead of children; gives ideas to children and lets children improvise on them.

writing and rewriting them on the empty pages. Boy, does their pride show through! We ended this period with the old standby alphabet-twister game.

V. *Just a regular sunny day, cold outside, children are content.*

It is on days like these that I hit them with the heaviest ideas. I stressed sounds of letters, and we worked in our preprimers. We learn sounds by first making sure everyone recognizes the letter. We then write the letter in our homemade books. I try to see if anyone already knows a word that begins with that letter. We then think of other words with the same beginning sound and look at pictures of objects whose names start with that sound. They can relate well with physical objects, so if possible, I have objects they can hold and feel.

Senses when children are ready for an activity. Makes judgments about the amount of imposition he must make in a given situation.

SYNCHRONIZING: The teacher keeps main ideas and events in focus.

Has materials ready for use.

* * *

My main thing in teaching is that at the end of each so-called lesson, I try to leave off at a high point, so that they will want to continue with it the next day. I try to be as consistent as I can with my lessons, because without continuity you have nothing to hold everything together with. I'm all for relating science with social studies, with math, with music, with reading. When we studied children of foreign lands we related this with all our activities. Otherwise it would mean nothing to them. It made learning more fun to play math games that the Indians played, to eat what the Japanese ate, to read a story about Africa. When things are coherent the children make more sense out of learning and enjoy it more.

Stops work before the saturation point is reached, when interest is high.

INTEGRATING: The teacher provides for integrating centers of interest and keeps main ideas and events in focus.

Allows no material or single activity to become an isolated entity in itself but integrates each activity into ongoing classroom events.

Basically, as choreographer of my classroom, I could sum up my attitudes in a collection of words, all of them equally important: flexibility, relationship, openness, freeness, acceptance, trust, sensitivity, opportunity. This list could go on and on and on. As for my role, I don't like to be the center of attention. When I take attendance, I like to sit on the floor with the kids. It can put them more at ease. If I sit at their table on the same size chair, it brings me closer to them. When we made our books, I made one too, and did the same work in mine as they did in theirs. I did many things the way they did them—but I was also the one who kept peace in the place. I did very little for the children as far as tying shoes and that sort of thing; instead, I had them find a friend who could do these things for them. That way, they learn independence and also how to ask a favor. Yet, when they needed me to do something that only I could do, I did it as soon as I could, so that in the future they would not be afraid to approach me. I liked to give them as much responsibility as I could.

The Choreographer's Aim

The teacher-artist choreographs his own behaviors as a relator, a mediator and a diagnostician with an eye to helping the child become involved in directing his own learning. In doing so, the teacher is sensitive to the amount of freedom, structure, guidance and direction individual children need and also to what the group as a whole can handle. In the illustration just cited, the teacher was working with young children; thus, she entered into their experience in a direct way. If the group is inexperienced or their past experience has been only with authoritarian control, the teacher-artist recognizes that steps toward freedom must be taken judiciously, and he does not upset the whole apple cart at once. Little by little, he introduces opportunities to choose from options and allows children to find their own direction.

SUMMARY

Because the choreographic functions of the teacher are based on intuition plus educated know-how and experience, no prescription for classroom management or teaching can be written. However, in thinking about the vitality of classroom life and the attitudes of children toward learning, the teacher may find the following inventory of choreographic behavior helpful in analyzing what may be going wrong (or right) in the total environmental milieu. He may ask himself, "Have I taken this factor into account? If not, is there something here I need to look at?"

THE TEACHER AS "CHOREOGRAPHER" IN THE AESTHETIC ENVIRONMENT OF THE CLASSROOM

I.   As a choreographer, the teacher structures an open environment, providing for personalization and individualization of experience; therefore, the teacher:

1.   senses the amount of freedom, structure or direction a child or group needs and provides for variations in structure to fit individual needs.

2.   arranges environment to enhance the possibility that each child may find his own structure for working and encourages children to find their own direction.

3.   arranges for individual progression, small interest and/or help groups and some whole-class activities; forms temporary groups on the basis of interests, jobs to be done, and similar problems encountered in learning.

4.   confers individually with children and helps them set realistic individual standards, goals and plans.

5.   senses the amount of guidance different individuals need and frees learners to become increasingly independent.

6.   accepts what the child is able to do as his best work in a given moment of time and provides encouragement for next efforts.

7.   provides for learning options—varying kinds of learning activities, materials and methods of learning—from which children may choose.

8. has children schedule some of their own activities and engage in independent study or projects that are self-selected.

9. encourages children to help each other.

II. As a choreographer, the teacher facilitates the integration of educational experience; therefore he:

1. lets his methods flow naturally out of his knowledge and understanding of the problems and goals he has in mind, the individuals and materials with which he works and his own personality and talents.

2. provides for integrating activities and centers of interest; assists the child in keeping main ideas and events in focus.

3. fits lessons and materials into the context of an open environment, so that the materials are fitted to the needs of the child—not the child to the materials.

4. allows no material or single activity to become an isolated entity in itself but integrates each activity into the ongoing events of the classroom.

5. lets authority and/or limits flow from the nature of the activities pursued by the children.

6. makes judgments about the amount of imposition he must make in a given situation; sets necessary limits within which children may explore and create.

7. anticipates problems children may encounter and prepares children for new techniques they will need to carry out an activity.

8. senses readiness for an activity, or whether problems need to be resolved before an activity can get underway.

9. handles routines efficiently and has materials ready for use.

10. organizes and arranges space for interest and work centers in a way that facilitates communication and the movement and flow of classroom activities.

III. As a choreographer, the teacher synchronizes the "here and now" of classroom events to bring about unity, variety, continuity and climax; therefore, he:

1. senses children's reactions to situations and adapts to moods, anxieties, fatigue, or other physical or psychical manifestations.

2. trusts his intuition when he senses things are not going right; adapts to events as they occur; makes changes and adjustments in his plans as the creative response of individuals emerges; abandons plans even though their development may have consumed time and energy.

3. capitalizes on teachable moments and improvises as he follows the lead of children; receives ideas from children and improvises on them; gives ideas to children and lets children improvise on them.

4. lets sequence develop from the nature of the activity and the questions and problems the child is pursuing; allows the child to follow a sequence natural to him.

5. takes a peripheral role as he moves children into the center of action.

6. controls the pace of activity when working with groups without calling attention to the fact that this is being done; allows children to pace their own individual activity and work according to their own rhythms.

7. watches timing, rhythm, repetition and pacing, and senses when boredom or overstimulation occurs; senses when to redirect an activity or when to stay out.

8. spaces activities and/or permits children to space activities to incorporate rests for integrating, for renewing one's self, and for changing pace.

9. moves smoothly from one activity to another and senses when children need to change from quiet to active or active to quiet activities.

10. manages time flexibly and moves with the mood of individuals or groups; stops work before the saturation point is reached, when interest is high.

11. repeats activities only so long as interest is maintained—leaves practice activities when interest diminishes and comes back with a new approach later; plans for repetition as a "variation on a theme."

Notes

[1]Clyde E. Curran, "Artistry in Teaching," *Teaching: Vantage Points for Study,* Ronald M. Hyman, ed. (New York: J.B. Lippincott Company, 1968), p. 352.

[2]Dorothy I. Seaberg and Wanna M. Zinsmaster, "What Can Teachers Learn from Directors in the Performing Arts?" *The Elementary School Journal,* Vol. 72, No. 4 (January, 1972), p. 169.

[3]See Jeannette Veatch, "Individualizing," *Individualization of Instruction,* Virgil M. Howes, ed. (London: The Macmillan Co., Collier-Macmillan Ltd., 1970), pp. 96-99.

[4]Dorothy I. Seaberg, "Experiencing the Role of the Teacher: A Case Study of Pre-Service Elementary School Teachers Practicing Role-Function Behaviors," unpublished Ed.D. dissertation, College of Education, Wayne State University, 1961, pp. 133-135.

Chapter 14

Choreography of Teaching

The Four Faces of Teaching has presented an analysis of the teacher's role in humanizing education. However, as the teacher choreographs the scene, his multifaceted role becomes a smooth blend of indistinguishable parts. No prescription, no set of directions, no wisdom of the sages can tell a teacher exactly what to do or when to do it. Teaching, being creative and intuitive like the other arts, has its laws but is beyond law. In the humanizing classroom many of the teacher's actions influence the child indirectly and are purposely designed to place the pupil in the driver's seat. But whatever the design, the actions of the teacher show a basic commitment to openness and trust in his relationships with children, and to the encouragement of their individuality and participation in the learning process.

To demonstrate the ineffable mood of the classroom—the rise and fall of action, the ebb and flow of events as teachers and pupils encounter together the ideas, problems, books, materials, people, feelings, actions, and even the space of the classroom—we have chosen four vignettes depicting teachers who stylize the classroom scene in an

open way. These word pictures convey more than a fat volume of didactic explanation, and from them we hope the reader will gain an impression, see a vision, or dream a dream of what he can do to make the classroom a place where humanistic education can occur. Illustrating open learning, the selections show classroom life from the view of a student teacher, a big city district administrator, a visitor of the British Infant School, and an advocate of the open classroom.

ENVIRONMENT FOR LEARNING
AS SEEN BY A STUDENT TEACHER

Glidden School is the first really "open" classroom I've seen. Experimentation and planning are going on all the time, as in all schools, but the attitude at Glidden is so positive that it's catching.

The day begins with a group meeting in each classroom. Special classes for the day are announced and the time schedules are put on the board. The class then breaks up into groups to receive their folders from their "teachers." Folders contain work completed the previous day. Some students need work assigned to them, but the majority of the kids make out their own schedules. They must include the required math, reading, spelling, and cursive. If they do not complete the daily work that they put on their schedules the kids are "grounded." They cannot leave the room, for any reason, without asking. This has a more profound motivating effect than grades, which these children do not receive.

There are two main types of schedules—"task" and "time." The kids are allowed to do what they want, when they want to. The task schedules contain a list of possible subjects to be explored, and the child can do any subject he likes for as long as he likes, provided he gets his necessary work done. A time schedule contains certain time slots throughout the day. The child puts down what he will do and at what time. This is an advantage to the teacher, because there should never be a time when a child has nothing to do. Some children, because of their personality, like to impose the time schedule upon themselves and some children love the freedom of a task schedule. It could be the exact opposite of what they have at home.

Special classes such as knitting and making popcorn balls or apple "turkeys" are held in the learning center. It is very difficult for the teacher to choose one or two children from her class to be in these groups. They draw so much interest that everyone wants to be in each group. There is only room in the learning center for a few at a time.

The art room has special classes each week. The kids usually have five classes to pick from. Everyone must choose one art group that they wish to be in. During the time I was in Glidden, Hallowe'en masks were made, corn husk dolls were put together, and objects were molded out of clay. The art classes meet three times a week with Mrs. B., who makes children's hands create.

During the day there are two 15-minute recess periods. This is a fantastic thing for both kids and teachers. The kids can go outside and run, or stay inside and play games. The teachers get a chance to catch their breath and talk out problems or ideas with other teachers. A day never goes by, though, when the teachers lounge isn't invaded by one or two kids with problems or complaints!

There has been talk of closing Glidden School. I'm not really up on all the facts but to me the atmosphere to the old building, the eagerness of the children to learn, and the attitude of involve-ment by the teachers make Glidden worth having open.

I've never seen anything quite like it!

ENVIRONMENT FOR LEARNING AS SEEN BY A BIG CITY DISTRICT ADMINISTRATOR[1]

How to Create an Environment

Life-space

During school hours the classroom is the life-space of the child. The various elements within this life-space consist of the following: the children and the adults who work with them; the instructional materials; the furniture; plants and animals; toys, manipulative materials, and objects; pictures, maps, charts, and globes; bulletin boards, chalkboards, easels, and project work areas; and special exhibits and realia on loan from museums and other resource centers.

The teacher further expands the life-space of the child beyond that afforded by the classroom through field trips, cultural field experiences, nature walks, and site visitations. The life-space of the classroom is also expanded by invitations to resource people and special guests to visit the classroom and share experiences with the children.

The classroom teacher arranges and distributes those various elements and experiences so as to create a learning and living environment for each child that provides for him a life-space affording growth in human relationships, attitudes, and values, as well as knowledge, information, concepts, and abstract reasoning.

"Learning the Children"

No matter how well a teacher knows learning theory, child development, curriculum, and methods and techniques, knowledge of each group of children and each particular child is essential to creating an environment. "Learning the children" is an ongoing activity for the teacher; therefore, creating an environment is an ongoing activity. A teacher sensitive to the needs, interests, life-styles, problems, accomplishments, hopes, gifts, limitations, and habits of the children may then artistically create an environment by selecting activities, blending human relationships through groupings, providing experiences, structuring a stimulating classroom, and introducing challenging concepts.

Knowing each child is a monumental task for the teacher. The cumulative record folder, the health record, the test data, and the personality inventory are nothing more than the prelude or overture to a continuing relationship with each child. Knowledge of each child comes from keen observation of children at work and at play, and from a sensitive response to clues in conversations, recitations, drawings, and discussions. The teacher constantly takes and files mental notes for future individual interaction with the child, and consciously builds a living thread of continuity in her individual relationship with him. Professional clichés, such as individual differences, differential psychology, motivation, reinforcement, discipline, readiness, and others take on a meaning and a human dimension when the teacher knows who needs the visibility of being monitor, who can lead a discussion on horses, who needs the reinforcement of the pat on the back, who is ready for the challenge of a new question, who needs some physical activity for the morning, who is too threatened by the new baby to concentrate on the morning story, who is ready to make a contribution in the mural, who can handle the easy question, who can handle the difficult question without losing face, who needs a restraining touch on the shoulder, and on and on endlessly throughout the day.

Use of Space

The use of space is another important dimension of environment. There is no greater visible clue to the teaching style in a particular classroom. Centers of interest, variable-sized groupings of furniture, individual nooks, supply and material stations, display of pupil work products, evidence of projects in progress, quiet islands for "reading" and reference, activity corners, art areas, nature shelves and window sills—the catalogue is as endless as the creativity of the teacher and the children. Furthermore, the stage is not set for the year—space is fluid. Its use is determined by a need for a temporary period of time, for as long

as the "assignment," the project, the particular interest, or the specific task requires.

The almost daily conversion of space to particular activities and tasks requires great planning, organization, and effort. The seeming lack of structure actually requires great structure. Without it, one notes only great chaos. The teacher, her aides, and helpers are constantly setting the stage, shifting the scenery, and arranging the props. This eventually becomes a routine which the children can absorb with almost complete independence by the end of the year. The children gradually learn where things "belong." The permanent "things" have a place and children readily learn where to put them if taught to do so. Slovenly housekeeping, clutter, obsolete exhibits, outdated displays, untidy work areas, and furniture in disarray reflect lack of planning and organization more than they do a creative learning environment.

One must also be careful of overstimulation—of clutter, of loading the space with more than can be useful and appropriate to the learning tasks at hand. If one uses the space and the environment for concept reinforcement, rather than just filling every inch of space with something, one can avoid this. Whatever learnings, units, concepts, and parts of the curriculum are currently in focus should preempt the environment for that period of time. There should be a relatedness, a sense of purpose, a focus to the scene. Children will sense this and respond to it. The incidental, the occasional, the accidental, and even the far-fetched have their places, but they are not the general design—they add a flair, a touch, an accent. One doesn't dismiss an idea because it doesn't happen to fit, but one does try to keep the main action front and center.

Pacing

Pacing is a third major dimension of environment. Each day has a life-cycle. At its beginning, the children learn what will happen that day. Where are we? What is our task? What do we need to do? Who is going to do which part of the job? Who is responsible for particular tasks? Who has unfinished business? Plan the day with the children. Make sure that active periods are followed by quiet activities, that a high point is gradually terminated, that great effort is rewarded with appropriate rest, and that the day is properly resolved and put to rest with some hint of what has been accomplished and a forward look to the next day. An occasional element of surprise, the intervention of the unusual, the rapid shifting of gears to accommodate the unexpected are useful, but a constant state of suspense is as frustrating and undramatic as a boring, repetitive schedule.

The Social Fabric

The social fabric of the classroom is the warp and woof which integrates the total life-space. The interpersonal relationships of the children and of the adults who work with them and the interaction of the adults and the children establish the values and attitudes essential to the affective growth of all. This process is critical to the cognitive growth of the children in the various subject areas. The adult models serve as object lessons to the children. The teacher who interacts in a courteous manner with them, respecting their individual worth and dignity, will find this pattern repeated in the children's interaction with each other.

Learning to share, taking one's turn, appreciation of other's abilities, respect for individual differences, and understanding for the problems of others are human skills which are part of the social fabric. The teacher has the adult responsibility for initiating, structuring, and planning for these skills to develop. This responsibility extends to prevention of situations fraught with negative consequences. The teacher is ever alert for signs of fatigue, which may lead to acts of aggression; she is sensitive to signs of frustration, which may lead to emotional outbursts; she is alert to the need for equitable distribution of materials, the lack of which may lead to unnecessary squabbling. Not all will be sweetness and light; however, an environment loaded with aggression, tension, and frustration will contribute to the unraveling of the social fabric.

The Teacher as an Artist

The concept of space becomes for the teacher a framework for her teaching style, an awareness which is ever present in her mind. This is the framework which undergirds her long-range goals,

which are extended ultimately to daily lesson plans and time schedules. The ability to translate philosophy to daily lesson plans is the art of teaching.

ENVIRONMENT FOR LEARNING AS SEEN BY A VISITOR OF THE BRITISH INFANT SCHOOL[2]

From the moment you walk in the door of an open classroom, the difference from the conventional procedures is striking. In most classrooms rows of desks or tables and chairs face the front of the room, where the teacher is simultaneously presenting material and controlling the class; the children are either quietly engaged by what the teacher is doing, surreptitiously communicating, daydreaming, or fooling. Even in classrooms using innovative materials, such as the Individually Prescribed Instruction, in which each student works on a math sheet prescribed for his particular level of achievement, the basic pattern is one in which all the children do the same thing at the same time, sitting at their desks with the teacher watching from up front.

But in an Open Classroom, there is none of this. There is no up front, and one doesn't know where to look to find the teacher or her desk. She is usually to be found working intensively with one or two children, or if things are going as they should, often standing unobtrusively aside but observing each child's activities with great diligence. There are no desks and few chairs—fewer than the number of children. And the children are everywhere: sprawled on the floor, in groups in the corners, alone on chairs or pillows, out in the hall, or outside in the playground if it's good weather.

How does the day proceed? As they arrive, the students check the Chore Chart to see what their housekeeping responsibility is for the day. They take turns doing chores such as bringing up the milk, watering the plants, cleaning the animal cage, mixing new paints, sharpening pencils, taking attendance.

Many Open Classroom teachers call a general meeting after the children arrive, focusing on some interesting experiment several children did the day before, something brought from home, an unusual item in the newspaper, or a sentence she has written on the board to be corrected by the class. The children squat on their haunches or sit cross-legged in whatever area most comfortably holds the whole group.

After the meeting, children choose the areas in which they would like to begin their day. Some prefer to start quietly reading, curled up in the over-stuffed chairs. Some like to get their assigned work out of the way first, but others may not have a choice if the teacher has noticed, for instance, that they have been neglecting math or need work in punctuation, and she tells them that they should start the day working with her. Soon the room is full of action, used as it will be for the remainder of the day, unless some special visitor or specialist focuses the group's attention for a special activity.

The child is free to choose, but whatever choice he makes he will be confronted with a wealth of opportunities for exploration and discovery. In the math section is everything he can use to measure and figure, including the Cuisenaire rods, balance scales, rulers and a stop watch, workbooks, and counting games such as Sorry and Pokerino. Similar riches await him in the language arts section, where he can read, make a tape recording or type, write, and play word-games and puzzles; or in the arts area with its paints, clay, dyes, and sand. Other corners are devoted to science, music, and blocks.

The child's freedom, autonomy, and independence—as well as his responsibility—are epitomized by the largest and most elaborate of the many charts and pictures around the room. It is the "Activity Chart," and it lists by word and appropriate picture all the possible activities in the room: from reading, typing, playground, painting, right through to visiting and gerbils. Next to each are several hooks, on which the child hangs his name tag to indicate what he's doing. A simple device, but it says much about the respect for the child and the relationship between the child, the teacher, and the room.

In the Open Classroom, each child's day is distinctive and different from every other day. To give him a sense of his progress, each child may keep a diary, which is also used to communicate to the teacher. Some typical entries indicate the flow of activity, and the frustrations and concerns of the children:

Today I read *Horton the Elephant.* I began the green series in SRA. Ollie helped me with the words in the *Horton* book. I helped John and Sara make a staircase with the Cuisenaire rods.

I played in the Block Corner most of the day. We were making a suspension bridge. We talked a lot about our water tower and how it got flooded by Jimmy and what we should charge for a toll. I'll do my math tomorrow. Okay?

We had a turtle race today. Mrs. White taught me how to break words down. I can read words, but I can't break them down. We timed the turtles with the stopwatch. They tried to climb over the side of the box.

We're making a book of fables like "How the Snake Lost His Legs," "How the Elephant Got His Trunk," "How Jose Got to Be a Genius," "How I Got to Be Invisible."

ENVIRONMENT FOR LEARNING AS SEEN BY AN ADVOCATE OF THE OPEN CLASSROOM[3]

The Learning Areas

The diagram on page 174 depicts the decentralized character of a classroom, serving eight- and nine-year-olds, that I frequently visit.

The areas are broken up by a variety of dividers such as movable screens (which also serve as display space), bookcases, and planters. There are tables in the room which comfortably seat five to six children; seldom, however, are all of the tables occupied. Shelves have been built to accommodate plastic storage trays in which children keep their personal belongings such as pencils, notebooks, crayons, and rulers.

The art area contains three easels which can serve six children, aprons, paints (water and tempera), jars, brushes, papers of various sizes, shapes such as egg cartons, glue, string, vinyl tile, wood chips, yarn, wallpaper, and magazines. There are times, because of particular interests, that the art center contains leaves, starch, styrofoam, rubber, twigs, dyes, and looms.

The reading corner is particularly inviting. It is

brightly carpeted, has a rocking chair, several pillows on the floor, and large numbers of books and magazines, which are freely accessible to the children. The reading materials cover a broad range of subjects and ability levels and include books written by the children. On display are "ideas for sharing," "new books in the center," and "books I especially liked." Such descriptions are all written by the children.

The language arts–listening center is adjacent to the reading corner and contains materials and equipment relating to the broad area of communications. There is a typewriter, a tape recorder, and record player equipped with headsets, records and tapes containing music for enjoyment, stories (sometimes associated with programed readers), and skill lessons in such areas as listening and spelling. There is also a variety of reading and spelling games (most of them made by the teacher), puzzles, a reading skills kit, and a box containing pictures and ideas for writing. Displayed are children's poetry, stories, and new words with some "fascinating" uses.

The science area is designed for active involvement with materials and typically changes more often than most of the other centers. In addition, it contains more "common," noncommercial materials than in the centers described thus far. This development typically occurs in classrooms when science is looked upon as an activity in which children learn more about their world through personal investigation and when children are encouraged to ask their own questions rather than wait to find out from the teacher what they ought to ask.

A variety of units from the Elementary Science Study ("small things," "peas and particles," "structures," "pendulums") are found in this center. These are open-ended units that stress such processes as analyzing, classifying, measuring, and predicting. They employ balances, lenses, microscopes (the $2.00 variety produced initially by

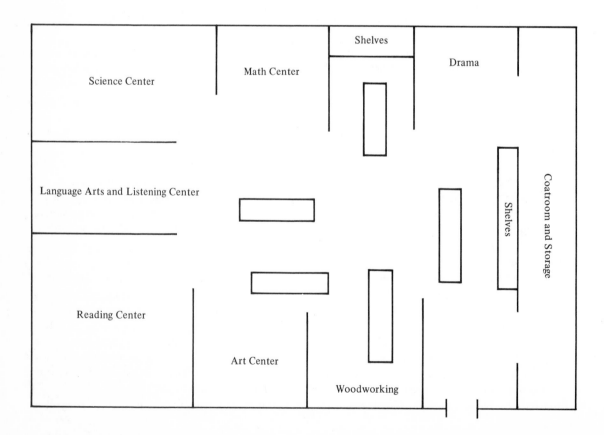

ESS), magnets, prisms, thermometers, plastic tubing, bottles and jugs, candles, rocks, and shells. A large incubator, motors, nuts and bolts, and pulleys are also in this particular science center. And there are living things: hamsters, an aquarium with a variety of water life, and a snake.

An electric fry pan is made available once a week for cooking projects. Cooking produces enormous enthusiasm because everyone can be successful at it; in addition, it provides an excellent opportunity for integrating the various curriculum areas. There are also science reference books on animals, plants, insects, rocks, astronomy, and engines. A filmstrip projector is available for use with the large numbers of commercial filmstrips pertaining to the physical and natural sciences. On display are projects that have been completed by individuals or groups of children.

The math area also stresses active involvement with materials and thinking. Measuring devices are prominent (tape measures, string, rulers, and jars of various sizes), as are counters (buttons, washers, and abacuses), Cuisenaire rods, blocks (multicolored and multi-shaped), geo-boards, catalogs, tangrams, dice, math games, puzzles, and flash cards, and a variety of math textbooks and workbooks. The teacher has prepared a large number of activity cards, which give some sequential nature to a variety of mathematical concepts that serve as starting points for children. The influence of the Elementary Science Study and the Madison, Minnemast, and Nuffield mathematics projects (the latter developed in England) is clearly visible. Evidence of their influence can be seen in the extensive measuring, weighing, graphing, sorting, and classifying activities in which children engage. Chess also is played extensively.

The drama area serves a broad range of the expressive arts from pantomiming, role playing, and puppetry to some limited forms of movement and music. There is a puppet theater and materials for making puppets. There are dress-up clothes, records, several recorders and drums, an autoharp, and a variety of rhythm instruments constructed by the children. Improvisation is strongly encouraged. (The broad opportunities for children to engage intensively in the creative and expressive arts is a sharp contrast to most formal elementary classrooms.)

The woodworking area attracts girls as well as boys. Local lumber yards supply scraps of wood, which children use to construct boxes, boats, rockets, and geometric designs. (Last year, in a classroom staffed by one of our intern-teachers, eight- and nine-year-old children designed and constructed a 6' x 8' x 6' playhouse. They even shingled the roof.) An old table serves as a workbench. There are hammers, saws, screwdrivers, pliers, nails, rulers, glue, wire, and sandpaper stored on a pegboard and in plastic containers.

A rich environment and easily accessible learning materials form an important dimension of the open classroom. Teachers in such settings consider it important that children know what learning materials—paints, brushes, wood, paper, scissors, batteries, masking tape, wire, audio tapes, and filmstrips—are available, where they are stored, and that they have open access to them. If children must ask permission to use the items, which usually involves waiting, or do not know what is available, they may well lose interest or have limited opportunities for exploring new areas. It should be noted, too, that the children do things for themselves—mix paints and clean brushes, and operate tape recorders, filmstrip projectors, and record players. These simple chores are part of the process of learning self-reliance and responsibility.

Structure and Organization

How does the teacher organize? What does she do? . . . The first hour of the day is devoted generally to "free activities." Children pick up where they left off the previous day or begin something else. After approximately an hour, the class gathers for a planning session. The teacher takes a few minutes to describe many of the activities going on in various parts of the room. Several children are asked to describe what they are doing that may be of interest to others, and a few others outline their plans for the remainder of the school day.

In the planning session everyone draws up a personal plan for the day. The teacher generally uses this occasion to call attention to new additions to the learning centers and new possibilities for using outside resources. She also takes this opportunity to organize a specific time to meet with particular groups of children (she names them) to work on a specific skill, for example, using reference materials, or using context in reading or number facts. These groupings come about as a result of her observations and discussions with children. They usually change from week to week.

In this particular classroom, there are some teacher expectations which children include in their planning. At a minimum, children are expected to engage in reading (recording for the teacher any new books they have begun), work in the math area, and do some writing. While these may appear to be rather separate activities, and the learning centers may well seem a reinforcement, encouragement is always given for integration of learning. The house-building project mentioned previously is an example. The children visited a lumber yard and arranged to get some old plywood. They developed quite elaborate plans which involved measurement and geometry. An architect demonstrated model making, which the children then tried. They viewed a variety of films on house building. A tape-recorded lesson provided additional information on the use of tools—the lever, plane, and gear—and two retired carpenters in the community gave some practical demonstrations.

Individual children pursued many different interests in relation to the house-building project. They wrote letters telling others of their experience. They took up individual projects including Indian homes, termites, trees, creatures that live in trees, homes around the world, workers who build homes, old and modern tools, skyscrapers, and doll houses. Such projects quite naturally move across the artificial separation of subject matter.

After the planning session, the children go into the various learning centers. The teacher then moves about the room, working with individual children and small groups. She asks questions, suggests other resources for extension of a particular activity, encourages, listens, and learns.

At the end of the day, the children come together again to evaluate and share what they have learned or found particularly interesting. At times there are dramatic presentations and readings of favorite poems. Often, the teacher uses part of the time to read a story.

There is direction—a structure—in this classroom, and it becomes obvious to most observers who remain for any length of time. Teacher direction and child direction are clearly balanced. Early in the year, teacher direction was greater, but it has decreased during the course of the year. By the end of the school year, the balance will undoubtedly have shifted even more toward child direction.

In subsequent years, as the teacher and children become more adjusted to an open setting, progress toward greater child direction should become more rapid. As all of the classrooms in this particular school become more open, such progress would be facilitated, of course, because movement from one classroom to another would not require major adjustments by the children or teachers.

Children need structures that provide a sense of order and meaningful options in order to establish a sustaining direction for learning. It is also clear that the teacher must be an active agent, not only as a provisioner but as a stimulator and catalyst for extended learning.

Notes

[1] "How to Create an Environment," in *Curriculum Guide for the Pre-Kindergarten: A Program of Living Experiences for Young Children* (Board of Education, City of Chicago, 1970), pp. 21-24. Used by permission of the author, Angeline P. Caruso, and the Board of Education, City of Chicago.

[2] Excerpts from "A Little Bit of Chaos" by Beatrice and Ronald Gross. Copyright 1970 by Saturday Review Co. First appeared in *Saturday Review,* May 16, 1970. Used with permission.

[3] Reprinted by permission of the publishers and the author from *Open Education: Promise and Problems* by Vito Perrone, copyright 1972 by the Phi Delta Kappa Educational Foundation.

STUDY HELPS AND INDIVIDUAL PROJECTS

Annotated Bibliography

In addition to chapter references, the following books are recommended readings:

Blitz, Barbara. *The Open Classroom: Making It*

Work. Rockleigh, N.J.: Allyn and Bacon, Inc., Longwood Division, 1973.

A practical sourcebook for setting up an open classroom. Excellent down-to-earth suggestions.

Ghiselin, Brewster (ed.). *The Creative Process.* New York: A Mentor Book from New American Library, 1952.

Paperback edition of a symposium of 38 outstanding men and women who reveal how they actually begin and complete creative work.

H'Doubler, Margaret N. *Dance: A Creative Art Experience.* Madison: The University of Wisconsin Press, 1966.

The philosophy expressed in this book may be applied to creative teaching in any field.

Hofstadter, Albert, and Richard Kuhns (eds.). *Philosophies of Art and Beauty.* New York: The Modern Library, 1964.

Selected readings in aesthetics from Plato to Heidegger.

Informal Schools in Britain Today. New York: Citation Press.
  An Introduction, Joseph Featherstone (1971)
  Towards Informality, J. N. Pullman (1971)
  The Pupil's Day, Ann Cook and Herb Mack (1971)
  Space, Time and Grouping, Richard Palmer (1971)

McNamara, Helen, Margaret L. Carroll and Marvin Powell. *Individual Progression.* Indianapolis: The Bobbs-Merrill Company, Inc., 1970.

The authors discuss the theoretical and applied aspects of individual progression and include the results of two research studies of individualized instructional programs.

Nyquist, Ewald B., and Gene R. Hawes. *Open Education: A Sourcebook for Parents and Teachers.* New York: Bantam Books, 1972.

A book of readings containing some of the best that has been written about open education.

Rasberry, Sally, and Robert Greenway. *The Rasberry Exercises: How To Start Your Own School and Make a Book.* Albion, California: The Freestone Publishing Co., Box 357, 1972.

A practical guide to starting a free school. Deals with people problems and the delicate problem of achieving freedom without license.

Rogers, Carl R. *Freedom to Learn.* Columbus, Ohio: Charles E. Merrill Publishing Company, 1969.

The student can be trusted to learn as the teacher serves as a facilitator of learning. The job of the teacher is to set up an environment that encourages responsible participation in the selection of goals and ways of reaching them. Examples are given of different educational levels.

Stephens, Lillian S. *The Teacher's Guide to Open Education.* New York: Holt, Rinehart and Winston, Inc., 1974.

Based upon her own experience and visits to many British Infant Schools, the author develops the philosophy of open education and then deals with the problems of organizing the open classroom, providing for the curriculum, and implementing the open approach.

Things to Do

1. Action project: Analyze the aesthetic effects of the classroom environment on children.

    a. *Description:*

    In your classroom, observe the effects of school activities and routines on the manifest behavior of individual children or groups of children. Keep a notebook handy where you can quickly jot down observations during the day. Then at the end of the day expand on your overall observations and make suggestions to yourself about things you might like to change.

    (1) Record observations in reference to specific periods of activity. Things to watch for:

    (a) Time of day and weather conditions.

    (b) Nature of the activity.
    Quiet or active.
    Teacher-initiated or pupil-initiated
    Skills and abilities needed.
    Kind of material being used.
    Did the activity require: Memory or recall? Problem solving? Creative ability? Repetition? Physical Activity? Cooperation or competition? Individual or group effort? Comprehension? Use of hands? Use of the senses? Everyone doing the same thing in the same way or everyone working on the same goals in their own way?
    Was the activity a "doing" activity or a "talking" activity? Who is involved in the doing or the talking?

Was the class ready to begin or to quit the activity?

Was the activity routine or fluid?

(c) The general mood of the class and of specific individuals. (Was the mood apathetic, gay, quiet, excited, involving, hostile, accepting, etc.)

(d) The success or lack of success children feel.

(e) The length of different activities within the same class or period of work.

(f) The pace of the activity.

(g) The nature of the roles of the pupils.

(h) The nature of your own role.

(2) Record observations about your own feelings both before and after a segment of the school day:

Did you feel rested? Tired? Bored? Excited? Depressed? Happy? Successful? Unsuccessful? Worried? Calm?

(3) Record observations in reference to the overall school day.

(a) As you moved through the day, were transitions smooth or disjointed?

(b) Were active periods interspersed between quiet periods, or was the whole school day of the same intensity?

(c) Were children on their own part of the day or under constant direction?

(d) Did you rigidly follow through on a plan, or did you make adaptations as you went along?

(e) Were you teaching "off the cuff" or by flexible preplanned design?

(f) Did you set limits for the children? What was the nature of these limits?

(g) Did you ever leave activities even though they weren't finished? Did you make children stick it out to the end even though they were turned off? Did you let them continue certain activities longer than you had planned for?

(h) Did you require all children to adhere to the same structure, or did you provide much closer structure and guidance for some and much greater liberty for others to follow their own bent?

(4) Physical plan:

What is the nature of the physical environment of the classroom? Are things organized so children can find things to do and the materials they need without too much supervision?

b. *Evaluation:*

(1) Look back over your raw data and try to analyze what has been happening in the aesthetic experience of children—how they feel or the quality of their experiencing. Describe what you think has been happening aesthetically to the group as a whole and to particular individuals. Document your description with notes from your observations. Did you discover any principles to guide your behavior? Did you modify your practice as you went along? Explain in what way you did this and what results you obtained.

(2) Fill out the *Pupil Perception Inventory of Classroom Environment* on page 129 in terms of your desired effects on children and then have the children respond to the questionnaire. Compile the results of their responses and compare them with your own idealized responses. What does this analysis reveal to you? How accurately have you been sensing the way children feel about things? Does this analysis suggest some changes you would like to make in your teaching?

2. Library Research: Consult *Education Index* to locate articles that refer to aesthetics and education. Also refer to the *Journal of Aesthetic Education.* Read selected books in the field of aesthetics, such as Hofstadter and Kuhns (eds.), *Philosophies of Art and Beauty;* Valery, *Aesthetics;* and H'Doubler, *Dance: A Creative Art Experience.* Write a paper delineating aesthetic principles and show how these principles can be taken into account in developing educational experience.

Epilogue

Analyzing the role of the teacher is like shaking a kaleidoscope. Each jostle reveals a new pattern, always intricate and wonderfully designed. In viewing the faces of teaching, we shook the kaleidoscope four times—and each tilt provided a fresh perspective. First, we saw a helpful "relator" creating an environment of growth-facilitating influences. We shook the kaleidoscope a second time and saw an intervening "mediator" putting the child in touch with himself and his here-and-now-world of ideas and sensory experience. We shook the kaleidoscope a third time and saw a "diagnostician" discerning the child's phenomenal self. Then we shook the kaleidoscope again and saw an environmental "choreographer" eliciting aesthetic response. As we shake the kaleidoscope a final time, we see a whole teacher emerge. Front and center in the viewer is a group of busy, smiling children. One beaming little lad looks ready to speak—and if he did, he would undoubtedly say, "We feel good about ourselves. After all, school is a pretty nice place to be!"